Edited by
Jan Fook and Renate Klein

# A Girl's Best Friend

## The Meaning of Dogs in Women's Lives

SPINIFEX

Spinifex Press Pty Ltd
504 Queensberry Street
North Melbourne, Vic. 3051
Australia
women@spinifexpress.com.au
http://www.spinifexpress.com.au

First published by Spinifex Press, 2001
Reprinted in 2002

Cover and book design by Deb Snibson, The Modern Art Production Group
Made and printed in Australia by McPherson's Printing Group

National Library of Australia
Cataloguing-in-Publication data:

Fook, Jan
A girl's best friend : the meaning of dogs in women's lives.

ISBN  1 876756 10 1

1. Women dog owners. I. Klein, Renate. II. Title.

636.70082

*For Gypsy and all our dogs we have not forgotten.*

# Contents

# Acknowledgements

In putting this book together we were particularly lucky to be supported in our task by Belinda Morris, research assistant and dog lover extraordinaire who, after an eight-hour non-stop work marathon to get a mailing out to all eighty-six contributors, happily proclaimed that anything to do with the dog book was not really work, just joy! Her great organisational skills and clear-headedness has meant that hundreds of precious family photos got sorted in an orderly way and no nightmare eventuated . . . a powerful testament to dog love and an invaluable support for both of us.

We also thank the women at Spinifex Press: Susan Hawthorne, Johanna de Wever, Maralann Damiano, Jo O'Brien and Laurel Guymer who, to various degrees, partook of our obsession with the 'Dog Book' but did their best to stay calm and accommodate our wishes re cover, design and publicity ideas. We had invited all of them to contribute but got some clear 'no's' followed by 'I like cats'. Nevertheless they all worked very hard — and two did contribute.

The cover and design posed a challenge: we did not want to have a 'cute' women-and-dog book — we wanted some humour and oomph. The first breakthrough came from our contributor Lyn Zboril who suggested that 'the girl's best friend' show her diamond — and indeed our cheeky cover dog now does: thanks Lyn.

Words cannot really express thanks to designer Deb Snibson who patiently tried to accommodate our wishes for 'radical' design and sat hours with us in front of the computer patiently changing colours and shades — without once losing patience. We love the result and thank her very much for her creativity.

A special thank you goes to Claire Warren who, whilst typesetting the contributions, lost Gypsy, her companion of sixteen years: it was our hope that the stories might support her in her grief and make it possible to write about her loyal friend. And she has and we're sure no eyes will remain dry whilst reading Claire's homage to her best friend.

We also thank Barbara Burton who helped with the book and felt inspired to write her own story. We were delighted and it is now included in the book. We think this probably doesn't happen often that people working on a book feel motivated enough to contribute themselves. Power to dogs, and women, we reckon!

Finally we greatly appreciate our partners Allan Kellehear and Susan Hawthorne for their support and encouragement in this project, and for taking dozens of photos of Minty, Nellie, River and us — no small feat given the growling and snapping of our darlings who didn't quite seem to understand that they too could be best friends and need not defend us from one another!

We also thank each other for a most joyful co-operation which not once was problematic and contributed greatly to reducing our work stress.

And last, but certainly not least, we thank Nellie, Minty and River for being with us.

Jan Fook
Renate Klein

# Preface

Jan Fook and Renate Klein

What do dogs mean to women? That's for you to find out in reading this book.

But if we tell you how this book came about, our experience might resonate with many of you.

We work together at the same university. We are both long-standing academics who derive a lot of meaning and joy from contributing to our disciplines and working with our students. Yet our work lives have become increasingly complicated. With cuts to funding in universities and an economic rationalist outlook, it is more and more difficult to find space for the creativity which once attracted us to our professions. In this climate we have developed a camaraderie, a profound support for each other as women, as people, as colleagues. In one of our commiserations, we asked each other what was MOST important in our lives, given that we often cannot control our workplace? What sustains us away from the petty yet often overwhelming daily tensions at work? Our answer was stunningly simple: River and Nellie and Minty of course! These dog friends provide a deep but often unacknowledged solace, different from the company of people, even our much loved 'significant others'.

Yet here we were, both prolific writers, and we had never written about this part of our lives that meant so much to us! And in looking through dog-related books, we discovered very little written by and about women regarding their relationships with dogs. Much of the classic literature remembered from western childhoods is stories of boys' adventures, shared with the companion dog. Adult literature often consists of stories about working dogs, bred by men for hunting or herding. In these, a dog is described as 'man's best friend'. Still other tales tell of great feats, of heroic animals remembered for special, life-saving deeds. Yet most of us (an average of 24 per cent of households in 21 countries as quoted in Rupert Sheldrake's 1999 *Dogs That Know When Their Owners Are Coming Home*) live with very plain but immensely lovable dogs. How do we ordinary people, particularly women, feel about our dogs, and what part do dogs play in our everyday lives?

That is how the idea of this book was born.

As we invited women and girls to contribute to this volume, we discovered the passion, the care, the dedication which females from all walks of life give to their dogs, and the often-even-greater passion, care and dedication that our dogs return. We were completely overwhelmed with offers to write for us (including offers of women-and-cat stories which might become the next book we do!). As a result we have finished with nearly twice as many pieces as we originally envisaged. Even as we go to press, offers to contribute are still flowing in. We didn't know what women would want to say about their dogs and we didn't try to influence what they wrote (we also respected UK/Australian as well as US spelling). The book grew organically initially from an invitation to contribute which we sent to dog lovers known to us, then via the spread of a few e-mail lists and finally by word of mouth. It became abundantly clear that the world consists of zillions of women who are crazy about dogs — as well as those (few) who probably thought we'd finally lost it and gone too far in our dog obsession.

Some contributors are acknowledged poets, story tellers and (non)fiction authors but, like us, this is the first time

they write about their dogs. For others it is the first story they ever put on paper. A few authors have long discovered the pleasure in writing about 'a girl's best friend'. The women and girls vary in background, country, and age — from eleven to eighty; they live in the Swiss and US countryside, in Calcutta, Melbourne and London's concrete jungles, the beaches in New Zealand and on farms in Wales and Australia. Their reflections on the meanings of dogs in their lives range from childhood memories to their current lives that are enriched by their furry friend(s). (There were even some dogs who took to the pen themselves!) We insisted on photos of the women — or girls — as well as their dog(s) which proved quite a challenge as we got many pictures of womenless dogs with enclosed comments such as 'it's the dog that's really important, not me'. But mostly we managed to get at least a snap of the female companions, as well as treasured old pictures from childhood, blurry images imbued with meaning, happy memories of special love.

Assembling this collection and dealing with authors was a pleasure from beginning to end. Boundless enthusiasm was offered as the pieces flowed in and every new contribution made our days — made us laugh, cry and wonder. The irritations at work faded as we excitedly shared a new poem, or story, and oohed and aahed over the cute pictures of dogs and their women that had arrived by mail and electronically. This continued as the book took shape and cover and page design eventuated.

In reading the contributions it became apparent that there were different themes emerging from the women's experiences. Whilst each story is unique, we thought it was fascinating to observe also the common threads about what dogs mean to women more universally. These themes suggested to us a loose way of ordering the pieces. Without detracting from the individuality of each piece, we think these groupings help us start thinking about what we might have in common as women with dogs. Many of us have childhood memories of growing up with dogs, especially perhaps of the one dog we have never forgotten. We start the book with these stories. Many of the pieces make us think about how we relate to our dogs, and in particular what might be women's ways of being with dogs. Then there is the ONE dog, 'the dog of my life' who stands out from all the others. Our fourth section is about Dogs and Home Life as, for some contributors, dogs are a symbol of a contented home life. For some women, their dog(s) have made a difference in their lives at a time of crisis, and perhaps in a way no other being or circumstances can. Lastly, we found that many contributors have loved a number of dogs, and often trace their lives through the various experiences associated with each animal. So we end the book with the dogs of our lives.

In these pages there is grief which is never forgotten; pure, simple joy and happiness; surprising vulnerability; cherished trivial and momentous events. There are affectionate, characterful and wise dogs. There are silly, boring, smelly and naughty dogs.

There are happy women — dogs are indeed our best friends.

And they make us smile.

In their many and varied ways, they do save our lives.

# Section One Growing Up with Dogs

# Sibling Rivalry with a Labrador

Kate Munro

**Some folks grow up** with a deep-seated resentment of a brother or sister they believe to have been favoured by one or both parents — not me, nothing so pedestrian in my upbringing, my brother and I were outclassed by a dog. An obese, ill-behaved, flatulent Golden Labrador named Cindy who shared a passionate devotion to my mother and Cherry Ripes in equal measure — which isn't so surprising because from the dog's perspective the two were pretty closely related.

In return for this unconditional love and loyalty, my mother indulged Cindy with a level of luxury that left our family wondering what more this dog could possibly want. For instance, Cindy was seldom forced to suffer the indignity of eating dog food; instead she joined the rest of us at meal times nudging the delicate floral Royal Albert China plate around the kitchen floor as she wolfed down whatever meat and three veg. was on the family menu.

Then there were the sleeping arrangements. Initially upon her arrival in our home Cindy positioned herself in the centre of the bed squarely between Mum and Dad. However as the months passed, the barrier between my parents grew with Cindy's expanding girth, helped along by the consumption of numerous chocolate self-saucing puddings garnished with dollops of King Island cream. Dad decided it was time to suggest alternatives and knowing full well that the bed was only big enough for two, he was intensely relieved to find that Mum and he were in agreement about which of them should sleep elsewhere. Cindy, on the other hand, was heartbroken at such rejection and sulked for months, refusing to be consoled even when Mum presented her with a luxurious substitute placed alongside the bed. I grudgingly conceded that at least the dog had taste; a hefty orange vinyl beanbag accessorised with a pink satin frilled pillow went well beyond the bounds of what might be disguised as 'retro'.

Nor were the comforts of a middle-class suburban upbringing confined to meeting Cindy's physical needs, indeed far from it, Mum provided Cindy with the kind of growth experiences that only travel can offer. The dog was always comfortably seated in the front passenger's seat with the window down so she could pant publicly into the wind and dribble great globs that blew straight back in the window onto we lesser humans confined to the rear seat.

However the true depth of Mum's devotion to Cindy was revealed on the fifth anniversary of Cindy's birth when a great celebration was planned to mark the event. I was appalled at the unfairness of it. Mum made me wait until my twelfth birthday to hold a party and then on my big day the entire class was struck down with measles so that not a soul came. Cindy on the other hand was being given the royal treatment and, as far as the rest of us could tell, she didn't give a toss about a party as long as she got her extra rations of Cherry Ripes.

However, as an experienced corporate hostess, Mum understood the importance of giving guests plenty of notice of forthcoming events. So in the tradition of classical social etiquette, Mum prepared a guest list and popped modest invitations in the letter boxes of all Cindy's canine 'friends' advising them of the celebration and reassuring their owners that she would personally pick them up and escort them home when it was over.

On the allotted day, Mum toddled around the neighbourhood of the small mining town gathering an odd assortment of pedigree and bitzer guests. Back at the house, everything was prepared and laid out beautifully on the dining table. There was a 'Happy Birthday Cindy' cake, fairy bread, pikelets, chips, Cheezels and, of course, plenty of Cherry Ripes. The larger

dogs like Sam the German Shepherd and Rocky the Ridgeback sat at the table without effort. Others, such as Benny the Beagle were seated on chairs so they didn't 'miss out'. They all wore party hats, some with more aplomb than others.

Just as things were beginning to get a little rowdy, I arrived home from the school bus with my best friend. We stood in the doorway of the lounge room staring in disbelief at the canine festivities before us. Initially I was motionless and pale with astonishment but then, as the eccentricity of this event dawned on me, I began to turn a shocking shade of adolescent pink. Mum was either oblivious or indifferent to my reaction, or perhaps it was a little of both. Whatever the reason, she ignored me and behaved as though doggie parties were a regular social event, apologising for the fact that she had forgotten the candles and that we had missed the cutting of the cake, offering us each a slice.

My friend politely declined the kind offer of hospitality and, making her excuses, left far too quickly for my comfort. This was a small town and I knew it wasn't going to take long for the details of this little incident to 'do the rounds'. However I needn't have worried, if I had initially had reason to worry about the rate at which

the tale would spread through the town, for my mum dealt with this swiftly. As promised, when the party was over, Mum escorted all of the canine guests home to their owners. With a beaming smile Mum returned each dog, with a small tray of leftover cakes and sweets and a note to the owners thanking them for allowing their dog to attend the party and wryly inviting them to share and enjoy the contents of their 'doggie bag'.

Compared to the rigid discipline imposed on my brother and I as we were growing up, the appalling behaviour tolerated in Cindy was in a stellar orbit all of its own and yet it seemed that my parents, and my mother in particular, loved this animal more dearly with each act of destruction.

Mum was away for a week and Dad, who was chatting to her on the phone, stopped and listened nervously to the silence. There are some moments when it is just too quiet to be peaceful, so that anxiety begins to seep from every second of stillness. He was right to be concerned. Cindy was not in sight and, from all evidence so far, she was not dealing well with the enforced separation from Mum. Earlier in the week, when he was at work, Dad had opted to confine Cindy in the laundry thinking that locking her up in this small room without furniture would minimise the opportunity for mischief. Big mistake.

This dog had one motto when feeling neglected — don't get mad, get even. She scratched and peeled the wallpaper around the skirting boards, tearing strips of sufficient length with her mouth to give her a really firm grip and progressively she stripped the majority of wallpaper from all of the laundry walls.

Mum and Dad were at this moment discussing the arrangements for the repair of this damage when the eeriness of the silence crept upon them. Dad called out to Cindy, who responded from the main bedroom with a playful yap. When Dad reached the bedroom doorway he froze in horror: the room was covered in feathers and down and the queen-sized mattress was torn down the middle, insides spread everywhere. Cindy lay on top of the remains of the duvet and several pillows looking at him with forlorn innocence. Dad returned to the phone saying nothing to Mum about the latest catastrophe, instead making the honest and understated observation, "I think you should come home soon love, Cindy seems to be missing you — *a lot.*"

*Kate Munro is a sibling survivor of a series of Labradors. She is now recovering day by day in Brisbane with Mr Spock, her Abyssinian cat. Cindy is pictured on these pages with Kate's mother, Roseanne Munro.*

# Sonja Jeanne Daly

**I too had a farm in Africa**, the farm where I grew up. It was bush country and the nearest town was three hundred kilometres away. We had to be self-reliant.

A leopard started taking the goats, dragging one each night over the thorn bush enclosure where they were penned up at night. One morning we woke to find that the leopard, sated by repeated kills, had just ripped the udder off a nanny goat and left her to die. "That leopard will have to go," said my father. "It's a bad one."

He disappeared into the house with a grim face and when he emerged he was carrying his .303 rifle. A hunt! Sonja and I panted in his wake. Sonja was the Rhodesian Ridgeback-cross who had been acquired soon after my birth to guard me from snakes. But now there were greater things afoot. She led the dog pack as we left the house. I too got my reward. For the first time, I was going along on the hunt in my little donkey cart, made from planks and a couple of bicycle wheels.

Two hours later the dogs had the leopard up a tree. As we approached, the leopard launched himself down from the tree and made a break for open ground. The dogs closed in, baying, and the leopard disappeared under the pack. The leopard snarled viciously and the other dogs backed off. But not Sonja, she had the leopard at bay. As she leaped for the leopard's throat, he ripped out her throat with a great swipe of his claws. She held on. My father shot the leopard right through the head.

Sonja was still alive, no arteries had been torn, but she was badly wounded. My father decided to take her home because my mother would want to bury her. She rode home with me in my cart. Her eyes were glazed and she struggled to breathe. We made a bed for her at the back door. When she managed, with difficulty, to lift her head to lap up some milk, the milk poured from the wound. So my mother and I sat with her for hours dripping milk through a straw that we inserted into her throat. She lived on, so my father stitched up her throat to give her a better chance of surviving. As we sat by the dog, my father sat under a tree skinning the leopard.

Gradually the wound closed and Sonja could eat on her own. The leopard skin had to be tanned. It was submerged in a vat of foul-smelling tanning fluid which stood near the house under a giant thorn tree. From a branch of this tree we had suspended strips of hide being made into raw hide thongs. The strips of hide were looped over the branch and a log of wood was tied to the bottom. The log was twisted up tightly and then left to untwist under its own weight. I rode that log as it spun around and around. Taking on her role of guardian once again, Sonja barked, and tried to drag me off the spinning log.

Sonja became a house dog, allowed to sit in pride of place on the tanned leopard skin spread out on the sitting room floor. Later she had a litter of puppies. Local people came in their donkey carts from miles around to ask for a pup from her litter. They wanted a pup from a dog tough enough to hunt a leopard. "Yes," said my mother, "this is a brave dog; the right dog for the bushveld." But we knew that she was more than that. She could fight, but when she was wounded she fought on, and she survived.

She was my Sonja, companion of a wild, lonely childhood.

*Jeanne Daly now lives in Australia where she teaches in the School of Public Health, La Trobe University. She is co-author of* The Public Health Researcher *(Oxford University Press, 1997) and editor or co-editor of* Health and Technology *(Oxford University Press, 2001),* Reinterpreting Menopause *(Routledge, 1997),* Ethical Intersections *(Allen and Unwin, 1996) and* Researching Health Care *(Routledge, 1992). She has three dogs, two children and a piece of land.*

# Max and Molly

Hannah Jones

**From the day I was born** to this present day, I remember our dogs, Max and Molly. Max, his black velvety fur coat shining brightly, his kind sweet face looking at you when he rested his tired, black head on your knees. He would never hurt a fly, and when I was young, he didn't touch me with any of his paws, or get nasty and try to bite me, from then until his death. Molly, her soft, silky, golden yellow fur, shining like a star. She was as kind as anything or anybody could ever be. She was like Max, she never, ever got horrible and she was like this to her death.

Those dogs were one of the first things I remember, in my whole life. They were full-grown when I was born and very, very sweet. They both had a wonderful life. Some things I remember doing with my dogs are these: once when I was two years old, I remember snuggling in between Max and Molly and giving them both a big kiss on their noses. I also remember taking them for long walks where they would run ahead then run back and run along beside us and when we got to this big river they would jump straight in. Whenever I came home from school, Max and Molly would come bounding up to me and give me a big kiss. Or if I had come home after being at one of my hobbies, they would come to the door and give me a big welcome. Even if we had a big party and a little child was hurting them, they wouldn't get angry they would just give the child a big sloppy kiss. So they were really, really lovely dogs.

But then came the deaths. One sunny morning, the first day of the summer holidays, we heard a cry. We rushed down the stairs and there was Molly. She was shaking and crying, and a few minutes later she was dead, after having a heart attack. She died at the age of twelve. From then on, Max was never the same. His missed Molly terribly. Four years later Max became ill. He had already been a bit deaf and a bit blind but he became deafer and blinder. A few days before he died he couldn't walk. It was very sad. He wasn't enjoying life much anymore, we decided to put Max to sleep. He was sixteen when he died.

But all together, they had the best life any dog could ever have. I will always remember our dogs as being the most kind-hearted dogs in the world. To me they were more like a brother and sister than dogs, for I loved them with all of my heart and I'm pretty sure they loved me with all of their hearts as well.

*I am eleven years old. I was born in England and lived in Devon until I was nine years old. Max and Molly were a big part of my life there. My family moved to Australia in 1999. We came here on a trip around Australia in 1997. When we got back home my dad was offered a job here. It was hard saying goodbye to all my friends but I couldn't wait to come. I have just started high school. It is a big step but it is a lot of fun. We now have a Golden Retriever called Harvey. He loves other dogs and he loves to play. I have a lot of hobbies. I play the piano and clarinet and play in a band as well. I also like to dance, act and sing.*

# Jazza, Monte, Ripper and Little Dog
### Melinda Tankard Reist

**In any recollections** from my childhood, there is always a dog. A lovely male Golden Labrador stands out the most, because he was with us the longest and the affection is therefore deepest. But other dogs contributed to my happiness, well-being and confidence as a girl growing up in the 1970s and '80s on a vineyard in country Victoria.

Jazza was the first dog I remember. The local city health inspector who ran the pound, delivered him to my parents' door, his jet black head protruding from the man's front coat pocket. He'd heard my father had lost his much loved Kelpie, Sal, hit by a car a few weeks before.

I really only remember Jazza as an old black dog (a bitzer, apparently), a bit unsteady on his feet, though photos show me with him as a pup. I do recall splashing water at him from a rickety blue plastic pool. And I have a vivid, disquieting memory of returning home from tennis with the family to find Jazza distraught, accidentally left in the house on an afternoon of rasping heat, the venetian blinds dented by his attempts to escape through a window. I can never look at venetians without thinking of him.

After Jazza died (at thirteen), my father brought home a lively brown Kelpie who we called Ripper (because he ripped things up: the Tankard children had not yet reached their creative heights). We adored him and he us, having many shared adventures, though he didn't seem to be with us long. I remember him being hit by a car. My mother found

him, days later, hiding in a cool, quiet trough of sand at the back of a shed, allowing his injured leg to heal. (What a clever dog! we all said.) And it did — until my mother backed over him in the ute not long after. She never spoke about it.

Then, of course, you didn't speak of anything which caused pain. Sick kittens — kittens dumped in hessian bags on our property who we kids tried to feed with eye-droppers of milk — were dispatched with a quick bullet to the head (at one stage we were trying to care for twenty-three cats and kittens). This was not for any cruelty on my father's part — it's just what you did

with sick animals. ("Min OK?" I overheard him ask my mother after ending the life of a particularly favoured black, blue-eyed and very ill kitten while I hid in my room so my tears would not be seen. We didn't talk about all this and the many other deaths, but his two-word question to my mother, using his pet name for me, gave me some comfort.)

My grandmother once told me how her first child drowned in an open irrigation channel. She told me she had never cried over this unspeakable loss. Tears'll get you nowhere, she said she was told. I heard it said my father had only cried twice in his life.

Yet the dogs in our lives provided an outlet for emotions and affection. My father might shoo away the mother cats who blocked the front screen door hoping for some milk, liver or the heads of freshly filleted fish, but the dogs were never considered in the way and words of endearment were rained on their heads.

I most remember Monte, our Golden Lab, black eyes against a cream golden coat. Howling with joy when we returned from school, accompanying us on long summer days exploring in the

nearby bushland, where we would disappear for hours and no one would worry — exploring rabbit holes, absorbing the cool beneath the orange trees, building cubbies, fishing in the channel. When I galloped my horse through the mist of the overhead irrigation sprays, down the columns of orange trees, Monte would often tear along beside, thrilled to be part of the adventure. Walking home in the dark of winter after putting the horse in his stable, my father's coat wrapped tight about me, I never felt afraid with Monte near me.

He seemed part of the life-cycle of the block, panting beneath the vines during grape harvest in forty-degree heat, running alongside the tractor on which we rode with our father, at my dad's heel when he headed off 'round the water' — checking the sprays in the middle of the night, driving a wire though them to clear dead fish and other blockages; nose frost bitten when accompanying my parents through pruning and 'rolling on'.

For my father, fishing from his tin boat on the Murray River was a sacred activity. While us kids often broke his meditation with poorly baited hooks, snags, lost sinkers, banging his fishing rod while he wasn't looking to trick him into thinking there was something on the line and me liberating some of the live bait over the side, Monte never caused such trouble and was a much more fitting boating companion.

Many in the town were daily amused by the sight of my mother making the quick trip to the local shop for the mail and papers in the ute with Monte, her front seat passenger, sitting upright beside her.

In my teenage years, Monte was a source of comfort. My parents may not have understood me — but the dog did. My plans to run away always included taking Monte with me. He was, without exception or qualification, insanely crazy about me. I may have written 'I love [the boy next door]' and 'Suzi Quatro forever' in my diaries, but 'I love Monte' was there too. I cannot see a Golden Lab on television or anywhere without feelings of warmth coming over me. I wish I could wrap my arms around him now.

When Monte, at sixteen, lost the use of his hind legs and became too ill to stand up and relieve himself during the night, my parents lifted him up and helped him in this task. A labour of love, my mother said. It was out of love too that my father ended his life and his suffering.

Little Dog (again, for want of a better name) was found behind the newspaper office where I worked as a cadet reporter — half dead, matted fur, eyes infected and stuck together, of questionable breeding (Silky Terrier perhaps?). I begged my parents to let her stay 'just a couple of days' until I could find a home for her. By then, she'd been washed, her eyes healed and, with the most endearing expression, she had grafted herself into my parents' hearts. I realised she was staying when some visitors asked if they could take her. "She belongs here," my mother stated firmly. It was one of the best things she ever said.

*Melinda Tankard Reist is a Canberra writer and author of* Giving Sorrow Words: Women's Stories of Grief after Abortion *(Duffy and Snellgrove, April 2000). Her children are all asking for a dog.*

# Rex

Lesley-Caron Veater

**I think I had no human friends** until I began school really.

Before that, of course, there was Rex.

And this was no isolated farm or the bush, but a popular seaside tourist town on the south coast of England. We lived above the garage, where my father worked, at The Grand Hotel on the seafront.

Rex was there before me and so we grew up together. He: a very handsome black-and-tan German Shepherd or Alsatian, as they were still called then, post-war. Me: a small carrot-haired girl baby who arrived to surprise my much-too-young parents.

Dogs like Rex sort of own you in some way I think. Early on he was pure guardian; left to sit by my pram while I got my 'fresh air' down by the garage workshop. I grew up around the fancy cars of the rich-and-famous patrons of The Grand.

Our playground was the seafront of course, no back garden for us; family walks along the seafront eating fish and chips from newspaper, cockles, and begging for fancy dolls from the seaside vendors. Rex was always close-by begging for my ice-cream.

I remember rides on Rex's back; private chats in Rex's ear, for him alone; awkward runs on pebble beaches, permission to go on the pier. He could speak that dog, with his eyes, bore into you with his message, no mistake.

I never saw Rex and our cat in the same room together. Tommy was a very large British Black who lived on the roof-tops. If I wanted to visit with Tommy I had to climb out the kitchen window and sit on the fire escape. Black iron railings, black iron grill, way above the world and our cat Tommy who lived among the roof-tops and was the best ratter in the neighbourhood. He never invaded Rex's territory, Rex had the spot at Dad's feet by the fire. Rex was number one in the flat.

Rex was the only one who could keep up with my father. Afternoon walks became route marches. Not long out of the army I guess, his stride was huge and the pace was brisk; woe betide anyone who couldn't keep up. My ally though, as always, was Rex, an easy distraction when a rest stop was needed.

He was well known around the garage and no one came near me if he was about. Rex had been trained with military precision; one word or gesture was all it took, but only from my father. He never snarled or snapped but would bark sharply if someone came too close. He was my best friend, playmate and guardian.

School came soon enough though and with it a year of great change. My parents decided to migrate. A coin was tossed one evening by the fire: would it be Canada, would it be Australia; heads or tales love? They packed up and bid farewell to all that was familiar, their sights set on a new land and new opportunity, in Australia.

Rex was sent to live with another family and I never heard of him again. Parents being what they are, they didn't think to ask me or Rex for our opinion. I used to see his so-intelligent face and imagine the big garden I knew he must surely have now. I used to feel with my hand for him sometimes. There was absence, loss, nothing to wrap my need for comfort in. I never have had another dog.

*Born in Brighton, UK, Lesley moved to Australia when she was six. Following secondary school and an extended stay back in the UK, Lesley entered the travel industry. With her two children she relocated to a self-sufficient lifestyle in the Victorian bush. Next followed periods of community development work and welfare work interspersed with studies in massage and alternative healing together with lots of organic gardening, baking and cheese making. Now working in social work, Lesley is a passionate gardener, artist, mother and traditional Witch with a zest for life, art, writing, good wine and good men, not necessarily in that order!*

# Every One of Them

Carolyne Bruyn

**I am staring at a photograph** of a Border Collie in a tutu and a tiara. The photograph came courtesy of my sister, the costume lent courtesy of her little girl, and the dog didn't see any of it coming fast enough. No doubt due to his impeccable lineage, he manages to look dignified in spite of the fact that he closely resembles one of the hippopotamus ballerinas in Disney's *Fantasia*.

In a long list of family dogs, my sister's Borders are the first to sport pedigrees. At the first opportunity, all former members of our happy yappy mongrel family would have dragged the offending articles a long way down the garden and torn them to shreds, rather than make the most of an embarrassing situation for the sake of a little girl with huge determination. Breeding will out.

I only just remember a shy, brown 57-varieties model appropriately named Heinz. Mum adored him, but then she was a sucker for any dog. I don't possess a photograph of her that doesn't include a dog. Her favourite photo is one of her as a toddler happily wielding bucket and spade on Narrabeen Beach. But where's the dog? She points to a smudge in the background. Two minutes after the photo was taken, she explains, the smudge materialised into a huge black dog which galloped straight over the top of her on his energetic way to somewhere else, leaving her howling in shock.

Our next dog was an accident — literally. One morning my father went off to the local Scout Hall to clean up. He came home with the inert body of a small brown terrier. "I found it in the gutter," he told Mum. "Must have been hit by a car. It won't live but I couldn't just leave it there." Hip not only lived, she lived for another twelve years. Her fierce loyalty to every member of the family more than repaid her rescue, and her example cemented strong instincts already implanted by our parents.

When my sister went to work for a local vet, we held our collective breath. We knew what would happen and, sure enough, a parade of all creatures, great and small, began arriving home with her. No creature would be abandoned or put down in her presence without an extremely good reason. The family accepted all refugees with patience and grace and interest. Home on holidays one year, I accidentally mentioned I was looking for a female kitten and flew back to Brisbane with the largest, fattest, male cat I have ever seen. She knew of course that deep down I knew I really wanted a dog but we accepted the inevitable.

For mostly she tried to rescue dogs. From the time she left home, wherever she took up residence, a succession of otherwise abandoned, unwanted dogs accompanied her. Mum lived vicariously in this never-ending campaign, egged her on and provided covert financial help as required. I was envious. I lived in units and flats and wasn't ever rebel enough to flout the rules, but she always managed to find a way around them. She reminded me of a girl I saw on television who was plotting to smuggle her two cats into a new animal-free zone. She didn't anticipate any problems whatsoever, even though the rules were strict. "They're identical," she smiled at the camera, "people will think there's only one."

Mum has no dog now and a husband who doesn't want an animal that might well outlive both of them. For her, the schoolgirl in the photograph cuddling up to a large shaggy mutt, the young married with the small Maltese Terriers, life without a dog must just be existence. I have a big yard and a husband who will have a dog only if it is a West Highland Terrier. He finds he is married to someone who once accompanied a friend to an animal shelter to drop off cat and kittens, and had to be forcibly dissuaded from returning home with a baby St Bernard which weighed nearly as much as she did, and ate twice as much.

But I'm not so sure I'd try it now. With age apparently comes caution, and a reluctance to take on any creature which demands time and energy and money. The media is full of advice on choosing the right dog and the best way to care for it. But when we were young, dogs didn't seem to be deliberated over or chosen. They turned up and stayed and we managed. The real difference then I suppose is that we enjoyed them. Every one of them. And all that comes back to me as I smile at that photo of a Border Collie in a tutu and a tiara. 🐾

*Carolyne Bruyn is an archivist who likes to write but won't give up her day job, who would probably be famous if she wasn't so lazy, and who lives in a creaky inner-Sydney terrace with an understanding husband and one-and-a-half bossy cats (the half being a male stray who can't commit).*

# Little River and the Big River

Susan Hawthorne

**Once upon a time** there was a dog called River. River lived next to a big lazy old river which meandered slowly across the plain.

River is a Kelpie. The word 'kelpie' is old Scots for the spirit of the waters, said to haunt rivers, particularly in time of a storm. Kelpie gives warning to those who are to be drowned.

On sunny days you would find little River curled up on the grassy banks of the big river in the mornings, or in the shade on hot afternoons.

I grew up on a farm near the town of Ardlethan on the south-west slopes in New South Wales. My parents tossed a coin on whether to call me or the dog Sally. I envied the Black Labrador her name. She and her pup Sonny were our inside dogs. Among the outside dogs were Kelpies and Border Collies, the working dogs of Australian sheep farms. The town now has a bronze statue to the Kelpie.

Little River and the big river got on fine until one day there was a heavy rainstorm upstream and the lazy old river became a raging torrent.

Ardlethan is in the middle of very dry country, and its annual rainfall is only eighteen inches per year. In 1956 the Mirool Creek, which passes around the edge of the town and past the golf club, flooded. The water came almost to the doors of the Land-Rover which my grandmother and I were sitting in as we crossed the bridge at the entrance to the town. Chrissie, a Kelpie, stuck her head through the window and the wind blew her ears flat to the head. Not long after this we brought home an Alsatian pup whom we named Prince.

Instead of flowing slowly between its banks, it rolled across the plain.

There were two things that little River did not like.

Getting her feet wet.

And thunderstorms.

As the big river rose it spread its waters across the paddocks, through the houses, along the roads, over the footpaths.

When I was twenty I witnessed the Murrumbidgee River bursting its banks and spreading out across the paddocks of my parents' farm near Wagga Wagga. The roar of the river was deafening. The dogs, a Rottweiler and a Beagle, crawled under the beds. The next day they stayed home as my brother and I brought the cattle to higher ground. The next time I visited my parents I brought a friend, a Blue Heeler called Miles, who grew up being carried in a rucksack on my back as I rode my bicycle through Melbourne's inner suburbs.

Little River wanted to keep her feet dry. So she ran ahead of the raging river.

Then came the thunderstorm. It roared and raged. Lightning struck trees, chimneys, powerlines.

Little River ran faster and faster.

She could hear the drumming so close behind her. She was frightened, very frightened.

As she ran, so ran the big river. They both ran for a full day.

Many dogs are frightened by storms, but Kelpies are famous for being terrified. River is sometimes calmed if you tell her stories about the history of the Kelpie. Because Kelpies are working dogs they have great stamina and can easily run twenty to thirty kilometres in a day. River has run away on numerous occasions, always during storms. She is capable of leaping a two-metre wall when she hears the thunder rumble.

Little River had never been so scared. She thought this must be the biggest river in the world.

Until she reached the beach. There before her was the biggest river she'd ever seen. And it roared at her and spilled fuming water on the sand.

I love watching River when she encounters something new. She was not at all keen on the ocean at first meeting. The waves chase her up the sand, then she sees a bird and chases it to flight. Although not keen on water, sand is another matter. She rolls in the sand, her legs kicking with delight, almost somersaulting with joy.

She looked around at the other river. It was flat. It was getting smaller again. Sinking back into its banks.

Little River decided she would go home. Since the river she had been so frightened of, was not so frightening after all.

River has a fine memory for the things she loves: bread rolls under a tree, the bone she buried a month ago, friends especially those who give in to her willing eyes.

She walked home along the banks of the big slow river.

When she arrived home there was a welcoming party. The whole family were out to greet her. The neighbours came too. They pulled down the signs saying, Have you seen our dog?

Once, I had to rescue River. We were walking on a Saturday beside a city creek. I called her, but there was no response. No River bounding up, tail to the wind. Just silence and stillness. We looked for her for twenty minutes. Then a couple came by with an Alsatian. As soon as the dog was let off its lead, it went straight to the creek's edge, where I'd stood calling her not ten minutes earlier. There she was clinging to a root at the edge of the bank. Scared, but alive. I tore off my shoes and long-sleeved shirt and leapt in fully clothed. Between us we lifted and dragged her up onto the grassy slope. She shook herself, mud flying like an expanding universe.

If you paddle along the big river you can see her lying on its banks. Curled up in the sun in the mornings, and in the shade on hot afternoons.

*When Susan Hawthorne was born, her parents tossed up whether to call her Sally and the dog Sue, or vice versa. Her life has been enriched by her relationships with dogs. She is also an academic, a publisher, and her passions are writing, aerials work, and circus performance. She is the (co-) editor of numerous anthologies, including* CyberFeminism *(with Renate Klein), as well as the author of* The Falling Woman *(a novel), and* Bird *(poetry).*

# My Puppies Clare Healy

**Ever since I was young** I have grown up with animals: guinea pigs, cats and horses. Best of all, I can remember one wonderful day when my friend came to school with a new litter of puppies. That day I fell in love with a little black pup that I got to hold all morning. As soon as I got home I told my parents the news, that I really wanted a dog and I had finally found one I really wanted. My parents had both grown up with dogs when they were small so they understood how wonderful it would be to have such a special pet that's such a great friend. We called by my friend's house ready to collect her, I found her immediately and my parents very happily agreed that we could take her home. On the way out, my brother was found around the corner holding a male pup with black-and-white patches. So we got to keep both the puppies.

Before we even got home we knew the boy dog was trouble; he cried all the way home. They were so small that you could fit both of them on a face washer. I suppose that I really wanted to take on the pups as their second mother, always caring for them. I feel especially close to our dogs and they soon grew to become like their owners. My brother's dog is more interested in food, very easy going and loves to relax. Mine of course is sneaky, cunning and smart with a passion for running. Tina (my dog) is especially smart, she picks up on our family communicating inside and can work out if we're going for a walk, giving her a bath or putting her in the dreaded car. She always seems to get her way in any situation.

Among the things that I like doing with my puppies are: sometimes I just sit nursing them like babies; I also love taking them for walks because it's wonderful to see their faces light up with happiness when I mention the word 'walk'; especially when I was smaller but still occasionally now, I like to dress them up in clothes and muck around with them. They always are in for a bit of fun with me as that's how they show their love. I just love my puppies the way they are. Growing up with dogs is like having a different best friend. I know everyone says that it's just an animal but such a loyal one that you get so attached you pick up their mannerisms and feel as if they are talking to you. I will always know my dogs communicate with me. Just being around my dogs when I'm sick or upset cheers me up and makes me feel a lot better. They have a sense of silent understanding and love.

I have many memories of my two pups growing into dogs. One thing that I will always remember is how one evening in summer, Patch (the boy dog), chased after a possum and followed it up a tree. When the possum leapt trees, Patch realised what had happened but, being a male 'wuss', he didn't know what to do so he started crying. I thought I'd help get him down but when I started climbing the tree he just jumped off, fell over and ran off crying. To this day he still ends up in trees.

Every Tuesday in the morning the dogs stay on their leads a bit longer to wait for the rubbish truck to come and empty the bin. If we don't let the dogs off any other mornings on time they let us know but somehow on Tuesday mornings they know the routine. The reason we do this is because they will run off and knock over our neighbour's rubbish bins. Of course they know not to knock over our rubbish bins. It's always Tina that does it by jumping up and knocking the bin onto the slope so that then she can run up the slope and drag out the rubbish. My pups are now dogs and they are getting old and going grey. I still call them my puppies even though they are eight years old and I just can't imagine what life would have been and would be like without my two best friends.

*I am fifteen now. We got the dogs when I was six. I go to Eltham High School and I am in Year 10. I play netball and basketball on Saturdays and I am in the school Concert Band (I play percussion) and I also do drama. I like all animals but other than our dogs the ones that I like are polar bears and zebras. We lived in Canada for a little while and I saw a great exhibition about polar bears. On the way back we travelled through Africa and I saw zebras and I love their stripes (they are all a bit different).*

Judy Horacek is a freelance cartoonist and writer. Her cartoons are widely published both in Australia and overseas. Her website at www.horacek.com.au features a 'cartoon topic of the month'. Dogs may well appear.

# Leash

Patricia Sykes

### 1. black dog

under the taming hand

you were ours          taking

every bit of kid trouble

we passed on

until the orphan year

the grief factory

then it was chilblains

and hard breath          it was

dolorosa behind the shed

as we poured into you

the terror we could not take

to the house where tall men

gathered          their clothes

the dark wings that hid

our mother on the borne stretcher

until the red japonica snagged

the green ambulance blanket

and she was exposed

to air cold and bloodless

among the thorns your tongue

as rough comfort licking

the wet salt from our faces

as a silent car arrived

to despatch us and you

were given to the winter

of drowned paddocks

though we did not know it

like all things abandoned

### 2. spayed

kids know what kids know     you were out there alright
tracking us like a ghost dog through layers
of orphanage bluestone     through the trams the traffic
the whistling factories     forgiveness as no dumb beast
your latest cub is handcuffs of saliva     her jaws
around my wrist a play on obedience     my wolfish ally
bought with a wife's allowance     now she's vet's bills
a pancreas that cannot digest     a bitch with cut ovaries
we wear the same surgical scar     the mammalian knife is multiple
with edges     (too much generation keeps the primitive alive —
*bitch beast animal :* the bared teeth of language     the toxins
of the chained life     it's all food in the dish     the death of her
as paddock ritual     dirt and shovel     the usual despatch

*Patricia Sykes is an Australian poet, editor and performer. Her first collection of poetry,* Wire Dancing *was published by Spinifex Press in 1999. While she is currently dogless (she shares an acre of a Land for Wildlife property opposite a forest), she is an honorary aunt to several of her friends' and relatives' dogs.*

# Emma

## Penny Jones

**Emma first came into my life** when I was ten years old. She came from an animal rescue centre in the local town. My father, an ardent dog lover since his childhood, had agreed the time had come for us to have a dog in our lives again (we had lost our last one Bruce, under sad circumstances). He had given my mother strict instructions as to the colour, size and type of dog we should return with. I can remember it well, "not a large dog, not white, not too hairy, and definitely not female" (my father was already the only male in an otherwise all female household). Emma was all these and had a few extra interesting characteristics as well — she was a mix of numerous varieties, a large, mainly white (with a few black splodges), female (of course!) puppy. I remember she had huge feet and a scraggy tail, and an increasingly strange shape. My father fell in love with her immediately, and she was to become a mainstay in *my* life for the next fifteen years.

When I look back on my childhood and teenage years it is punctuated with snapshots of Emma at various stages in her and my life. She was always there for me and is inextricably bound with all my later childhood memories. In particular, the house that we lived in for fourteen years, all through my teenage years, was Emma's castle. When I picture the house or a room in it, she is always there, just as she is sitting in the garden, or wandering around on the road outside, as she did her whole life through. I am amazed, looking back, that we allowed her to roam so freely. I can remember clearly the regular sounds of screeching brakes as she ambled out across HER road. We smiled — I suppose somehow we always thought she was untouchable, certainly in all her fifteen years she was never hit by a car (or as far as I know, ever caused an actual accident, for which we should be very grateful). I know she often lay in the road and cars would stop and beep their horns and wait for her to heave herself up and amble away, with a look of disgust on her face at the cheek of it all.

My parents owned a caravan where we spent many happy holidays in the late 1960s and '70s. Often, Emma stayed behind with my grandmother (who lived with us) while the four of us went away. I can remember whenever holidays came near and preparations began, Emma would gradually become more and more sulky, refusing to look at us, indeed having nothing to do with us at all on the final day. On our return she would always perform the same ritual; with the front and back doors open, she would run through the house and round, over and over again until tired out, when she would collapse into happy sleep, relieved we were all together again.

Emma had her own settee in the kitchen. I don't think it began as hers, but it became hers over time. She slept on one end curled up in a ball, the other end available for anyone who wanted an audience with her. As she became older, she spent more and more time asleep on her chair, but she was always there for me when it felt like the rest of the world was against me, as it can so often seem in those teenage years. I suppose, like all dogs, she had that rare human quality of being a 'listener'. She never appeared to judge me, and we never 'fell out'. In retrospect, I can see she was the rock throughout that period, always constant, always a lick and a nudge, and a sympathetic glance, and I daresay she fulfilled the same sort of function for my sister, although we were unaware of her stoicism at the time.

After my sister and I left home, she remained with my parents and my grandmother, part of the welcoming party when I returned for holidays or weekends. When I was desperately homesick during my first days at University, I missed her comfort. She was so much a part of my growing up that I never imagined there would be a time when she would no longer be there.

My grandmother died after a short illness in 1980. I was, fortunately, at home at the time. The phone call from the hospital came in the middle of the night; my mother and

I took a long walk in the early hours of the morning, talking, crying, laughing too. It was my first great loss — she had lived with us all my life and was like a second mother to me. No one though could have foreseen the impact on our dear old dog. The night after my grandmother's death, after never having a day of sickness in her life, we were awakened in the middle of the night again, and this time, Emma was having the first of many fits, which she then continued to have until her death. I thought we would lose her too, that night, and I realised that we would do, one day.

Not long after my grandmother's death, my parents bought a much smaller house, in the same area. Emma moved with them, but she never settled in the new home, and her fits increased. I phoned one day to hear she had gone. I can remember it clearly, I took my driving test later that day, and failed — my heart just wasn't in it.

Now, I look back on those days of Emma, and wish I could sit with her for just five minutes again on that battered old chair of hers and tell her what a special friend she was to me. She was a wise old dog though, so I'm sure she knew.

*I have lived most of my life in England, where I married and had my two children. In 1997 we travelled extensively around Australia and New Zealand for nine months and subsequently we moved here early in 1999. In the UK I trained as a social worker and most of my working life has been involved in the area of childhood disability. As a family we have had many canine companions; our first Australian dog is a Golden Retriever called Harvey. My interests are reading, and music, but also playing tennis and travelling with my family.*

# Cyrano de Dogge Carol J. Adams

**Cyrano de Dogge was the trickster** of my childhood. He adopted us one day in the early '60s and throughout that tumultuous decade he rattled institutions at a most intimate level. We lived an hour outside of Buffalo, New York, and people who no longer wanted their dogs would drive to bucolic settings such as our town, and drop off their dogs. Cyrano had high standards for himself, and immediately picked one of the biggest houses in town as his own-ours.

To gaze upon Cyrano was to gaze upon mongrelization at its best — or worst. "Dog by committee," my sister recalls. More positively, he was a veritable melting pot of canineness. A long pointy terrier nose at one end and a long pointy tail at the other with bristly, wiry hair in between. When people called him homely, they thought they were being generous.

Cyrano was no respecter of boundaries; nothing was not his if he desired it. Cyrano would rob the grocery man of his best cuts of meat. "Who let that d—n dog in!" would resound throughout the store. No one really let him in; they just couldn't keep him out. We never knew what he would be chewing on in the back yard.

A long-practising car chaser, he was hit by several. Once a car broke his leg. When Cyrano returned home from having his leg set, he trotted proudly, cast, leg and all, to the nearest puddle and lay down comfortably in it. His leg had to be reset.

"Go home Cyrano," were the most disobeyed words every spoken, well, next to those words about the tree of knowledge.

"Go home Cyrano," we would implore as we headed off to school or to a friend's house. "Go home Cyrano," but he had other ideas. Tail to the heavens, he trotted along, importantly sniffing out our trail. One time, in fifth grade, I was so proud of my job as a member of the safety patrol at my elementary school. I arrived early, and was wearing my badge and directing kids. I felt very important! Cyrano could sense an ego in need of deflating, and arrived to do

his part. He got into a fight with another dog on the school steps. The principal appeared, towering over me and said, "Whose dog is that?". Everyone pointed at me. "Take your dog home!" he commanded. Shamed in front of my peers, dismissed for that day from my high status role, I had to return Cyrano to our house, a mile away. I walked home defeated.

Unfortunately for me, there was no one to counsel me about how one responds when a trickster thwarts you, exposing the needy child behind the façade of the proud and institutional one. After getting Cyrano inside the house, I lay down on the couch and never wanted to go back to school. The phone rang. I knew it was the school. I was not going to answer it. A voice sounded from the second floor. "Carol, are you down there?" "Yes, Daddy." "Well, you are supposed to be in school."

Cyrano provided excitement. Climb a ladder? Why not? But return down it from the second floor of an old barn? No way. My best friend's father had to carry him down.

Cyrano died the month after I became a vegetarian. I try not to read anything cosmic into that, but there is this: what is a vegetarian in a meat-eating culture but a trickster — pricking at the (virile?) ego that thinks it needs meat, exposing the institution to critique. He was the dog of lost causes, or impossible odds — and I guess I am attracted to lost causes, impossible odds. Yes, sometimes I feel like a dog who has climbed up a ladder. How did I get here? But unlike Cyrano, I know how to get down again.

As a child, I loved Cyrano deeply. Was it unconditional love? I don't know if a child can give an animal that, an animal at least like Cyrano who was consistently undoing the child's world order. But he absorbed as much attention as you could lavish upon him, and wasn't beneath causing sibling rivalry among us sisters, depending upon who gave him the most attention, he returned it to her. As I began to write this piece, I realized I didn't just love a dog, a scrawny, mongrel concoction of a dog, but a male, indeed, extremely male dog. I was embarrassed by his sexuality — which in keeping with his personality was a very public sexuality.

After I began to write about Cyrano I realized I needed to confront my assumptions. So many of the stories that came to mind recalled his distinctively male way of being. Part of his outrageous behavior was connected to his not being neutered. And my stories, too, revealed a more fragile 'Carol' than I usually recall. I yearned to connect them theoretically, to understand it all, to find one explanation, and left this piece for several weeks of simmering. But I now think I understand. I loved his dogness. I loved his freedom. I loved his affection. That wag of his tail. His 'telos' — his purpose — included snooping things out, even if this meant discovering a skunk on the Cape Cod beach the very morning that we were leaving or having that long nose filled with porcupine quills when he lost in an encounter with that unusual animal. (He had to be sedated to have the quills removed.) His telos made him seem outrageous to us, outside of the sphere of such behavior, such freedom. During those years, before Cyrano was banished off our beds at night because he carried fleas throughout the house, Cyrano was a nightly comfort. His affection, as well as his outrageous behavior, was boundless. We created stories about him; we had to shape his life into our verbal world. It was that verbal and perceptual world that was weighted toward conventional interpretations. But at night, as he lay on my bed — with a pillow for his head, of course — that time was wordless. The shames of the day — even those he had caused me — were swallowed within something more palpable, more vital — a dog, breathing, and wagging his tail at the foot of my bed. Cyrano was home and so was I.

*Carol J. Adams is the author of* The Sexual Politics of Meat: A Feminist-Vegetarian Critical Theory, Neither Man nor Beast: Feminism and the Defense of Animals *and most recently* The Inner Art of Vegetarianism *and* Living Among Meat Eaters. *After Cyrano, another dog, Demeter, adopted Carol and her family.*

Section Two Ways of Being with Dogs

# My Baci Dog — A Love Letter
### Renate Klein

Dear River,

**I'm sitting in a café** at the Piazza dell' Duomo in Florence and wish so much you were here. It's a gorgeous summer day and the Italian cappuccino is excellent. I even got a complimentary Bacio. But that made me miss you more: what's the point of eating Baci when I can't give you that tiny piece at the end (yes, yes I know, chocolate is poison for dogs).

Ever since I said good-bye to you down at the farm in Ocean Grove I've been missing you terribly. I'm sure you're having a lovely time at Thelma and Morrie's as always, but seeing you stand in the den with your paws on top of the gate with that expression on your face almost made me cry. In fact I stopped once I'd driven on to the road with my heart thundering: would you be good and stay, or turn into Kelpie mode and climb whatever obstacle there was in your way? You seemed to say, this couldn't be true; I couldn't be leaving you behind? Not again.

But it was true: the once-a-year ritual when your mothers go overseas — you turn into a well behaved dog again, and we pine for you for four weeks. Of course you were good and stayed and I drove off with a heavy heart just hoping that the weather wouldn't be too cold — no electric blanket for a month — and that no thunderstorms would drive you into a mad frenzy and into running away.

That was only three weeks ago and there hasn't been a day when I've not wanted to talk to you, cuddle you, give you kisses, play with you . . . all the things we do so well together and which make us both smile and happy and content with the world. At the airport in Sydney, there was a Dalmatian in a BIG cage checking in, ready to travel to Los Angeles. Her companion happily told me that it was no big deal, her dog didn't mind the trip. The regal composure of the spotted canine who was holding court and attracting quite a crowd confirmed her words. (I have to say that this 'Dalmatia' was much cleaner than your favourite toy at home who really needs a wash.) So what do you reckon? Being an old hand at flying to Queensland, would you brave a thirteen-hour flight? But then there is the quarantine at the end. Not worth it for a mere holiday.

The dog scene in Boston wasn't that flash; not many hounds around on the streets, a couple of Poodles with bows and ties accompanied by ladies looking just like them. London was better, lots of dogs romping and frolicking around on Hampstead Heath. I indulged in wild fantasies imagining you with us, having a lovely old time —

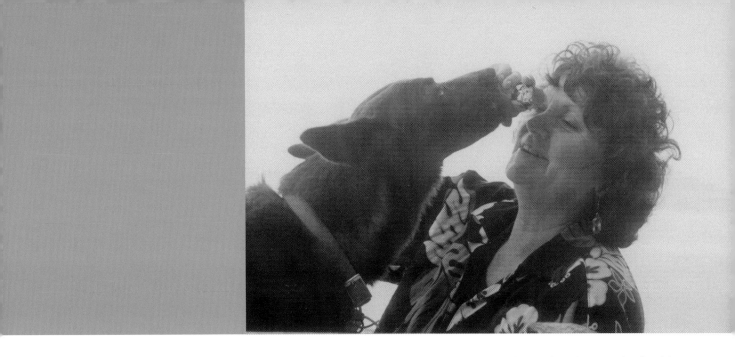

I'm sure there are still rabbits to chase in the wilder parts of these gorgeous parklands. Having a few leisurely days in between conferences made me miss you even more: I have to admit that I become quite pathetic and relate every conversation to dogs (oh yes and there was the dog movie on the plane . . . that improved my mood). Anyway, sitting in High Street and again longing for you, there came this woman with a cute Jack Russell-type-of-dog happily eyeing everyone around her. I must have looked so dog-bereft that she asked me would I hold her dog while she went to the shop next door. Would I hold her dog!! Of course I would (sorry preciosa, she was of course nowhere near as cute as you), and so I was in dog presence heaven for the next five minutes. The dog was really very nice, jumped on my lap and seemed to instantly know about you. She gave me a big lick when she departed with her friend — and I was seriously thinking about flying home right away.

But reason prevailed — conference papers need to be given, friends wait to be met: the whole hoo-ha-ha of people-centred living which allows little time and space for dogs. So the road show went on as did the pining — and I should say very clearly here that your other mother misses

you as much as I do — it's just that she contains it a bit more and doesn't moan and groan as loudly as me. I mean there are some pluses in having a doona all night long and not waking up freezing because one dog cleverly rolled on to all of it . . . ditto not being (almost) pawed out of bed by one dog needing to stretch . . . or waking up with a fright because the bed is shaking as one dog has wild dreams . . . but oh, what empty pluses compared with the lack of having the tail-wagging laughing exuberance of all of YOU affectionately convincing us that it really is time to wake up, time for a kiss, and (more importantly), breakfast and a walk.

Sometimes I wonder why it took me fifty years — half a century — to make the commitment to share my life with a dog. What pleasures missed out on, what incredible love relationships forgone. It's not that there were no dogs in my life; there was my mother's dog Bessie (and our cat Tiger); there was a little bitzer named Pichu who helped me study for my biology exams one long summer; and there were my best friend's successions of dogs from Gnocchi, the endearingly stubborn Beagle and her children Ravioli and Spaghetti to Mephista, the beautiful Labrador, and the many bitzers my friend smuggled into Switzerland from

Italy and Spain. I 'borrowed' them for walks and holidays and we had great times. But with living in different countries and travelling a lot for most of my life, having a dog just didn't seem the right thing to do. In fact I had begun living with a dog in the '70s — Risotto, one of Gnocchi's pups — and had to give him up after a short time when my plans unexpectedly changed and I left Switzerland. I still remember my deep heartache and the guilt I felt looking at his sad brown eyes . . . in spite of the fact that the home I found him was far better than living in a tiny fifth floor city apartment with an erratic woman quite unsure of where life would take her next. I think I learnt then, that starting a dog relationship is as serious — or even more so — than a human love affair; perhaps because the responsibility one takes on is greater and more one-sided: after all most adult human beings can fend for themselves however hard that may seem at the time, but what happens with a dog when her or his most beloved person(s) leave(s)? I often look at you and would give a lot to know where you came from and what sort of childhood you had: I'm pretty sure there was abuse because you trust uneasily. And why was such a beautiful dog found abandoned in Melbourne's streets and not claimed. Writing all of this makes me worry even more: I hope you know that we'll be back as we always are . . . but what if you don't? Or might it be that the missing is really mostly on my/our side and you are enjoying farm life to the hilt: not least of it the five kilometre walk a day — and the animal life, the ducks, horses and other dogs?

Be that as it may, reservations about travelling overseas and having too complicated lives all melted away in minutes when you came into our lives. A refugee from the Lost Dogs' Home, it was love at first sight: not that we found you ourselves but a friend did and introduced you to us when her dog Elvis didn't like you (his loss, our gain). Never mind all the trauma we've since had with you: from the first roll in fresh cow shit while travelling (and us smuggling you into a motel to wash off the mess in the shower) to the tick invasion which had us dreaming of these creatures who invaded our house on you; to the three months with a neck brace you had to wear to heal a broken neck after bashing into a car whilst excitedly eyeing

another Kelpie; and the almost drowning in a muddy creek that you slid into while chasing birds . . . (and I won't mention the barking at trams and motorbikes and occasional nipping at people's legs if for some unknown reason they appear to not exactly be your types . . .). Not for one moment have we regretted having you join us, and continuously delight in the myriad joys you bring us which far outweigh the little annoyances (yes my dear, there are some . . .) and the BIG pain of longing when we are apart — which brings me back to our trip.

After England, Switzerland came and went: not a bad place for dogs to live these days, restaurants and shops teeming with dogs of all sizes and types. Gone are the days from my childhood when 'no dog' signs appeared on shop and restaurant doors — my mother never went eating out again — they didn't last long as even Swiss people revolted against leaving their best friend at home. So back in are the pooches, lots of furry persons to pat and talk to wherever one goes. I think Australia could learn from them and change some of their dog-unfriendly behaviours.

Of all countries, Italy would have to be the dog paradise on earth. In the old towns whiffs of garlic sausages and salami float through the air. Dogs are everywhere, lying in the sun, running around in packs and having big smiles on their faces as they enjoy their dolce vita. There are also pictures of dogs in the museums and on the doors of the baptistery of San Giovanni by Ghiberti. (But they are not allowed in churches which is very canist.) As I sit and write and miss you so much (your other mother is being cultured and stands in the queue for the Uffizi), I'm joined by a brown dog with cute sticking-up ears and a piggy-like tail who must have been feeling my dog thoughts . . . or is it perhaps the second Bacio that has arrived with the next cappuccino — what else than indulge in chocolate can a missing-her-dog-girl do? So I will give her a small piece and imagine it's you. Meanwhile my darling, I send you oodles of pats and whoof whoofs, meaty smells and of course baci — lots and lots and lots of them.

With much love,

Your best friend R

*Before I realised the joys dog love can bring into one's life I used to be a boring academic and editor/author of eleven books (none of them, I ashamedly admit, are on dogs). I still care passionately about social justice for women, particularly in the area of reproductive and cyber technologies, but River makes me laugh much more these days and experience pure joie de vivre.*

# Confusion

Katharine Coles

Not even a decent pack. Just a pair,
though in small rooms they move to multiply.
A piebald dog. A dog with golden fur.
One who herds. One who gulps each fly
that buzzes her, cracking it in snap jaws.
Tonight, stretched out on oriental rugs,
a relaxation of dogs, dog tired; a doze
and snoring. Then absolution: a bliss of dogs,
a conflagration, a swarm, unspooled. Odd
dogs, chasing the invisible. Like me. A fool,
a blaze of dogs, a plight, an inspiration
of frenzied tongue and paw; two dogs in a pod,
mathematic. An education. Love's school
in wilderness, its muzzled exultation.

*Currently I teach and direct the graduate creative writing program at the University of Utah. My third collection of poems,* The Golden Years of the Fourth Dimension, *was published in August 2001 by the University of Nevada Press.*

# Sublime Beings

Mandira Sen

**Dogs have always** brought a sublime extension to my life. Who else but a loyal affectionate dog will match your mood to hers or his? Accept you as you are? My earliest memory of myself as an individual is at age three, playing with Jolly, my grandmother's dog. We were sharing a tangerine together. I would break off a piece and moisten it in the water from a waste pipe. The pleasure was short-lived as soon an aunt, shrieking with horror, prised me off to have my mouth rinsed. The adults attempts to keep Jolly and me apart did not work, and we were beloved companions for many a burning hot summer in Jaipur. Children do not feel the heat and Jolly and I would spend the late afternoons in the hot back veranda while the rest of the household barricaded themselves in cool dark rooms.

Jolly was a mongrel of medium size, with silky black-and-white fur, a bushy tail, and a round intelligent face. My grandmother too thought he was wonderful too but was more discreet in her affection. She made delicious pound cakes, the smell of which would draw Jolly to the threshold of the kitchen, which he would never cross. He would get the scrapings of the baking tin and also a piece. Jolly loved payesh, an ambrosial dessert made with milk, fragrant rice, molasses and raisins, not bearing the remotest resemblance to the lumpy English rice pudding that I was to encounter later, and which I believe was inspired by it. I think that my interest in cooking started from this time. It seemed a good idea to learn to cook what you wanted to eat and to share it with someone you liked made it even better.

The summer I turned six, Jolly was attacked by a rabid dog. An uncle managed to pull him to safety. I rushed out to cuddle him, offering what comfort I could, and as a result I too was given fourteen shots of the anti-rabies vaccine. People were surprised that I made no fuss. I had learnt that you must accept the consequences of your actions. Jolly died of old age a few years later. My grandmother had to be away during his final illness and telegrams went back and forth so that she could keep in touch. Sadly, he died before she returned. She never kept another dog.

My mother's dog Bibi was of a different temperament. If Jolly was engaged with life, Bibi had a serene detachment. She seemed to indicate that life's blows will come whether you get frantic or not, so why not let it all flow over you. She was a jet-black Labrador and loved her creature comforts, which were considerable. She ate whatever my parents ate, and as often, and when the vet indicated that this would have to stop, my parents were thunderstruck and uncooperative. They did try to get her to go for longer walks, but Bibi would simply sit down at a comfortable spot when she felt that she had had enough. Bibi had two litters and was a dutiful mother if somewhat detached. There is a lesson here for many middle-class Indian parents who tend to be interfering and clinging. Bibi preferred human beings and was very fond of me, though a bit suspicious that I might haul her off for more exercise. Bibi died suddenly when she was twelve. My sister Lipika was visiting our parents and she said that that day Bibi was climbing the stairs, perhaps in search of our mother, when she suddenly lay down halfway and died.

Kaju (cashew nut) was my mother's last dog. His ancestors were offspring of a Pomeranian and a Retriever, and the mixture was very handsome. Kaju was large like a Retriever, with silky white fur, two brown patches on his back near the tail and his ears were brown. He had a Pomeranian pink eye and a black-lined retriever one. He was two when my father died, and became fiercely protective of my mother, who said that he seemed to understand her grief better than anyone. When she died suddenly six months later, Kaju was shattered. He would whimper and search the whole house for her. He decided he would live with me. Amit, my husband, and I brought him from my mother's house in Delhi by train. Upset and forlorn, Kaju calmed down the moment he stepped into the car that was taking us to Old Delhi railway station. In his happiness, at the station, a beautiful colonial building, he wrapped his leash around one of the tall Corinthian pillars, entangling himself and me too in the process. The railways let us take him in a first class coupe and he enjoyed the journey. He took just a few hours to settle into our flat in Calcutta and win Amit's mother over. Some years later when Amit and I wanted to adopt a child and the social worker wanted to know why we thought we could be suitable parents, I wondered whether I could talk about Kaju and how he had accepted us and loved us the way we loved him.

Kaju established himself in the neighbourhood as a regal dog who had a lofty air with other dogs and humans. When owners of pedigreed dogs would say "nice looks for a mongrel", Kaju would look bored. He knew his self-worth. This is good strategy for humans too. When Amit's parents died after years of illness, we felt drained and weary. We wanted something that would bring hope and life. In December 1988, we adopted our daughter, Sucharita, then seven weeks. Kaju was shocked by her arrival but knew that he would have to be mature and curb his jealousy.

Less than two years later we adopted Arka, our son, also at seven weeks. By this time Kaju knew what to expect. He loved the children and was their friend and protector, rearing up on his hind legs if he thought someone was going to scold them. The children would fling themselves over him and he would endure it patiently, looking a bit sheepish as if to say, look what I have sunk to. When he died on 7 January 2000, he broke our hearts. I was away at a conference and still grieve that I was not there for him. The children buried him like a Pharaoh with his belongings around him, his beloved old blanket and winter coat.

Amit said that he could not go through this again. He had held Kaju in his arms till he died and closed his eyes. Some of our friends knew what it was like. The world, as we know, is divided between the besotted and those who are untouched. After some months, Sucharita and Arka said that having known Kaju all their lives, they could not live without another sublime being. They looked up an ad for Labrador puppies and one came home with us on 19 April 2000. He is called Badam (almond). He has filled the house with joy and no one cares about the trail of destruction he has unleashed on our material possessions. Like Bibi, he lives to eat and especially enjoys the doggy birthday parties he gets invited to.

A life without a dog is no life. A dog takes you out of yourself and gives you unstinting love, tells you the daily grind doesn't matter, but you do. For a stressed woman, a dog is the undemanding companion who makes the least demands, at the most wants to go for a walk, which is just what she needs too. Sublime Beings make life sublime and we, not the dogs, are the lucky ones in this relationship.

*Mandira Sen lives in Calcutta and is a publisher of two imprints:* STREE, *which publishes women's studies, and* SAMYA, *which publishes on social change, social protest and the construction of culture. She is married with two children and a Sublime Being called Badam.*

# Talking Toby

Anne Beech

**First, let's be clear.** I'm a cat person. Always have been, always will. So what's with the dog stuff?

Toby is a terrier — of sorts — and he isn't even mine. He belongs to my oldest friend, like me a woman of a certain age, whose house over the years has been filled with an almost unseemly variety of children and associated pets. Some pet residents have been long-lived, others (accidentally) all too fleeting (we remember and mourn the stick insect, the Australian tree toad, serial hamsters, the odd white rat — very odd, now I come to think of it — and a variety of other species whose brief moments on this earth were celebrated and marked in a series of shoe boxes, duly decorated and laid respectfully in the earth: her back garden is crowded).

Of the higher mammals (apart, that is, from her children and the husband), however, she has always maintained a dual allegiance: cats and dogs in what passes for harmony. The cats were kind enough to produce a small feline surplus, two of which, Baxter and Smudger, passed into my hands. The dogs were just the dogs. Quite big, quite hairy, very noisy. Lots of barking and wagging. I liked them well enough. But I was still a cat person.

Then Toby arrived.

He had all the standard attributes. Everything was more or less in the right place. But as well as bad breath, he had the canine equivalent of that certain something — not poise or elegance, to be sure, for he is a stranger to both — but SOMETHING.

We bonded almost from the start, once he'd learnt the full range of toileting skills and stopped throwing up. In my more mystical moments, I'm convinced that in an earlier life, we must have been related. He's messy, untidy, disorganised, over-enthusiastic, too loud and very undignified. This much we have in common. He finds mud ponds in arid deserts and rolls in them. I don't — but I understand. He comes when I call, which is more than anyone else I know is prepared to do. And he offers hysterical amounts of unconditional love. I reciprocate. We're the Mutt and Jeff of North London: absurd, unlikely, even ridiculous. We are both (in his case, quite literally) barking mad. My friend, her husband, their children and the cats — not to mention my own family — indulge me with a roll of the eye and a despairing sideways glance. There have been murmurs of treatment — even certification.

But Toby and I don't care. I am, as I have occasion to remind him and his family, his (unofficial) guardian, his step-mother and his great-aunt, all rolled into one — and the only person on the planet who laughs out loud when I look at him.

*Anne Beech is editorial director of the London-based progressive publisher, Pluto Press. She has worked in publishing for the best part of more years than she cares to remember or divulge. She lives in Stoke Newington, London, with Rab MacWilliam (a writer and publisher himself), two cats (inappropriately named after a former Arsenal striker and a Scottish footballing legend) and the occasional visit from Rab's son, Nick.*

# Irreconcilable Differences

Trudy Griggs

**I used to love him.** He used to be my companion. We walked together every weekday lunchtime during my study leave. I could confess to him, as to no one else, that the thesis was going nowhere and I was in deep trouble. He would trot contentedly beside me, a perfect listener, never interrupting with unwanted advice or passing judgement. And part of getting to live by the beach was for him, because he always loved it so when we brought him down here. He would canter to the cliff edge, tongue hanging out, grinning — if that's possible for a dog.

And now we are here, and I never walk him. These days I can hardly bear to touch him — or for him to touch me. He makes me feel unclean, and I want to erase the smell of him from my hands. He smells, slobbers, leaves hair and shit everywhere. I am afraid of the germs and diseases he could give my children. I am afraid that he could hurt them.

I'm talking about Jed, a lean, athletic, Blue Heeler-cross. He is almost ten, but still a powerful runner. He is at his best on the beach, tearing along at the edge of the water, ears flat, tongue hanging out, radiant with joy. Sometimes, he looks at me sadly with those soulful dog eyes. I feel sadness too, but no interest. I have moved on.

Jed came to us as a three-month-old foundling from the local RSPCA shelter. He needed calcium supplements to make up for the malnourishment he suffered before he was rescued. He was excessively timid and cowered frequently. We felt fiercely protective of him and committed to making him feel loved and safe. Years later, on a holiday, I missed Jed so much I felt like patting the wallabies that hung around our accommodation. Now, I look back on such feelings with disbelief. At some point I ran out of love and time for him. I do not want to give time to him, I don't regret not having time for him. I would just rather not have a dog; life would be much cleaner and more peaceful. My children fill up my life so much.

How did this happen? How did my boon companion become my bitter enemy? Somewhere, in the process of becoming a mother, I became unable to love or give time to our dog. I conceived a distaste for pets.

When I was pregnant, the childbirth books I consulted gave strong warnings about the dire consequences of contact with pets for the unborn child. I became afraid of Jed and of any dogs and cats; afraid of the toxins that could give my unborn child brain damage. I was afraid he would jump on my stomach in affectionate exuberance. I was too weak and exhausted to cope with his strength as he dragged on the lead. I resented being pregnant, sick and having to drive to playgrounds so my son could play outside, because Jed owned our outside space. I resented that my husband did not see what the problem was and left me to struggle with a barking dog waking up children I had only just got to sleep. So you can see how our relationship got poisoned. Jed became the whipping post for all my pregnant anguish. I thought I would be 'normal' again once I was no longer pregnant. But our relationship has never recovered, and I don't think it ever will.

I resent his colonisation of one yard. I resent the smell of his turds on the grass before they have been cleaned up. I resent having to feed him when my husband is away. I resent not being able to grow vegetables and herbs in the back yard because he reigns there. I resent all the unfenced and unleashed dogs in our town that make it hazardous for my children and I to go for a walk.

There are lesser evils too. I am tired of having to clean dog shit off my children's shoes. I am tired of us having to watch our feet when we walk, because dog owners are too lazy to clean up after their animals. I am tired of strange dogs bounding up to my children to lick their faces. Yes I know there are responsible dog owners and well cared for, lovable dogs. But I feel besieged.

Some people nurture their dogs as if they were small children. And I know women who have children and love their dogs just as much as they always did. They seem to be able to fit the dog in, somewhere along the spectrum of maternal solicitude. But for me, for some reason, it is a situation of mutual exclusion. It gets down to the children or the dog. Of course, therefore, I choose my children and Jed has become somehow 'illegitimate', unwanted by me at least.

Could I will to love Jed? Could I make him part of my life again? Once or twice I have made myself touch him, talk to him, squat down and rub his belly, speak softly and lovingly to him; the babbling nonsense you croon to a dog when you are just hanging out together, not really unlike the way you communicate with a very young baby. He always responds to any meagre attention I give him. His need for love is heart wrenching. How can he still respond after these years of indifference and sometimes outright anger? And yet he does. Such is my shame.

When I try to make an effort with him, it usually only lasts such a short time, because life crowds in again. I have a family, a job, a house to run, books to write etc. It is all too easy to forget him out in the back yard where I can't see him unless I specifically make the effort to go out there. And would it be better to leave him alone? What good does my inconsistent attention do? Isn't he better off with just my husband and the kids, because then the love is real, consistent and unconditional? But maybe to Jed, I am not such a termagant. Maybe a dog can be patient, understanding and loyal in ways that a human being cannot.

*Trudy Griggs would rather not take life too seriously but can't seem to get out of the habit. She is (at the moment) a part-time, temporary women's studies academic. She is married and has two pre-school children. She studies classical guitar and is embarking on part-time study to train as an editor. She would like to be a writer and lutenist but can't seem to find the time. With regard to dogs, Trudy has always been a serial monogamist. Jed is her third relationship.*

# Landscape Photography with Dogs

Coral Hull

the park is inside my dogs/ we hop out of
the holden on the edge of a picnic area/
ignoring the signs that prohibit dogs to
run without leashes/ kindi & binda release
themselves from the hot back seat to bound
through grasses wallaby related/ to vanish
above & below its tracks of dry waves as
though it were flowing/ past the flaky
grey bases of gums & old ten gallon drum
bins toppling over with drumstick wrappers/
the calm gradient of city parkland carries
their bellies along to the creek's hidden
edges/ i want my dogs to experience many
landscapes/ as dusk nuzzles up to my ankles
& to my dogs' noses turning damp & cold
fogging up the camera lenses/ they will
swallow or be swallowed by foreground
objects like barbecues or boulders/ they
will fade out over the round cupped edges
of hills into clouds that sink behind
themselves/ & appear like black specks on
the watery grey endings of dirty rainbows/
or disappear completely before emerging
again from forest darkrooms/ my dogs will
be unleashed so that they may contain the
landscapes inside themselves/ in australia
shadows of blue heelers, red kelpies &
photographers ignite along its huge crust
& vanish in an instant/ leaving behind
projected movement & dust-filled film
equipment/ & they may have left a passing
footprint in the sand/ & they may have left
a story for the rock

# Dogs & Gods

*Coral Hull is the author of thirty books of poetry, prose, and photography. Most recently is* Zoo *(poetry with John Kinsella) published by Paper Bark Press and* Inland *(photography) published by Zeus Publications. She is the Editor of* Thylazine: *http://www.thylazine.org*

in the city botanical gardens i placed myself in the company of unleashed dogs/ & as the dog turned its cheek to view the blue sky so my cheek was turned/ a shadow from its jaw bone cast across my cheek bone/ then a flock of tawny birds fluttered up from the grass & garden sprinklers/ & i soared within their flight & was on fire with their wings/ wings which cast a shadow before the sun/ & so i knew of birds/ their lighter spirits within the heavy breast of flight/ & so i became a flightless bird in the eyes of god/ what do dogs dream?/ in the rise & fall of breath/ a twitch of soft tan bristles, back pads trotting & a deep inside woof?/ do my dogs dream about me?/ if i were to disappear would i live on in the eyes of them?/ would i be reflected in the purpose of their wandering?/ in their legendary search for origins?/ i have heard that it is best for dogs to view the body as its spirit passes on/ so like anger or fear it can be passed through the heads & hearts of dogs/ & our emotions pass through dogs like the open hands of god/ they are not held nor trapped nor stored/ they are grasped & then gladly let go by the dog who gladly loves you/ if i were to commit self murder who would look after my dogs?/ they are the reason i exist/ i was going to cut my wrists/ but i had to get their dinner/ take them for a walk & scratch them under their chins

# The Dog Trainer
## Finola Moorhead

**The dog trainer sat** at the edge of the circle, seeming to brood. Every woman at the party had a dog and each of these bent its gaze longingly in the direction of the dog trainer merely to receive a returning glance or an imperceptible nod. After this exchange took place, the philosopher noted, the canines settled down and slept. Even the true-bred Shih Tzu curled on the lap of the nurse registered the presence and mood of the dog trainer. Various mixtures of hounds and working dogs comprised the mongrel majority. Tied to stake with a rope was the beloved puppy of the scientist, a Border Collie-Dalmatian-cross. Except for the dog trainer's Rottweiler, all the other dogs were without leads.

While the women behaved with jocular equality, their four-legged companions needed to establish some kind of hierarchy, a correctness, before they rested. They usually cruised around women in a group sneaking a pat or two from non-owners. Tonight they were very quiet and still. The dog trainer seemed burdened with message; a message she had no means to fully convey. Whatever was happening in the world of silence was beyond the fervent philosopher and she was inquisitive. Her clever articulation could find no words to prize it out. As she had no lively question to discern the menace, the nature of the truce, she moved.

The young film maker joined the circle. Her Scotch Collie was a dead ringer for Lassie. Pretty in the pointy-featured, tall, slim style of energetic youth, she gave truth to the old saying that dogs and their owners look alike. The company shuffled to accommodate the new arrivals. The Rottweiler now lay with her heavy head between parallel paws. The astrologer sat on the other side of the philosopher and began to talk about the stars. Ever inclusive, the philosopher engaged the astronomer in the discussion. The clear night sky untainted by civilised lights was moonless. They stood up pointing and soon began splitting hairs. The philosopher shrugged and glanced at the dog trainer, who was smitten. Her intense eyes had latched on to the bubbly young film maker as she expostulated about her project.

Dogs got up and sniffed and growled and went about the business of establishing the strength, age, sex and eventual position in their pecking order of the Collie. Even the pampered Shih Tzu leapt off the lap to prance his short-legged power. The black-and-tan, German, attack-trained bitch at the dog trainer's feet moved no more than her eyes amidst the general scurry and chatter.

"Gidday," chimed the philosopher to the film maker, "Where's your girlfriend?"

"Coming," she answered. "She decided to jog from the gate."

"This is Shiralee," the philosopher of life said.

The dog trainer having been introduced to the woman of her dreams with the professional and artistic skills she needed to offload her burden, spread her message, launched into speech. "You could come and live at my place and bring your camera. We can start with just a digital video and you can film me training. You can bring me any dog. Ask me any question. I reckon the end product would be at least an hour long, maybe two, but in that time, with editing and you know how to do all that, it could be brilliant. You would have to leave a lot on the cutting floor. I've thought about this for years. It's the only way. There would be hours and hours to edit. My place is okay as a background. There's a training yard with jumps and things and few houses in the distance. My home, I'm afraid, is a bit of a kennel, but you could sleep with me."

The sudden, collective silence glistened with the frisson of embarrassment as each woman listened, horrified at the social ineptness, anticipating the worst. The male Shih Tzu with the introduction of a new female to the camp was busily marking territory with his urine while the other dogs settled quietly near their owners.

"With the depth of my knowledge," she finished, rustily clearing her throat. "We'd have to have a wide distribution. It has to be an international hit."

The philosopher of life felt she should save the situation but she couldn't think how. The school-yard-bully-cum-teacher-cum-recent-convert to Buddhism said sarcastically, in a voice as soft as warm poo, "Why don't you try television?"

The young film maker missed the irony and grinned, nodding. "What a great idea," she said. She was of that age when daydreams have the emotional impact of an ordinary ambition. "Anything's possible, but I'd have to hire the equipment. From college . . ."

There was a commotion.

An over large Rhodesian Ridgeback-Weimeraner-cross had loped into camp, pounced on the Shih Tzu and was shaking him in her mouth as if he were a fluffy toy. His distressed yelping brought women shouting to their feet. The Ridgeback's owner finished her jog with a sprint and was puffingly imploring her dog to stop.

"Drop it, Dinah. There's a good girl. Here give it to me."

But the Ridgeback had played with teddy bears and animal slippers and sheepskins and took off, begging to be chased. Teasing the jogger and leading a pack of barking bitches, she ran about. The nurse became hysterical. The philosopher of life and most of the others endeavoured to control their own dogs by calling their names and grasping leashes. The Rottweiler stayed put. The dog trainer got up and stood in the path of the Ridgeback. When the bounding hunting dog was close enough, she simply grabbed her by the ears and lifted her off her front paws. The Shih Tzu fell from her jaws and slunk off simpering. Rather than being indignant or mortified, the Ridgeback, after her squeal of pain and surprise, sat in front of the dog trainer looking up and wagged her tail. The dog trainer met her eyes for a moment then turned away. Her signals were minute but clear, the philosopher noticed. The Rottie was now standing, eagerly watching, waiting. Casually her owner slipped off the choke chain, a second later she was over the Ridgeback-Weimeraner, smoothly growling. The sleek, long-legged, golden dog grovelled, first

circling, lowering her nose, putting her front half on the ground, then her back. Completely cowered, she rolled over. The other bitches either strained at their collars or dived in for a sniff of her belly. But that was too much. She leapt up and bounded away.

"Dinah!" commanded the jogger. "Come here."

Dinah came, panting with a wide, happy mouth, showing her teeth as if she were laughing. She looked very pleased with herself. Now the Rottie was free, she wandered into the dark, checking out all the scents and adding her own.

"How could you do that?"

The dog trainer responded with a sermon.

Order achieved by the control of the fittest among the canine contingent left most of its members quite content. Although, the philosopher noticed, Dinah's muscular back legs were still shuddering. Chaos, however, burst across the conviviality of the lesbians. An anarchy of righteousness, of individual love of individual creatures, of intelligent women having their say broke out in response to the lecture begun by the dog trainer.

"But that's totally fascist," whined the school teacher.

"But I don't want to suppress her nature," cried the jogger.

"I don't believe in the violence," stated the scientist.

"It is being exactly like the boys," opined the nurse. "Might is right, and all that."

The timbre of the dog trainer's voice expressed the stress and strain of knowing she was right and having to explain. She interrupted. She made a fist and impressed her points by thumping it into the palm of her other hand. She shouted. She became frustrated, and angry.

The dog lovers felt insulted. While some taunted, others became impassioned. Full-blooded argument ensued. The philosopher of life, with her eager curiosity, should have been entertained. But she was disturbed, saddened. The wall of silence she had wished to pierce had cracked like an eggshell and the contents were spilling out all over the place. The mystery of the outsider's mute communication with the canine world had transformed into a flurry of harsh words. The level of aggression was rising. There were no bones of contention, it wasn't a feud, nor was it warfare. There were not two sides, rather the expression of hurt feelings falling from lips like soft yolk.

The dog trainer stood. "Silence," she screeched. "Listen to me!" She used her hands in a flattening motion. "You're all full of bullshit."

But the other dog women were defensive, sincere and savage in their love. They did not like being told that their pets were unhappy. Not being tied up. Not being disciplined. Being spoken to as if they were human children, not being handled and cuffed with short, sharp pain if they erred. The philosopher felt the lesbians wanted to learn what they didn't know, but were not prepared to become different people, to differ from their normal warm, cuddly personalities. They needed to express the huge gratitude to their dogs for the amazing loyalty and companionship, for the joy they gave them. The dog trainer seemed to challenge them with her firm methods, but it was her manner that really got their backs up. Raised their hackles, as it were.

The school teacher jumped up and thrust her chin in her face and began to murmur threats.

"Don't get too close," said the dog trainer. "Just don't."

The philosopher suddenly saw why she

should be obeyed. The Rottweiler was waiting for one more aggressive move against her mistress. Her black coat shone with brown light from the fire on the lines of power packed onto her stocky frame. She eyed the situation, ready to lunge in a flash. The dog trainer did not want to step away from her argument, from making her point, but she had a killing machine dedicated to guarding her to control. Someone else had to put a stop to the bullying, the philosopher realised. One more misunderstood sign and the dog would attack. The school teacher was not aware of the tension she was creating, or, indeed, the danger she was in. The young film maker was.

"Okay, calm down," she said.

The philosopher handed the dog trainer her choke-chain. The leashed Rottie looked even more threatening, and the school teacher took a step back. All the words in the world could not describe the essence of the dog trainer's truth, certainly not the dog trainer herself. Not only had she the gift of understanding the species, she had studied and practised, sacrificed herself, given up money and relationships, attended courses and trials, to extend her expertise. And after all that there was still more. Yet in the face of what she knew, she felt humble. What had been a lecture, a sermon to the others, was an expression of her quest, her findings. She sagged and the Rottweiler bitch stood tall and protective beside her. The philosopher realised the wall of silence she encountered and wanted to break down not a wall but silence itself. Some things that can be done cannot be said. Or talking can only mean anything in the context of doing. The dog lovers' dogs still looked at the Rottweiler's owner as if she were some sort of deity to them, with fear and respect. She could command their attention even though she seemed diminished in her personal carriage. The film maker's eyes were similarly bright and

alive to the next change in atmosphere.

The party settled like water in a swimming pool, quickly. Chattering, murmuring, drinking. The philosopher addressed the young film maker, saying, "I really do think you should do that film. At least get video footage."

"Yeah, so do I. I reckon it'd be great."

The dog trainer picked up her bag and flung it over her shoulder. She was leaving. The pull of her mission in life made her hesitate. "Here," she said, as she felt into her hip pocket, "Take my card." She gave one from a small stack to the film maker. Then turned away.

"May I have one, too?" requested the philosopher of life, putting out her hand.

"Sure, why not?"

She watched the outsider and her bitch walk into the night. No 'heel', no 'come', no word was said, no action, no eye contact. The Rottweiler and the dog trainer moved as one.

*Finola writes: As a kid I was always wandering around with my dog, Tatts. There were times when he saved me and others when he embarrassed me. He savaged others, especially men in uniform. When TV came and I saw the show, I wished for a Rin Tin Tin. Anäis, my Rottie, was highly trained, kind and intelligent, she was ten when she died of liver cancer. My present dog is called Rin Tin Tin, though I didn't name her and took her over when she was three. She's a Blue Heeler, and suits my bush lifestyle as I have to get cattle off the land a lot. She's ten now and she is always with me, but when she's not, it's not hard to find someone to look after her as she is an obliging and affectionate bitch.*

# Django

## Susanne Kappeler

**By anybody's standards,** I am a cat person. If today there is a dog in my life, this too is due to a number of cats.

When I was asked by the animal refuge in my neighbourhood if I would work with a wild dog, it was not because of my experience with canines (I had none), but because I was known to be willing to invest a lot of time to save a cat from euthanasia. And that was what was needed now, someone to work intensively with this dog who would otherwise have to be put down.

Django had been brought to the refuge by the police. How they had managed to get him into their van remains a mystery, but they certainly did not dare take him out when they arrived — this fell to the refuge's sixteen-year-old trainee, sent in to put a collar around his neck. Once outside, it proved impossible to walk him to the kennels and he had to be carried by all available staff, the trainee getting bitten on the shoulder for her efforts. After that, no one managed to do much more with him, the vet having had to resort to an anaesthetic to be able to vaccinate him, and to replace his collar with a flight-proof metal chain — a so-called 'choker' or, as the French put it, a 'strangler'.

Beth, a refuge worker, took me to his kennel. I saw a lovely black dog, part Labrador, part Setter, gyrating. When we went inside, he went to the outside run of his box, when we went out there, he went inside. He did not look at us, but simply ran his circles with concentration. Impossible to get his attention, the only sign that he was aware of our presence was his flight into the part of the kennel where we were not. I was distressed at his distress, and terrified.

Beth asked me not to look into his eyes — I needed to be told basics. Kneeling down and looking to the ground, she soothingly called him. Django turned round and round, apparently impervious. Round and round, round and round. I was holding my breath, while Beth heaved a deep sigh: was it justifiable to torture an animal in this way 'for his own good'? And *was* it for his good?

Finally she asked me to block the way to the other half of the box. Cornering him, she extended her hand to touch him. He stopped in his tracks, crouched and pressed against the fence, a posture of terror and stationary flight in face of the inevitable. He gave no sign of having been touched, he was as if hewn in stone, petrified. Her caressing hand worked its way slowly up to his neck, finally snapping the lead on. It was a heavy metal chain — it had to be, any other he bit off within seconds. I took him on our first walk.

Terrified myself, I tried to soothe us both by talking to him. Walking, he continued to gyrate, drawing circles around me clockwise. I was told a dog had to walk on my left. I clung to my end of the lead, talking. The slightest rattle of the chain sent him flying; if I trod on a dry branch or waved a fly away, he jumped a yard. When I sat down for a pause, he went from left to right the length of the lead and back again, restless.

I could not but think of what he might have experienced. Some

thought he had lived in the wild all his life, others that he must have been very badly mistreated but, in any case, his behaviour was judged 'untypical'. If I didn't know anything about dogs, I knew something about abuse. It seemed obvious to me that the most important thing was not to be violent in any way: not to force him, not to impose on him, showing him that I was not going to do anything against his will. It is how I relate to cats and in fact to anyone.

This meant that I ran up straight against established Knowledge About Dogs, the dominant theory about how to construct the relationship between 'man and dog'. The parallels with patriarchal lore about 'how to deal with women' are disconcertingly obvious: a scenario of dominance and submission, based on a structure of power and dependency. "You have to show him who is boss. A dog needs to surrender to you. Be tough and rough, a jerk on the lead here, a stern word there. Be sparing and above all entirely strategic with your caresses. No more talking than is necessary: give orders (once), and praise if they are obeyed. In case of disobedience, punish him. If he seeks your attention or reassurance, ignore him altogether. It's the only language a dog understands: he needs to be dominated and he wants to submit to you."

The dog experts around the refuge didn't hold back with good advice, nor with hints that they thought me too soft, not assertive enough, too hopelessly indulgent. To say nothing of the menacing predictions about the dog's future development: if he lost his fear, his real problems would emerge, he might bite, hunt, kill.

Things got worse when, one night, he managed to slip out of his collar. Putting a lead on to a bit of chain hanging from his collar had been difficult enough, a daily ritual governed by mutual fear. Tying a collar around his neck or slipping one over his head was out of the question: a hand approaching his head made him recoil and, if it came too close, snap. I spent a week sitting daily in his box, letting him draw his circles around me. I talked to him and I contemplated the difficult task of imposing a collar on him without imposing on him. I resented it as much as he did. Slowly, he began to let me touch him on the side of his body, at arm's length, or to rub his ears from behind so he need not see it. Yet approaching his head frontally was out, to say nothing of two hands at a time.

I started playing with a piece of string with a tiny snap lock on one end, having abandoned the chain lead and collar. I showed it to him and waited for inspiration. I threw it down in front of him so he could sniff it or bite it to bits if he wanted to. He continued to gyrate. I playfully threw it again, when I suddenly realised that he was showing me how to do it. For he neither winced as I threw it nor as it touched his body, sliding over his back. So I continued to throw it across his body or neck, eventually taking both ends and snapping the lock around the other end, a yard or so from his head. He watched, unflinching. And he rose to come with me as I gently pulled the sling towards his neck. We went out again, walking.

He had got used to my voice and refrained from biting the string through. He let himself be caressed by my voice and increasingly by my hand. As I sat down for a pause during our walks, he no longer yo-yoed at the end of the string, but stood in front of me sideways, out of reach, then inching closer to get to arm's length. The stroking sessions got longer and longer, but he never sat down, his legs ever ready just in case. And he never accepted any goodies, which eliminated the traditional method of dog education by means of recompenses. He was unbribable.

The dog experts watched. "It cannot go on like this, you've got to go in, snap the lead on and out. And he needs a proper collar and lead." I tried to tie a collar with a buckle around his neck — no way. Finally, I put a noose-collar around the string which served me as lead, lifted the latter and let the collar slide over his head. No sweat. He looked at me expectantly. The collar was on, but it was impossible to pull the ring on it to fix a lead on. As soon as a hand approached, he began to snap, though early enough not to snap my hand. I desisted.

The dog experts were itching to have a go, to show me how it is done. And eventually they did. Yet none of them managed to take him out of his kennel, snappily or otherwise, unless they went in in twos, cornering him. I took him out my way, with the string, and brought him outside the compound, where one woman wanted to snap a lead on to his collar, determined not to give in. "It's very important that if you want something,

you see it through. Never give up, or he'll know that he has his way instead of you having yours." I looked the other way. I heard a violent scramble. I just saw the metal lead slap over his head and then her bleeding hand proffered to me. He had bitten her.

While a colleague bandaged her hand, Django let me put on the lead. He sat by my side. I was shaking, I detest violence. And I was terrified on a different account: I knew that if a dog was known to bite, he might be put down.

The woman who got bitten had the grace to recognize it as her fault and decided not to tell anyone. Grudgingly, she agreed that force was no use in this case. And Django, it seemed to me, after that decided to stick to me and to trust me bit by bit. Together, we figure out ways how to do difficult things like putting on leads and taking them off again, it getting easier by the day. And although he is considered a dog with no expression, he is beginning to show his joy. He approaches me like my cats, of his own free will, the more confidently so as he knows I will not take advantage. He has adopted me, and although I am a cat person, he is soon coming to live with me where he will continue to have his way.

*Susanne Kappeler lives in the French part of Switzerland, working as a freelance teacher, writer and translator and volunteering at the local animal refuge. She has six resident cats, two from Morocco (where she used to live), two belonging to a Swiss friend, a former mother cat from the refuge who raised her young at Susanne's house and a young blind cat adopted at the refuge.*

# To Kill a Mockingbird: Something Too Precious

Tara Middleton

**I was twenty-five** when Scout allowed me to be her partner and companion for life. An abnormally tiny puppy, half the weight of her brother and sisters, she instantly aroused a nurturing instinct I'd never expected in myself. We started a love affair I'd been craving since early childhood.

I'd wanted a dog in my life, as long as I could remember. Growing up, I adopted neighbours' and friends' dogs for hours at a time. I loved holding their attention with a mixture of gentle pats, strong scratches, teaching them new tricks, or just sitting with them holding their paws and adoring the silky softness of the hair on their ears, or the gaze of their eyes. Shape and size didn't matter to me because I admired their one common trait — their absolute loyalty to their human partner. No matter how much attention I lavished on them, they deserted me when their human called, instantly bounding away. Those obliging borrowed dogs were my first childhood lesson in loyalty.

It was the simplicity of pure devotion that drew me to dogs. I admire the innocent canine ability to attempt to befriend everything. Their utter glee in meeting new people unfettered by social boundaries of class, attire, gender, odour or dress size. Anything different is interesting and worthy of inspection, but their pure love is never divided from one special person in their lives. And they love that one person with complete and unconditional naiveté. It's a quality I aspire to and something I want to be reminded of daily — a lesson that can never be too often demonstrated. And so when I was finally independent and in a position to share a home, I sought a furry friend.

Scout immediately taught me there was more than mutual adoration required for a canine-human friendship to succeed. Understanding and respect were necessities, too. As a baby puppy, her need for companionship was so deep that she woke miserable four and five times each night for the first few weeks. Patient with her need to grieve the separation from her family, we rocked each other to sleep on the floor in the laundry. And when she woke at midnight (and 2 a.m., 4 a.m., 5.40 a.m., 6.30 a.m.) with toilet needs, we'd run out the side door and dance about on the wet grass until she found the right spot. My feet grow numb now with the memory of Melbourne's winter charm.

When finally ready to accept she needed to sleep outside in her kennel, I found myself pining at the window looking for a glimpse of her shiny black nose and furrowed brow. There were nights she empathised and we comforted each other with a compromise as I crawled inside her kennel and stayed with her until she slept.

As she grew, we explored the neighbourhood from corner to creek. I, through new eyes, Scout through inquisitive ones. We battled periods of refusing to walk when I was too tired from work or she frightened by a swooping magpie. We faced an even longer period of not being able to walk fast enough to the point of Scout's tongue turning blue from pulling, and my face glowing red from exertion. Two years later it's still something we debate at the beginning of every stroll. But we've found middle ground where I recognise she wants a walk, and I need one. Not only for the exercise, but for the pleasure of feeling the day melt away behind me, and getting the opportunity to see the world through those liquid brown, inquisitive canine eyes, and perpetually wriggling nose. Grotty commuter traffic forgotten, boring backyard forgiven. Just us and what we discover.

Even with the tender and affectionate memories of our beginning, it is the present I adore the most. We walk and run together as a team revelling in each other's commitment — absolute loyalty to the other for life. Scout wears a soft red collar for our fun walks. No time for formal training on our long treks about the neighbourhood. When it's safe the lead is unclipped, and Scout roams nearby. Her own rule seems to be that all exploring through puddles, fields, mud and long grass are only perfect if I'm right behind her. And if I lag more than 100m, she gallops back towards me with ears flopping, coat rippling, an expression of absolute, pure, unadulterated joy at the sight of me.

I think she understands the tears in my eyes express the same love in return.

*Tara Middleton, 27, has a Bachelor of Science, and works as a sales management professional for an international consumer goods company. She lives in Victoria with her two-year-old Golden Retriever bitch, Scout. They're members of the Victorian Golden Retriever Club, and the Geelong Obedience Dog Club where they train towards titles of Companion Dog, Agility Dog, and Professional Hair Shedder Dog.*

# Ayla, the Fur Person

Regula Langemann and Suna Yamaner

**Almost a millennium baby,** I was born on 5th of January 2000 in the suburbs of Zurich/Switzerland and am now a little bit more than a year old. I don't remember much of my earliest puppyhood. I was just playing, racing around, kissing, eating and sleeping with my four other Border Collie sisters and brothers. I have a black coat with long hair and a white bunch around my neck. That's why my name is Ayla, which in Turkish means moonshine. I love my name.

My paws are white with grey spots. Also I have a few spots on my nose but, unfortunately, I can't see them. My two mothers have told me though.

They wanted a girl from the beginning. At first I was a bit worried that they might take my much larger and rowdier sister. Already then I knew how to get them, looking sheepishly and wild yet at the same time lovable and intelligent. That worked and has been working since. It was the right match from the start. They are crazy about me and I am crazy about them. We do find each other gorgeous, nuts, funny and very playful.

When I came home to them I was just eight weeks old and full of mischief. That of course hasn't changed, but I don't tear at the fringes of the rug anymore. They didn't like that. I am never bored though. You should see my basket: I have everything from a stuffed pig called Babe — you may remember the movie — to a small duck that gwägwägs three times in a row when I push it on its belly, to a squeaking plastic sausage and a bumble bee with a string to pull at. Plus, I know everyone, including my huge colleague, the velvet lion, personally by their name.

Besides, I have a myriad of different balls in all sizes and colours. Balls are my absolute favourite. Balls are so fascinating that I forget all I have learned when I see children play with a football. How can I let them know that I can play soccer myself? They don't believe it till I prove it to them and then they scream with joy and excitement.

And then there are the frisbees, at least seven different kinds. My favourite is the one that flies as far as sixty metres so I can run like the wind and jump far into the air to catch it. It is actually made for humans, not really for dogs. Being a fur person though, I often like people more than other dogs. Next to all our wonderful people friends who come to my office and to my house, I do have at least six really fabulous fur-person friends. When our mates have to work too much or go out to concerts, we visit each other regularly. There we get to play wildly, race around the furniture, jump on the sofa and the beds and run up and down the stairs. After such days I am usually so exhausted, I can hardly manage to walk up to my sleeping place. Then my mothers carry me on their back and I am very grateful.

Often I can hardly wait till my two buddies wake up so we can go outside. Sometimes they want to sleep in, especially when they went dancing the night before. I then throw myself on their bed, wag wildly with my tail and lick their faces till they are wide awake.

We have so many games together when we go out into the woods and across the meadows in the morning. We practice all kinds of wonderful tricks. Each fallen stem, each bench, each fence gives me the opportunity to practice agility skills and general fitness. Paired with high speed, high jumps, dexterity and imagination, this makes for a wonderful beginning of our days.

For my first birthday my two playmates gave me ten private training sessions for circus and public events. My trainer, a woman who is the manager of an adventure zoo, has been running circus shows with five cats, Scottish Highland cows, minihorses, minipigs and chickens. She is absolutely floored about my high work motivation and eagerness. We will eventually create a show which would give me the opportunity to earn my own food.

My spiritual development is daily challenged by the two cats who have had green cards long before I was born. Particularly with one of them I get to learn the divine love for all beings despite the fact that she often teases and scares me intentionally. My life would be paradise if only the vacuum cleaner wouldn't be so popular in Switzerland. The stupid sound as well as the hot smelling air that blows in all directions scares me to death. Also the fireworks could have stayed in China where they came from also.

I see that we are getting ready to go home, where we will all play some more before we call it a day. So I stop here with my story although there would be so much more to tell. We truly enrich each other's lives in a most beautiful way and so we are very happy and grateful for each other's presence and joy. 🐾

*Suna Yamaner (right): born 14 April 1957 in Ankara/Turkey. Daughter of a Central Anatolian Watchdog and a Central Swiss Noble Retriever. No family trees available on both sides. Migration to Switzerland at the age of four. Obedience 1 to 23 successfully completed. Most recent diploma as a Trainer for Non-violent Communication.*

*Regula Langemann: born 14 October 1956 in Zurich, Switzerland. Daughter of a mixed breed Alpine Toller and a Giant Cardigan Corgi with a very complex family tree. Freelance emergency help and therapy dog in different disaster areas such as California and downtown Zurich. Most recent diploma as an agility facilitator and conflict resolution.*

# Kuri  Susan Rhind

**The dog poked a blunt nose** into the pile of sausage scraps lying by the fire. E kuri, the woman smiled, that's good, eh? You like it, dog? I give you everything I got. Better than a husband, eh? She emptied the bucket over the embers and the steam hissed swiftly. The dog gulped down the rich gobbets, yawned, stretched and ambled over to the hollow in the pine needles where, curled together, they had slept the previous night. Round and round he pawed and trod, and settled with a gusty sigh of content.

The morning heat soaked through the branches and the cicadas sang ceaselessly from the lupins throwing their flowers to the sun. E kuri, said the woman, we can't sleep now. We go fishing. For our tea. She looked at the surf line with a seasoned eye, out to the curve of the horizon and back again over the green stretches of the water. Kahawai for tea. Or maybe snapper. Depends what bites. Come on, dog. And together they stepped out into the morning leaving the nest of pine needles, empty for now, warm from the dog's body. The steaming embers guttered into silence and the beach laid itself open at their feet.

The dog paused, sniffing the million scents of the day, and leaped over the marram grass, shouting and shining in the sunlight. Down down down to the water, flinging his limbs as he raced before the wind, scattering flocks of gulls wheeling and turning, springing arched in the clear air. The woman tied her line to a log lying in the sand and leaned against it as she watched the dog dance and run, pirouetting, turning. His movement pleased her. She forgot her line, and it twitched lazily in the waves.

Back he came, returning as always to his source of food, his warmth and his shelter. He pushed at her arm to rouse her, to share his joy in the wide beach and the sandhills. All right dog we go. We get our kaimoana later. We walk, you and I, eh?

We two together. Always together. You, dog, you're better than a family.

And together they went down the beach towards the distant hills and the village lying in scattered pieces below them. You can't really see the houses, she thought, it looks like a shell heap where the fishermen left it long ago. But I like my line best. You know what you're getting if the tide's right. You can't tell with shellfish these days, e kuri. Sometimes they're rotten.

The dog erupted from the surf and ran to the woman where she waited in the shallows. He braced himself, splay-footed, and shook a torrent of salt water over her. With all this beach to shake on you have to do it all over me, dog. Go and chase the gulls. Find a stick, you wet bugger.

Barely pausing for breath the dog turned, his attention caught by a passing tumbleweed running ahead of the wind. And he ran, skimming the surface as he fled through the marram grass, back again to the beach through the strands of blackened seaweed and the pale driftwood that had known a hundred nights in the sea. Away and up and over after his spinning tumbleweed, or myriads of other tumbleweeds running under the sun, far into the distance where the long curve of the beach met the arc of the sandhills and the two merged into one.

Her fishing line abandoned, the woman watched him go. She lay on the shore looking at the waves breaking and the wheeling flights of godwits rehearsing their coming migration, a sudden launching and the great spiral of birds overhead. Then the equally swift collapse of the turning helix into a huddle on the sand, the calls and squawks, the shuffling for position, and after it the long lonely cry heralding the coming departure. You'll go soon, she thought. But you'll always come back. Maybe battered, maybe tired, but you'll return. You'll never leave us for long. That's what I like about birds, you face the wind. Not like my dog, who runs after it like the tumbleweed. My dog. She smiled.

And then she slept while the sun moved slowly through the long afternoon and dropped towards the sandhills. Endlessly, pointlessly, the tumbleweeds raced, coming from nowhere and vanishing along the sand where the shattered light jangled in the silence. As she woke she moved her hand to feel for the warm bulk beside her. The sand was cool and unresisting. That's odd, she thought, he'll be hungry and I haven't got my line in. She stood up and looked along the beach where the shadows had begun to lie, at first curiously and then with a growing foreboding. Kuri, e kuri, she called, and only the wind called back to her. She ran out of the sandhills to the edge of the sea. The lamps in the village came alive one by one as if in answer, each doll's house a single point of light a hundred miles away. Kuri, kuri, she called as she ran towards the lights, where are you gone? And the wind blew her words, uselessly, with the spinning tumbleweeds into the gathering dusk. O god don't leave me you bastard you wet shaking bastard o god I can't see. Where are you gone, kuri, kuri?

But no answer came as she ran up and down calling, crying, into the long grass through the piles of driftwood out again to the sea and along the beach through the falling night. She stopped. Perhaps he will come if I wait, she said, and she shouted again to the sea. And slowly, slowly, she began to move in smaller circles, and dropped on her knees. The village gathered the cloak of the night about it and settled to sleep under the high incurious stars, and still she knelt. He is gone, she whispered, he is gone. He will not come back like the spring birds. He is gone.

She began to weep, at first noiselessly and then in great karanga as she called the flood of pain into her heart. Aaiee aaiee kuri, where will you sleep this night? Come to me, kuri. Aaiee, my heart is breaking and I am alone. You are gone, and I am alone. And at last she sat motionless, her arms wrapped around her knees, holding her body together as the clouds moved across the face of the moon. Aaiee, she cried, kuri, kuri. The lamps are gone out, and you are not returned. The fires of day are done and the darkness has begun and it will never end. You are gone. You are gone.

And the sea stirred restlessly as the stars went out and the voice on the beach cried once and was still.

The first light of dawn touched the water as the tumbleweeds began their endless dance, and still she sat alone in the river of her grief. No sound came, not a voice, not a movement. Only the dull thud of the waves breaking below her.

Only the seabird's call.

The seabird's cry.

And the wind blowing in the long grass.

*Susan Rhind lives in Northland, New Zealand, where she teaches music. She has been a schoolteacher, labourer, university lecturer and public servant, and has won awards in several short story competitions. Throughout her life she has cared for many very independent (and often scruffy) mutts and loves them all dearly.*

60

# Nipa
## Meg Lees

**My dog Nipa** has been a devoted companion for nearly fourteen years. She is, according to the people we bought her from as a pup, a Fox Terrier-Chihuahua-cross.

Technically she is my daughter Tegan's dog — a present back in 1987, but she soon became very much part of the family. In latter years Tegan has taken on a much bigger friend, Ridge, and Nipa has become my constant companion whenever I go where dogs are allowed.

Ridge is a Ridgeback and Bull Mastiff-cross but his size, at least thirty kilos more than Nipa, is no problem for her, she stands her ground in games and moves him out from in front of the fire when she wants to.

Nipa is up and ready of a morning, waiting by the door to see if it is a day when she can come with me. Whenever I am in my Adelaide office she spends the day keeping me company, disappearing from beside my desk only when someone else has lunch or rustles a sweet wrapper. She insists on coming shopping on a Saturday morning — even though she has to stay in the car for much of the time.

I don't think we have ever driven to Mallacoota without her. On the way over, when we stay in a motel rather than camp, she happily sleeps in the car. Once at our mud brick cottage, she is at her second home and anxious to go to the beach. Trotting along a beach is one of her favourite activities; she has always enjoyed the water.

She gets bored when I am gardening, usually choosing to find a comfortable spot where she can sit in the sun and watch from a distance. As a pup she was taught not to chase birds so they are allowed to come and go — looking through the weeds and freshly turned dirt.

Christmas 1999 holidays she came down to Tasmania with me. Travelling over on the Devil Cat in high seas for several hours longer than usual was not much fun but she bounded out on arrival just happy to have company again. While I went bushwalking or kayaking she stayed in kennels, or with kind caravan park operators who had secure yards.

As a child I had a golden Cocker Spaniel, indeed one of my first memories is of Beauty hiding on the porch in a thunderstorm. Thunderstorms are one of the few times that Nipa becomes irrational and difficult to calm or control. She has to find an enclosed dark spot — a cupboard or under a bed — as soon as she hears the first rumble. Often she will tell us when a storm is about. The few times we have lost her are when, in her search for a spot where she can't hear the thunder, she has got out and run for miles during a storm.

I miss her company the many days I am away from home, but always feel very welcome and pleased to be back when she greets me at the door with great enthusiasm.

People who have never had a canine companion have missed a marvellous experience.

*Meg Lees joined the Democrats in 1977 and became a Senator in 1990. In 1991 she became Deputy Leader, in 1997 was elected Leader and at the 1998 election she led the party to a record number of nine Senators. Meg is a former Physical Education teacher. In her spare time she enjoys bushwalking, canoeing, and reading.*

# Sully's Eyes Angelika Aliti

**He is a face with flapping ears** behind bars. Eyes without hope, eyes without expectations. The confidence to be alive still unbroken, but the eyes — hopeless, dull. For over a year I have been passing his cage when I go for a walk with my dog Tipsy. Summer, winter, day and night he is squatting in a small square of mesh wire that contains a dog pen, not isolated. Exposed to rain and snow, sun and heat. Sully with the eyes of despair.

I immediately knew that he hadn't always been a caged dog. Something about him told me that he had seen better times. There were periods when I chose a different route so I didn't have to see him. Other times I visited him regularly although Tipsy didn't like the look of the kennel as it reminded her of her own time behind bars when she was at the dog pound.

Yesterday I'd had enough. I passed his cage and saw him freezing and trembling in the cold winter air. So I took him with me. I left a note for his owners as I live far too close for there to be a chance that my deed would not have been noticed. On the way to my house Sully had the most wonderful olfactory sensations. He couldn't stop sniffing. At home it took him only about half-an-hour to cope with this big excitement. After that his eyes lit up. They twinkled and radiated the whole day as he said hello to the cats, discovered my snoring pig in the stable, got to eat the

best cat food, as I played with him, as Tipsy raced him around on the meadow, as we all went for a walk.

Sully with the radiating eyes. When we passed his cage he turned his head away. His eyes went on glowing until the evening when his owners came and demanded to have their dog returned. Nothing would move them to give him to me. They left with Sully.

However, this is not the end of the story, just the way things are right now. Dogs have their own magic and so have I. Sully will not remain in his prison. He and I have something that his owners don't know: the capacity to love. Love works magic and Sully will be with me because I want his eyes to radiate, shine, glow, laugh. His owners have given me permission to take him for walks as often as I wish. This gives me hope as it means that on another level, on the level of energy, they have already agreed to a change of dynamics from holding on to letting go. My next task is to concentrate my strength so that they no longer wish for Sully to return to them. Only persistence will succeed and the magic of one small step at a time. How Sully is going to work his dog magic now that he knows where he can go I don't know. When you read this story of Sully and me please send him and all caged dogs in this world your love. They need it.

P.S. Five minutes after I emailed this story I got a call from Sully's owners. They told me I could have the dog. They asked me to take him for a walk and not to return him. I can hardly believe it. I really think love is the best magic and cannot be countered. Early tomorrow morning I'll get Sully and after that a few beings on this planet are going to be very very happy together.

Translated by Renate Klein.

*In her youth, Angelika Aliti studied social work and worked as a journalist and actor and at one time had her own travelling theatre troupe. She then became a feminist therapist and practised in Vienna, Austria. She is a best-selling author of crime fiction and non-fiction books on women and myth, and women and power including* Mama ante portas! *She lives on a remote farm in the Austrian countryside with lots of animals including her pig friend as well as dogs and cats.*

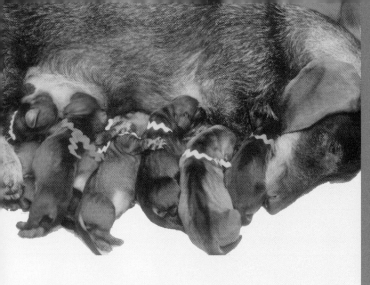

# First There Were Four

Cristina Biaggi

**One Saturday morning** our Dachshund Dandelion's temperature dropped, a sure sign that labour would start within twenty-four hours. All of Saturday she appeared restless and walked around the house with a worried, anxious expression on her face. Around eight o'clock in the evening she began to pant and mild contractions started. She chose the location for the birth of her puppies: our guestroom bed (the most comfortable in the house). We stayed up all night, with the contractions and the panting continuing but nothing happening. We fed her small meals of goat's milk and raw organic honey to keep up her strength and help her milk come in. At six on Sunday morning the contractions ceased and Dandelion fell asleep.

All of Sunday Dandelion stayed in the guestroom, periodically wandering around the house looking anxious. We took her on several walks to try to help the labour start. At around seven in the evening, the contractions began again and at eight o'clock the first puppy made his appearance, feet first. It was a difficult, intense birth; I had to literally pull the puppy out, worrying the whole time that I would break his tiny legs or his fragile back if I pulled too hard. Pattie was coaching Dandelion, telling her to "push, Dandelion, push". Dandelion seemed in an altered state, her eyes were huge and glazed, her body was rigid. Finally the puppy emerged. Giglio, an 11 oz. male. She gazed at it with an amazed uncomprehending look and for the first

few moments did nothing. I freed the puppy from its sac and cut the umbilical cord. Finally Dandelion sprang into action and started licking the puppy and cleaning up the afterbirth. We cheered her and felt ecstatic with joy! We were finally in the process of birth.

An hour-and-a-half later Coriopsis, another 11 oz. male, emerged, again feet first. Then Hillary arrived, a 10 oz. female, head first. Silvius William appeared next, a sweet small 9 oz. male, again feet first. Our son Aidan had assisted at two of the births, tenuously at first and then with compassionate interest. His brother Noah saw the fifth puppy born and seemed a bit freaked out by it. It was past midnight and we thought the end was near when Miosotis, another 10 oz. female emerged. So we had five puppies and thought, "surely it must be over". We congratulated Dandelion and left her looking much more peaceful and suckling her new brood. At long last we offered ourselves the luxury of a glass of wine and started announcing the births via email to our friends. We noted the interesting difference that all the males had emerged feet first while the females had been born head first. We commented on the fact that Hillary had a short crooked tail and the deep significance of that. We laughed a lot and then decided to go and see how Dandelion was doing. As we walked toward the 'birthing chamber' we mused, "what if she has another puppy?" If she did we should call it Codicil and so much for the medical profession and their sonograms — an earlier sonogram had told us that Dandelion was pregnant with four puppies.

When we walked into the room all was not well. Dandelion looked terribly worried, another puppy was on its way: its body was out and its head still inside her. We felt horrendously guilty; we had let Dandelion down. I quickly pulled the puppy out and discovered that it was lifeless and cold. It was another large male that had come out feet first. It was not breathing and its little pink tongue was sticking out of its tiny mouth. We felt extremely sad. Pattie said, "Let's call it Blossom." I started rubbing the puppy vigorously, trying to stimulate its circulation. I rubbed and rubbed, talking to it, praying that it would start to breathe. Pat was weeping and kept urging me on. "Come on Blossom, you can do it. Come on Blossom, Blossom, Blossom . . ." Suddenly the puppy took a spasmodic breath, and after a while another. It was like the reverse of seeing someone dying. The spasmodic breaths became more frequent and soon the puppy was breathing in a very laboured way, but breathing nonetheless. It still felt cold and there was no movement except the breathing. I kept rubbing. The breathing became more regular and small twitching movements appeared. We warmed up some goat's milk, put it on my finger and put it into the puppy's tiny mouth. All of a sudden the puppy started to suck and then its legs began to move. It was alive at last! Then it started to scream. A lusty high-pitched little scream which went on for a long time. Finally we coaxed it to start nursing from its mother. By this time it was four in the morning and we were exhausted. As all seemed finally under control we decided we could go to bed. We fell asleep on the bed next to Dandelion's whelping box, so that we could keep in touch with her and the puppies.

When in the morning Jovelina arrived I greeted her and said, "Mira, Dandelion tiene six perritos!!!" I took her to Dandelion's box and showed her the puppies. "Aqui ay seven perritos," she commented. "Cristina conta, uno dos, tres, quatro, cinquo, seis, siette!!" and sure enough Dandelion had given birth to another puppy after we had gone to sleep and we had not even heard her doing it!

This one was another male (we didn't know whether it had come out head or feet first), a small 9 oz. puppy which we called Cal Ripkin Jr.

We now all decided that it would be a good idea to make an appointment with the local vet to have Dandelion checked out. The vet thoroughly palpated her uterus and pronounced it puppy free. She gave the dog a shot of oxytocin to make sure that all afterbirth would be expelled and we all got into the car to drive home. Less than two minutes later, Noah noticed something coming out of Dandelion and Pattie said that it was just fluid and was normal. But then suddenly Noah yelled, "No, Mom, it' s a puppy!" Within seconds the puppy was howling in the back seat of the car. Pattie made an instant U-turn and sped back to the vet. This time we insisted on an X-ray to make sure there wasn't going to be a ninth puppy. It looked like Dandelion was finally finished. Eight puppies!!!! This one, a small 9 oz. male, we named Makolino in honor of Pat's car (the puppy's birthing room) whose license plate is MELMAKI in honor of our dearest dog Maki who died three years ago.

And so ends (for now) the story of Dandelion giving birth to eight puppies. She is well, as are all of the puppies, and is getting adjusted to her new role as super mom with a little help from all four of us. We take turns supplementing the feeding of the puppies with tiny baby bottles to help out Dandelion. It's like having eight little new babies because that is what they are. Birth is such a miraculous event!

*Cristina Biaggi is an artist, lecturer and author of* Habitations of the Great Goddess *and* In the Footsteps of the Goddess. *She is also a pilot, mountain climber and fourth degree black belt in Tae Kwon Do. She is passionate about all animals especially dogs (she has six of them).*

# Entente Cordiale

Suniti Namjoshi

**As Suniti and River were sitting** side by side staring at the waters of the muddy Yarra, it occurred to Suniti that the Kelpie didn't in the least resemble a river. She said as much, and added politely that River's coat was a far richer and more reddish brown. River shrugged and asked Suniti why she was called 'Suniti'. "Oh well, it's Sanskrit, you know," Suniti replied trying to look as modest as possible. "It means beautifully behaved or well conducted."

River didn't say anything. She just looked at Suniti until at last Suniti mumbled, "Oh yes, well, I see. Yes. What's in a name? Oh yes, quite. I take your point."

River yawned and Suniti stared at the water a bit. Suddenly she shot a question at River.

"Why do you chase trams?"

River was startled, but she gave the matter due consideration. "I expect it's a neurosis. I dislike trams. What about you? Why do you dislike loud music and flashing strobe lights?"

"Oh, but I don't run at loud music and flashing lights."

"But you do run," River replied.

Suniti thought of saying that she didn't think it was neurotic to dislike loud music and flashing lights. Indeed that it was rational to do so. And to run away from them was also rational. But then would River make her admit that chasing trams made perfect sense? Indeed, did chasing trams make perfect sense? Had she not in her time — when she was younger and fitter — chased a tram or two herself? It made her feel confused.

"You're so argumentative," she said crossly to River. "Why don't you just think what other people think? And why don't you just do what other people say? It would be so much easier, you know."

"Well, why don't you?" River asked. She liked Suniti, but she seemed to need so many words before she understood anything.

"Because it's a fallen world," snapped Suniti.

"Well, there you are," River grinned. And after a while Suniti grinned back. After all, it was pleasant by the riverbank.

*Suniti Namjoshi was born in India and is the author of poems, fables and academic articles, amongst them* Saint Suniti and the Dragon *and* Goja: An Autobiographical Myth. *Suniti writes: "This fable is for River; but there's very little that's fabled in it. It's pretty much what the Kelpie said. I just wrote it down."*

# Pipi Sue Barber

**Pipi was so tiny,** the smallest of the box of dumped puppies, hunched up in a corner, half sat on by her boisterous big brother, with his tail flicking in her face. She looked pleadingly up at me and I scooped her out to safety and that was it really, there was no decision to make, no choice in the matter, she had chosen me and I was happy with that. I wasn't going to get a dog, as we had just shifted and really weren't prepared for a dog, leave alone a puppy, but she snuggled up to me, stopped shaking and I called her Madeline.

Names have a habit of changing in our household. I reckon it is another thing that our dog friends do and that is choose their name, or at least get nicknames that change with their moods. Madeline became 'Pipi' when I took her home and I hid her in the bedroom ready to break the news to the rest of the family. However in true style, before I even had a chance to speak, she whipped out from the bedroom, darted across the lounge under a chair, leaving the others somewhat surprised and amused. "What a pip squeak!" was the remark and the name stuck and she was allowed to stay.

The night she came home with me I stopped at the supermarket and bought a range of canned food, biscuits and fresh meat to tempt her.

Her little nose went in the air as she wandered away every time I put something new in her bowl. Not until I had cooked and removed the chicken off the bone did she choose to eat and from then on she knew I was a push-over! So chicken it was until I was able to please Madam with other gourmet delights that she so desired.

One day she was hanging around me looking for something to eat and it wasn't hard to get the idea that she was hungry, as she had this habit of holding her bowl in her mouth and following me around, walking in my way and nudging the bowl against my legs. Once I noticed, she'd put down her bowl ready for it to be filled. One time I held up her milk carton in one hand and some dry food in the other and said, "OK, which one, milk or dry food?" I said it again, this time shaking each one in turn, I asked again and she put the bowl down for dry food. Now she was able to tell me not only that she wanted something but what she wanted because she wouldn't put the bowl down until I got it right!

I spent a lot of time in the car travelling around and I used to take her with me almost everywhere because I couldn't bear the little wet nose pressed against the window as she watched me drive away. So into the car we would go and when she was still a puppy she would sit on my shoulder curled around under my hair and watch out the window. She was contented just to sit there. When she got bigger, she would go into the back seat, after flying through the car door or in through an open window, in one bound, every time I picked up the car keys. As we drove, she would bounce from one side of the car to the other sniffing deeply all the smells as they blew into the car and sticking her head out the window to bark at the cows and other big scary creatures as we sailed past. I would have to say that travelling in the car was one of her most favourite past times.

She was tennis-ball-mad, but as the tennis balls were too big for her little mouth, we introduced her to golf balls which were just the right size. Her eyes would fix onto the ball, poised and ready to fetch, waiting for the hand to move into action to throw the ball. Anticipating the direction in which we would throw it, she would be off; sometimes she got the direction wrong and I ended up doing the retrieving, under Pipi's disappointed gaze! Empty soft drink bottles were another hit and she would be for hours attacking, destroying and demolishing these bottles, but her favourite was logs of wood with lots of bark. When we were cutting up fire wood, you knew if she had found one of these logs because she had this high-pitched bark that let

us know when she was pouncing on and stripping the bark away. There would be bark all over her face, all over the yard, and she became the ferocious Pipisaurus Rex!

No matter what I did to try and not let her know I was going out without her, like putting the keys in my bag in the bedroom and walking to the front door without my shoes on, she always knew and made it so hard for me when it was impossible to take her with me. Pipi would jump up and wrap herself around my shoulders hoping to come along, pleading with me. It was always heart wrenching when I pulled her down and left her to breathe on the bedroom windows with those big accusing sad 'you always leave me' eyes, as she watched me go, especially if I was gone for longer than a day.

One day I was outside and I heard barking. It was a worried bark and I couldn't get to her. I tried, but I couldn't get to her in time. There was a snake nearby and she was warning it off, trying to keep it away from us. I stood helpless, the snake attacked; there was nothing I could do. The vet was rung and we rushed to the car but I knew — and so did she — that the vet was too far away, not enough time, only time for good-byes. But I drove and drove. I was on automatic pilot, not thinking only feeling numb — this

couldn't be happening. Half way to the vet I knew, I had an overwhelming feeling of peace and love that was so strong and final.

The vet confirmed my worst nightmare. I took her home and cried and cried. We wrapped her in her blanket and put in a few favourite toys and then buried her in a special place on the hill which overlooks our home and down the valley. Later we drank champagne as the tears continued to roll down, to celebrate life and a beautiful friendship.

A friend gave me a rose to plant in her memory, a beautiful pink tiny rose just like my Pipi. The Pipi rose is always in full bloom. I don't believe that Pipi and I crossed each other's paths by chance. We had a connectedness that just doesn't happen through chance. A special relationship; intuitively knowing how the other feels; a friendship that lasts forever.

*I am currently studying theology and social work at university. My best four-legged friends are Jimmy my seven-year-old Terrier-cross, Claire our three-year-old Kelpie-cross, Mavvy our fifteen-year-old Labrador-cross; and Jack the Brat, my baby Jack Russell Terrier, all of whom like chasing tennis balls, rolling in smelly things and are second-chance dogs!*

# the visitor

Miriel Lenore

Irrunytju the dingo is back
she fed him as a pup
thought he'd left for ever

'bring him meat
get his rug
he might need water'

he sits on her foot
his strangled yowl a conversation
& leaves the meat

why has he come if not for food?
surely he's a father now out bush?
perhaps he missed us after all

that night black clouds & wind
thunder a mighty storm
Irrunytju sleeps on his blanket

in the morning he's gone

she checks each track
recalls their desert walks
epiphanies he helped her see

she only gave occasional food
he never was her pet
they always met as equals

both still choose to be free

Miriel Lenore grew up in Northern Victoria with Border Collies and the occasional Kelpie. Her family even owned a Border Collie in Fiji. Adelaide is now her base (no dogs or cats). Her most recent book is travelling alone together (Spinifex Press) which describes a group of older women following Eyre's route across the Nullarbor.

# Thelma

## Suzanne Bellamy

**I had a dog called Thelma**. I had a farm too, not in Africa but in Bredbo. That's where we met, Thel and I.

Just at the difficult end of a relationship with a human, into my life came a dog who stayed with me for twelve years until she died a couple of years ago at our new land in Mongarlowe. I still miss her daily and treasure all we shared. Our great joint contribution to the planet was our loving creative partnership, and that is what I want to begin to walk back through here.

She was a perfect dog for me, right size, right attitudes, right smell and already adult. A Beagle-cross (what with?), she arrived at the farm either dumped or lost, off the back of a truck perhaps. I never found where she came from and at first I was panicked about having her in my life. Really panicked. Someone else to look after when I was so fragile myself, I thought. As it evolved though, she looked after me, this mysterious Beagle with a hidden past.

Long after her arrival, we met an old man in Cooma one day who thought he recognised her as a dog that had grown up in a public bar, belonging to a woman who left town in a hurry. That explained some of her ways. I never met a more sociable dog, she had a way of making friends and really connecting. People around here and in Bredbo still talk about her with a smile. She had character and humour, she had sincerity too, in that great George Burns way, you know, where "the most important thing in showbiz is sincerity and once you can fake that you've got it made . . ." Thelma had that one in spades. People would say to me, "Oh, she remembers me," after they got the big greeting, and I went along with this line every time. I adored her, I adored hanging out with her, I thought I was so lucky to be in her company for so long. From her I learned so much, about me, about dogs, about love, the free offering and giving of trust, how to share the bed and the shopping and all things that were special, how to smell, pay attention, not pay attention, keep routines, break the rules. Bounty was always shared, as were the sometimes terrible times, not to mention every kiln firing deep into the night. Work and play fused seamlessly in the expansive life of a great dog and her true friend, me.

A dog needs work, and beyond that three things that matter a great deal to a dog are physical exercise, bones and a good car. Thelma set about achieving all these requirements immediately. We walked every day, all over the place, on other people's land and our own, into difficult and dangerous places. Our rules were that she could chase rabbits and foxes (never caught), but never chase our friends the kangaroos and definitely not sheep and cows. Tough rules, mostly kept. It just never occurred to me to leave Thelma out of adventures, she was always there, even when she clearly thought I had lost my mind. The time I decided to do a twenty-four-hour vigil for the Summer Solstice on the local mountaintop, Thelma was there watching the stars and planets, and freezing in the sleeping bag with me. She certainly had a strong spiritual side, she ran with the Great Dog Mother, no doubt about it. Somehow though, I knew she was a practical mystic who would stop me from going too far.

Some of the years at Bredbo were emotionally abrasive for me, handling surfacing tremors and reconstructing a strong inner landscape through the practice of my creative work. It's a truly thrilling place to live, up there on the high Monaro, wild winds and weather, a place of extremity in all ways. Being in partnership with Thelma truly made it all possible, she was solidly there, and as I see her now she was a heroic figure in my healing and my creative life.

Having to make a place for the enormous energy field of animals is very corrective for the human ego. Thelma arrived with her own troubles, just as I had mine, and we both sought transformation and belonging. Simply and slowly, we learned to be together. We were true partners, but I made the decisions (well mostly). My great source of importance was that I drove the truck. The truck herself was the Goddess, and the ownership of the passenger seat was Thelma's inalienable right. When my sister came

to stay they would race each other to get that seat. It was Thel's, no question. When she sat in that truck and looked out the window there was a special look on her face, ownership, thrill, intensity. We both loved the truck, and we loved our life in cahoots with the truck.

About the question of bones. Life with Thelma happened in a co-operative manner, inspired by the great nineteenth century utopian anarchists I have always loved like Fourier and Kropotkin. This involved sharing space and respect, some boundaries and some clear lines of autonomy. I bought the bones, she ate them, but it's what she did with them over time that was the great Mystery. The ritual patterning and burial of dog bones had escaped my notice until I paid attention. I think it's related to Geomancy and land management. The very best bones were used to create an elaborate and deliberate system of alignments over the land. If she thought I saw her during these practices, she would return later and move the bone. Secrecy was critical.

Some of her other patterning rituals were more open but just as arcane to me, especially her barking places, performed and repeated like a passion play in sequence through the landscape and around the house. Barking-in-the-car practices were an area of dispute between us, although I tried not to interfere in her pursuit of the great census count of all cars that ever passed us by.

From our first year together walking the creeks, climbing rocks and exploring, I would sit at some stage and do a small meditation. Thelma always seemed to love this time and would return from her wanderings to sit on point duty behind me. One day I was sitting on a big flat rock in the middle of the dry creekbed, with my eyes closed. I felt a soft wet doggy nose gently run along my arm. I opened my eyes to see a wombat in front of us and Thelma standing right up against me, having chosen to tell me what was happening without drama. I was greatly impressed by this care and sensitivity, as we sat together for an hour watching the wombat decide to come out of her house and drink. When we came across wildlife like that, generally I would indicate a soft ssshhh sound and we would stand motionless together watching an echidna or a lizard, with Thelma sitting or standing on my foot.

Thelma made an elaborate study of wombats in particular, possibly because they were a similar size to her and were elaborate display poopers. She learned to back her bum up to logs and poo just as they did. I began to wonder if she was in fact a Beagle/wombat-cross, but I think it was more a linguistic/anthropological project. She taught me how to smell the path of a wombat crossing, even hours old. I learned from her every day, and she really wanted to show me her world and to contribute equally to our joint world. That link didn't stop with her death. She walks with me every day still. I smell things as she showed me, but I don't bury the bones or bark.

Because this is a tale about Thelma, I am not even mentioning Cinnamon and Smiley, the cats who also lived with us. They chose to regard Thelma as a lower form of life, until they too ultimately grasped her contribution to our magical delicate ecosystem as a household. She did the George Burns number on them too, feigning elaborate respect, and they totally fell for it. Ah, sincerity. She took their outrageous displays of attitude in her stride, and all our other hardships, in the end, because she and I went off in the truck. From it we repelled shooters and intruders, went to town, got manure and seaweed and hay, cut wood, went to the coast to swim, visited the city and made a life. I could not have, nor have I ever, loved anyone more than Thelma. We created a personal legend together, and it saved and changed my life.

*Suzanne Bellamy is an Australian feminist artist and writer living in a print and sculpture studio on land near the tiny village of Mongarlowe in southern NSW. Originally from Sydney, she lived previously for ten years on an old sheep farm at Bredbo (1983 to 1993), where this story begins. After the death of her great dog Thelma, Suzanne became involved in wildlife rescue and wombat release work on her land and now has a wombat friend called Sweet Pea living near the house. Other wombat work is ongoing, with little Freckle currently in intensive care waiting to come home to her country.*

# Section Three The Dog of My Life

# Nina

Kaye Moseley

**She wandered into my life** when she was six months old, a stray. Lost and thin, almost fully grown, she was friendly but aloof, and I named her Nina Wolf.

She was given to gazing at ephemeral things, like shimmering leaves in trees, the dappled reflections of light on water, the sinking moon in the western sky. And yet she was a hunter and caught seven rabbits in our walks along the river.

Once on a windy day in summer, she loped in the grass with her nose to the wind, the call of the wild in her veins, and I saw the spirit of her ancestors, Lupa on the plains.

We lived for a long time in a chapel in a garden, enclosed by grevilleas and wisteria, jasmines, ginger lilies and lemon blossom. We were visited by wattle birds, rising moons and possums, while she kept guard over our home and her bones.

With her, I discovered secret beautiful places. With her, I was free to roam and explore the waterways of the city. In summer when the heat became intolerable, we escaped to the creek, under the willows where the air is cool. I would read, and she would wade in the water to her belly.

Sometimes at dusk we would steal down to the grove of gums along the creek to watch the tawny frogmouths take flight, hunting in the night.

She especially loved the beach and the dried up delicacies the sea left for her. Once she saw seals on the rocks, and never forgot. We sat in the dunes while I sketched and she watched: the clouds, the sea, the horizon. In the balmy evenings we explored overgrown tracks and hidden paths. So much to smell. Once on the beach, on a dark and starry night, the phosphorescence in the sand twinkled at our feet, and we were walking in the stars.

She was fussy with her food and never left a mess. She split pistachio nuts before she ate them and left the shells in neat little piles. She never took food from strangers unless she was being polite and then she disposed of it thoughtfully, out of sight. She had a lot of grace.

She was a smoochy dog. Loved having cuddles, having her ears stroked. She liked to nuzzle into me and bury her head under my arm. She devised a way of holding me with her paw, the way I held her, and I loved how she did that. Whenever I was sad she came to me and comforted me. She was always so aware. We were companions of the heart.

We shared nine years of our lives, and she let me understand the world in a different way. She was singular, passionate and strong, and she was my guardian, in more ways than one.

I had no warning of her death, no time to prepare. The rites of loss for a dog maiden are heavy to bear. I thought my heart would break. I buried her beside Diana, goddess of the hunt, and now I guard her bones.

And always, at dawn and dusk, and when the wind changes course, I miss my girl, my Nina Wolf.

*Kaye Moseley is in her late forties and has enjoyed the companionship of dogs since she was a toddler, when she frequently wandered away from home with her grandmother's Fox Terrier Trixie, who protected her. She is a teacher, writer and artist, and lives in Melbourne with her partner and two canine companions.*

# Gypsy

### 28.10.1984 – 5.3.2001

## Claire Warren

**We're quite similar, Gypsy and me,** and that's partly why I came by her. Xmas 1984. When I heard Grimshaw's puppies would be little Scorpios, I was tempted. We would already know things about each other. Grimmy was brown and curly, half Poodle, half Curly Retriever; the father, a grey Schnauzer. I visited them — six fluffy balls. The others tumble-ran to the front of the box. "Pick me! Pick me!" Gypsy hung back, just watching. My heart went out to her. That's the one: the little shy one; the tiny ball of black wool with big brown eyes and the cutest nose shining from within a windmill of fur.

When we brought her home, she didn't cry, just sat quietly, looking and learning. She was always with me: she became my shadow — sometimes in front, but never far away. At night when I would call her, thinking she had wandered off, she was there at my feet; a soft touch on my leg with her nose to announce her presence — my shadow even in darkness.

She has put a lot of joy into the world in sixteen-and-a-half years; caused a lot of smiles and softness. She has a particular way with little old ladies. So many of them have had a small dog just like her, who lived to a ripe old age. "I love scruffy little dogs," perfect strangers would say, and she would beam back up at them. A friendly little bunyip, and multi-faceted: serving as hot-water bottle, clothes and seat warmer, rug realigner, cushion scatterer, doorbell alert, chief catbowl washer-upper, burglar disperser, tour guide — she even played guitar at Bridget's wedding. She's been acknowledged in books; had her photo in the *Age*, seated among nuns; and been mistaken for both a handbag and a cushion.

We were so in tune that she always knew when I would be home. About ten minutes before I arrived, she would go to the front door, or climb onto the back of the sofa to look out the window, on full alert. That's Scorpios for you. When I started working from home she was overjoyed, but also aware of the need for balance in life. So if the day had been too single-mindedly work-orientated, she would remind me with a touch on my leg so gentle that, if I were totally focused, it would not disturb me but, if I were at all open to a walk, I would look down into those expressive, soft, brown eyes, and a deal would be struck.

Without her, I never would have walked in half the places we explored: back lanes, parks at dusk, quiet brooding places. She let me know if they were safe or not, whether people approaching were goodies or baddies — she was quick to pick up vibes.

She was a non-demanding dog. On our walks she was happy to do her own thing while I solved the problems of the world in my head. She didn't need to be chasing sticks or balls and, if she did, she seldom brought them back. Why should she? But she did like me to throw pinecones, which presented a challenge with their unpredictable bounce. She often claimed one as a souvenir, and would keep it for those idle moments when she was guarding the car. Of course, pinecones have seeds which fall out when chewed, and old Volkswagens often leak. A pine forest along the back window-ledge of my blue VW reached five centimetres before dying in the summer drought.

She was perceptive and learned quickly, sometimes from a mistake: for instance, baths are hot, and weight is better IN the car than out the window. Prickles in foot: stand still and hold up to show me which one. Flea-hunting: roll over to show me where to look. I spoke to her as if she should understand every word, so her vocabulary was huge. Sometimes she wrestled with the concepts, but she pronounced the words "Good morning" and "Hello", with exactly my intonation.

And she worked out some things that truly amazed me. One night we were sleeping in a loft reached by a vertical ladder. I carried her up, holding on with one hand, but she herself solved the problem of how to come down. I climbed down a few rungs so my shoulders were level with the loft floor. She put her front feet on my shoulders and I scooped her up with my free arm.

She had never run with horses, but knew to stay clear of their hooves and show respect. On a day ride, when I'd been in the saddle for hours, she sussed out how to get a pat. She ran ahead to some high ground then, as we came by on the track, there she was waiting, at arm-height. Once she followed me about fifteen feet up a huge laurel tree — oh sure, it was an easy climb, like a staircase, but she did it. And when I took her to meet an elephant at a circus, I think she thought she was in the shadow of a tall building. When she realised this was an animal, she freaked totally and dived between my legs. Mind you, this was after the lion had unexpectedly roared at us.

She could count to at least ten. I played cricket in summer and, on one stinking, scorching day far too hot for a sensible black dog to run out to the wicket to join the celebrations, she slept in the cool pavilion. Only when the last wicket fell, did she come flying out on to the pitch. That boggled a few minds.

There were just a few points on which we differed. She never liked the way I kept rugs straight: preferred instead to scruff them up to provide a couple of layers of softness between her poodleness and the floorboards. She decided early that she'd like to be a bit scruffy. Even so, she loved being brushed — particularly if it interrupted my cat being brushed — though she was really precious of her moustache and beard, so forget-me-not seeding was a horror time of year.

I adore that little dog and, in all those years, we spent only fourteen days apart. Because she went everywhere with me, she became remarkably socialised. At book launches and exhibition openings, I tracked her progress around the crowd, listening to her recognise the legs she knew. I love the way she greets her friends — such boundless, unbridled enthusiasm. Her especially favourite people cause her to scream with delight. I love the way she insists people acknowledge her with eye contact and a hello. A pat makes her happy.

She's amazed me often and taught me a lot, and from me she's learned the etiquette of dinner parties, exhibitions, cricket matches; and how to behave on trams and in shops. She had a wicked sense of humour, thinking it funny to bark in the library-quiet of the bank and watch everyone jump. In pet shops she loved window shopping — sniffing along rows of dog food and treats. Once she shop-lifted some rabbit pellets.

One day we were walking in Studley Park in Melbourne — a huge park, wild in spots, tracing the Yarra River around the bottom of the Kew hills. Gypsy rolling in lush grass. I walk on, expecting her to gallop past me. After a while, I turn. No little black curly person in sight. Walk back to where I'd last seen her, rolling on the bank. Nothing. She's gone back to the car. Climbing to the top of the hill and calling. No sign of her. Calling. Calling. Desperation. Thought I heard a noise — like when she's asking to come in the back door. Another call and she responds. Down the hill, running. "Gypsy!" A moaned "He-e-elp". Keep calling to get location. Mostly she responds. I'm quite close now. I'm nearly back where I last saw her. Where IS she? Calling, calling. Nothing. Call again. There! She answers.

I've passed her. Go back. Call. From below me, she answers. I lean over the bank to look. There she is perched on a snag in the river like a mountain goat, all four feet bunched together. She had been so into her rolling that she rolled right off the bank into the river, and couldn't climb back up.

She loved surprises: that little face lit up at the first smell of ozone or the eucalypts heralding her farm birthplace. But best of all was our ritual after-dinner hunt for the hidden dog treats. There were only ever three, but she would always look hopefully for more — and once or twice there were.

On her last day she did something truly amazing. She could hardly walk, and the need to go outside for a wee came on quicker than she could manage. But this time she waited at the front door for me to open it, stumbled to the front gate and waited, then walked to the grass for the wee. Then, she walked to the end of our fence and sniffed where it joined our neighbours'. She turned and walked back past the gate to where our other neighbour's fence joined ours and checked that out. Once inside again, she went out the back. We carried her down the steps and she looked up the side of the house, then walked to the near corner, under the lemon tree. She paused at that spot and came back the long way, past the vegie garden and in behind the fish pond to check out the hidden corner. I think she was making a map of our home, so that her soul can watch over us from heaven.

My eighteen-year-old cat Polly has kept a vigil beside the grave since Gypsy landed there. It may be that that's the best spot for catching the winter sun, but perhaps their bond was greater than even I knew. Anyway, I know where I'll bury Polly.

Gypsy had a wonderful sense of humour. Exactly a week after she died, she sent me a white cat. I know it was her, because he has one blue and one yellow eye, the colours of the *Dianella tasmanica* (flax lily) flowers which I planted beside her. This Mr Alby Fluffybum has lifted me out of my sadness and made me laugh. A good present. Perhaps when he is two years old, as Polly was when we brought Gypsy down from the farm, I will be ready for another little dog.

I can see Gypsy's place from the window — a mound of brightly-coloured gumleaves, petals and flowers, brought home for her, to let her know where I've been — today, a spray of wattle and a cockatoo feather from Studley Park. For when we'd been out together, she'd always brought home a collection of assorted flora stuck to her hairy little legs.

The she-oaks are whispering; the wind plays tricks on me. It causes the bead curtain at the back door to click and I look up expecting to see Gypsy come out on to the verandah, checking what I'm up to. I miss playing hide-and-seek with her in the park, and driving on winter nights when she climbs onto my lap and leans her whole body back against mine, head on my shoulder, sharing body warmth.

I miss my little black shadow and the soft nudge of her nose on my leg saying, "I'm here." Ancient Egyptians believed that whenever you say a person's name, they are still alive. "Gypsy. Gypsy. Gypsy."

*Claire Warren was born in the Chinese Year of the Dog, and lives in Melbourne with three cats. She has a large part of her heart and brain reserved for fond memories of her beloved Gypsy. Although she appreciates thumbs, she has sometimes wished that humans were bred with tails.*

# My Wonder Dog

Doris Kartinyeri

**I look at my dog** with some sadness. She is old now. I have had her since she was a puppy.

Her name is Sharah. Sharah is sixteen years old. I watch her carefully. She does not hear me approach her as she is deaf. She also suffers with arthritis.

My Wonder Dog has had a stroke but she fought back and fully recovered. She is a smart dog. Sharah is a Border Collie-Kelpie. Her colouring is black-and-white.

She has the right to live. I would never consider putting her down. She is faithful and she is my best friend. Sharah is my companion. Once a fit dog, with energy so strong, she has slowed down a lot.

She looks at me with sad eyes and I adore her heaps.

P.S. My dog Sharah is no longer with me. I still feel her presence, particularly when I am hanging clothes out or when I am sitting on the back patio. She really was my best friend.

*Doris Kartinyeri lived with her dog Sharah for sixteen years. Of Ngarrindjeri heritage, Doris was removed from her family when she was one month old. She grew up in the Colebrook Home on the outskirts of Adelaide, and later suffered from bipolar disorder. Her autobiography,* Kick the Tin, *published in 2000, tells of the legacy of being a member of the Stolen Generation.*

# My Life with Marx

Karen Lane

**I remember childhood** as a pretty miserable time. Mum and Dad fought a lot but this was in the 1970s before the divorce laws changed and people just stuck it out. Inevitably their tensions were redirected to the kids and we ended up feeling the weight of their unhappiness. I didn't realise then that parents took out their frustrations on the kids and just ingested it all as my own inadequacies.

The one oasis in this world was that they let me have a dog. I discovered then that what a girl really needed was her own dog. We got the puppy from the Lost Dogs' Home and called it Socks. It was a black-and-white Border Collie with all of the characteristic markings. Unfortunately, Socks got distemper and had to be put down, but I learned in that short time that the world was bearable if you had one good friend and that could be a dog. It was not until I was married, too early in my life, I must add, that Socks was replaced by Marx. By this time, I had left the workforce as a secretary to the head of a government department to become a university student. The addition of Marx, another black-and-white Border Collie but crossed with something like a German Shepherd,

occurred in my fourth or Honours year. This was the year of changes in other ways. My premature marriage strained under the weight of different career trajectories and the question was raised of who would keep the dog. It seemed as serious as who would get custody of the kids, although there were none, just the dog. I decided that he should keep Marx because he seemed so bereft at our failing marriage. However, Marx was used to my company because I had been at home studying. When he tried persistently to follow my husband to work we decided that he should live with me. I was joyous.

At this time, I had decided to undertake a PhD. This meant four or five years of hard, relatively solitary slog. I had resettled into a communal household of people studying for PhDs but who also possessed a range of ancillary domestic responsibilities. Our household comprised four adults (but often there were eight for breakfast, or more), three dogs, two cats and at one stage six kittens. There were also two children on some weekends. This was a wonderful featherbed transition from an early, failed marriage into the insecure world of academe. There

was no surety of getting a job, or even of finishing the daunting journey through a PhD. I had left my job and money was scarce. We were poor, but a very happy and supportive 'family'. The dogs and kids and cats seemed to make it all bona fide, even if we were only bound together by circumstance and temporary alliances.

It didn't last, of course. I met the new professor who had come to Australia from England and we fell in love, almost instantaneously. Before long, it seemed like a good idea to set up house with him. We had very similar values and goals, at least then. I made it clear to him that I would move in, but it was definitely a package deal. The dog had to come. So Marx and I moved again and after a few years we got married. Marx looked wonderful at the wedding. He had a cream silk bow around his neck and I had shampooed him the day before so his coat was gleaming and smooth. The ceremony was conducted in the very pretty front garden under a huge leafy tree. It was a still, hot January day in Adelaide. We all dressed up but in a self-conscious way. Marriage was not fashionable in academic circles then, so it felt like a renegade act when 'Left' social scientists eschewed the ostensibly conservative conventions of marriage.

I didn't recognise it then, but my new husband was a pathological mover, driven by the vista of personal fame and fortune, preferably fame. Within three years of marriage, I had finished my PhD, he had resigned from his post as professor and had accepted a prestigious fellowship offered by the German government. Now there was real pain. I had to leave Marx for a whole year and I didn't know when I would be able to see him again or when I could send for him to join us somewhere in Europe. We had no firm plans. His reputation was such that we anticipated that a job would emerge, but the question was where and until I knew that I could not take Marx with me. There was also the huge anxiety of knowing where to lodge him safely. None of my friends was in a position to take him and the only possibility was an elderly neighbour whose husband had suddenly died. Gretta agreed to take Marx for twelve months but then came the time of preparations to leave. I cried copiously. It was a tortuous time because it was like leaving a child, but I knew that I could not stay in Australia because of a dog.

We did our stint in Germany. I rang and wrote to Gretta periodically to check on Marx. He remained in good health, but I suffered at the thought that he would not understand why I had left him. As we had envisaged, a job offer did emerge — from Holland. We moved there and after six months we bought a house and sent for Marx. I set about making arrangements to have him flown to Holland. It cost a fortune, but my husband knew that I would only settle when the dog was restored to me. We were reunited. Luckily the Dutch government imposed no quarantine period on dogs imported from Australia because the Australian government had controlled for rabies. Flying the dog over to Holland was an apparently seamless event, although I realised much later that it would take its toll on Marx.

Two years on we had our first child. I was thirty-nine years old and my husband was forty-four. Marx never really understood what the new baby was. He was never aggressive towards Adelaide, but he was rather disdainful and distant. I was happy with my domestic life; a new baby and Marx and my husband. It seemed idyllic. Inevitably, however, my husband again felt the pull of glittering new horizons and again I confronted the pain of separation from Marx. The new job was in England which had strict quarantine regulations because Europe had not been able to control rabies. The tunnel under the North Sea was then only a concept which meant that I faced tight bureaucratic processes for importing livestock. This was an expensive nine-month stay in a quarantine station. My husband never questioned the money, which was merciful. But the thought of yet another separation caused me great anguish. I tried to make arrangements to have Marx shipped to England and then transported to the quarantine station but every time I tried to speak on the phone I would be overcome by distress and tears. The recipient would only hear incoherent sobbing. Finally, I did manage to carry out the contract for his departure.

The same process occurred all over again. Renting a house, then looking for a house to buy and then settling down to new jobs, friends, doctors, dentists, hairdressers, strange culture and shops. It was exciting in its own way, but also a great timewaster and very emotionally disruptive. Marx was boarded in some kennels which took us about an hour to reach by car. We visited him dutifully every week and he did remain healthy and well looked after at least in terms of the restrictions of dog kennels. We had to be punctual to see him because this was not a private business but a bureaucracy. They didn't have to treat us well or be conciliatory so we were prevented from seeing the dog if we failed to observe visiting hours.

The day came again when he could be released. Strangely, it was a disappointment. Marx had bonded with his young female carers and so coming home with me was not the joyful reunion I had envisaged. This was trivial though because within a few days we had restored our relationship. Adelaide was then two years old and Marx tolerated her as a respected rival, although he never really came to accept her graciously. He was an older dog now; ten years old. We had bought an historic cottage near a railway line, which was used only once per day. When the train did pass the noise endured for only sixty seconds which was predictable and temporary to the human ear. However, Marx obviously found this a trauma. I wondered if the noise of the plane had compromised his equanimity because he clearly disliked the thunder of the train. One day it became too much. I didn't see the turn, but I found him in the sunroom in a peculiar pose. He had suffered a stroke and was unable to get up or focus properly. He was also quite frightened. I called the vet who insisted that we take him to the clinic, but he was such a large dog I couldn't move him. After several phone calls and persistent pleading, the vet did come and said that with some treatment he would recover. A few days passed and he did get better, but the reality was that he had lost his mobility and faculties. He could barely stand and was unable to take himself outside to the toilet.

I rang the vet again, who eventually came to the house. This was a different vet who now proposed that he would not recover. I had always remembered a farmer saying that every dog owner has to take the responsibility to put their dog down when the time came. This was the time. I held him in my arms and whispered to him how much I loved him and how grateful I was that he had been my friend through so many changes, troubles and lifetimes. I stroked him gently, saying all the time how good he was while the vet administered the fatal injection.

After that I became very ill. The grief had lowered my susceptibility to the prevailing viruses and the following weeks were a blur of sickness and sadness. It was December in England which was quite cold and miserable and although Christmas was near I felt bereft of family, friends and Marx. But something very odd happened. Although I really cannot remember the event, it was during this period of great sadness that our second daughter, Mathilde, was conceived. Out of the ashes, a new life.

Time passed and it was clear that my career was stagnating in England. We returned to Australia when Mathilde was one year old and when she was three my husband decided to keep moving on. He announced his departure to live with a younger woman. Soon after they married and returned to England. My girls are now eleven and nine years. They have said for some time that they wanted a dog of their own and, of course, there was no denying on my part that a dog is a girl's best friend. With their father gone they needed something of their own to love and cherish. I had broached the years without a dog by borrowing two black Labradors from around the neighbourhood to go jogging each morning but the yearning to have our own dog had never subsided. We looked in the papers each weekend but it was difficult to find just the right crossbreed. I inquired at all of the lost dogs' homes whether they had a Border Collie and German Shepherd cross. Apparently, this is an unusual combination and all replied that this was very unlikely. Eventually I found a cross between a German Shepherd and a Labrador, at least that's what they said at the pet shop. Nine months later I'm not sure he's either of those but he is very beautiful; probably a cross between a tiger and a wolf-hound. His name is Casey.

*Karen Lane is a single mother of two girls and a lecturer in Sociology at Deakin University. We have a dog called Casey and two cats named Tiger and Lilly.*

# Hector

## Eileen Bailey-Styles

He was born in high summer
In a valley of lush green fields,
And he tugged at a bitter-sweet memory
Because he looked like beloved Henry.

Although his eyes were sad for days
He ran and tumbled and grew to love us,
And slept at night beside my head
Safe and secure in my big empty bed

And he crept stealthily into my heart
And chewed my house and ravaged the cats,
And jumped and romped all over the chairs
And collapsed and tumbled down the stairs

And he grew in strength and stature
So too grew his love of life,
And waited hours for my return each day
Full of impatient desires to play

And so I released him to more freedom,
To another valley of lush green fields,
And I will never forget his yellow eyes
Looking at me with enquiring surprise

And perhaps one day in the heat of summer
He will catch the sudden scent of a marigold,
And as he lifts his noble head — I wonder whether
He will remember me, as I will him, for ever.

*Eileen Bailey-Styles. Born 1921.
Educated at Boarding School near
London, left school and joined the civil
service. Was married during the war,
and later attended art school. She
raised a family of two daughters and a
son, working in art establishments and
later became a professional
photographer. On retirement, at
seventy-five, she travelled for a year
round Australia, where one of her
daughters now lives. Presently lives
alone, in Devon, where she is still very
much a part of the art scene.*

# Cassiopeia: Queen of the Night Sky

Janice Raymond

**One cold day in January,** 1988, a creature bounded out of a field filled with snow at least one foot deep, and followed us home. I was enjoying a long winter walk with my partner, Pat, and in sighting the approaching animal, we couldn't decide whether she was fox or dog. As the creature came nearer, she confirmed that she was definitely dog — mostly German Shepherd-looking with a slight hint of Husky.

I had always wanted a dog, but not right at that moment for, quite soon, we were headed to Europe for several months. However, this beautiful dog decided to adopt us but on her timetable, not on ours. Once we took her in, she declined to leave. I tested her steadfastness in several ways. Foolishly, I put her out in the cold one night when we left for dinner with friends, thinking that she might wander home. When we returned, the foundling lay on top of the woodpile! Somehow, this baby dog had managed to climb onto the stacked wood, position herself on the pinnacle of the pile, and all this without disturbing a log! Having no idea how she could have managed this feat, we took this as a sign of creative commitment.

We put a notice in several local media to find if anyone was missing a dog, phoned the regional animal shelter and even asked the town dog officer to come to our house. When he finished listing what happens to dogs who are unclaimed and not taken in by anybody (ten day limit in the dog pound, on a cold cement floor, after which she would be euthanased), we knew that we could not bear to hand 'our dog' over to this fate.

Our next problem was whether she was female or male. This took about a week to determine, a fact on which I shall not comment further, since both of us should have known immediately! The final problem was a name. For weeks, she responded to various names, among them Chien and Canis Major, until we agreed upon Cassiopeia.

When I published my book on female friendship in 1986, I would never have believed that a dog would become one of my best friends. But that is what happened. For twelve years, Cassi was my constant companion. She took long walks with me, nudging me out of the house when she thought I was too preoccupied with work. She helped me write, often coming upstairs to my study where I would be glued to my computer. And there, she would put her paw on the keyboard, sometimes managing to tap out a word or two! No matter the quality of her tactile intervention, I would always be very amused by her attempts to join me at the computer and divert my attention to her.

When Cassi first adopted us, my mother, who was afraid of dogs, declared she would never visit me again. With canine charm and grace, Cassi managed to win her over the first time they met. From that point onward, my mother loved Cassi and would comment that Cassi seemed to know what she was thinking. She could tell by Cassi's eyes, she said, and was convinced that there were worlds in those eyes. Mother felt that Cassi protected and stayed by her side when I would be at the University working, and my mother would be at my home alone — i.e., without the company of another person.

My mother took her exercise every day by walking through the rooms of my house, and up and down the stairs, sometimes five or six times, praying the rosary. Cassi would accompany her from room to room, and up and down the stairs. Mother was convinced she was a Catholic dog! When my mother died and I was filled with grief, Cassi would put her ubiquitous paw on my knee. Whenever she sensed sadness, inevitably this paw would pry me free from sorrow.

After twelve years of being with us, Cassi died on 27 December, 2000. For several weeks, she had been listless and refused most food. Every day she looked sicker, with eyes glazed over. On Christmas Day, she would not move, so I phoned the vet on call who told me to take her to the somewhat distant animal hospital in our area. I left her there in the morning and in the afternoon, a very nice woman vet called with the diagnosis. "The good news is that she looks better, some of her energy has returned, and she is eating a little. The bad news is that she has advanced lymphoma." My father, brother and sister-in-law were at our house for the Christmas holidays which were holidays no more. The day after Christmas, I retrieved Cassi from the hospital and brought her home to die. We called the vet who came to the house the following day and put Cassi to sleep as we held her in our arms.

If anyone had told me before Cassi (B.C.) that the death of a dog could be as overwhelming as the death of a close human friend or relative, I would not have believed it. But that is what happened. Pat still cannot part with Cassi's ashes. So far, she will not bury them, even in the vegetable garden which was one of Cassi's favorite spots. Cassi would lie precisely on the periphery, paws slightly into the vegetable patch, never venturing into the garden unless we gave permission. As for me, I find it hard to contemplate another dog. Cassi was the best of friends — unique, herself, irreplaceable.

*Janice G. Raymond is Professor of Women's Studies and Medical Ethics at the University of Massachusetts in Amherst. A longtime feminist activist against violence against women and sexual exploitation, as well as against the medical abuse of women, she is Co-Executive Director of the Coalition Against Trafficking in Women. Janice Raymond is the author of five books on issues ranging from violence against women, women's health, feminist and lesbian/feminist theory and bio-medicine including* A Passion for Friends: Toward a Philosophy of Female Friendship *and* Women as Wombs: Reproductive Freedom and the Battle Over Women's Bodies.

# My Prince

## Bette Guymer

**I always knew I would meet my Prince** one day. In all the fairy stories my many aunts told me as a child during the War, the main theme was that my Prince would one day come to save me from a life of drudgery or worse . . . I often wondered if he would be tall, dark and handsome — or short, blonde and dangerous! I never ever imagined that he would come in the form of a big lumbering Labrador, just five years old.

He came to us from the Blue Cross Society which is an organisation set up to find new homes for pre-loved pets who have lost their owners. His name was Prince and he became a family member immediately . . . I loved him and I'm sure he loved me too. Each morning I would wake to see his happy face and lively eyes looking at me as if to say, "What will we do today?" Prince always agreed with any decision I made and was overjoyed if he was included in my plans for the day. His lovely face and intelligent eyes showed me all his different moods, such as the mischievous look, the whimsical look, the petulant and guilty look and, of course, the loving look. I never saw an angry or leave-me-alone look. Prince was a people's 'person'; he needed to be with people as much as possible. I have never had such harmony, joy and understanding in a relationship and possibly will never have it again . . . it was marvellous.

Prince was my loyal friend, a playmate for the children, our protector — and another mouth to feed. He seemed to have an insatiable appetite and would often sneak under our dining-room table during mealtimes and accept nibbles handed to him by my children Rob, Stephen and Laurel. This led to an extremely funny incident: one evening when we were entertaining overseas guests I disappeared from the dining room for a few moments. When I returned, much to my horror I was greeted by a strange silence and an appalling odour. Our guests seemed to be looking at each other quite strangely and reaching for their handkerchiefs. Suddenly it dawned on me that my Prince was under the table. Very sheepishly he crept out, head down and his wonderful eyes were saying, "Please forgive me, I am only *human*". Our dinner party was a great success. Amid fits of laughter my friends have often reminded me of that night.

*Bette matriculated from University High School as Bette Kracke, then went on to nurse at the Alfred Hospital in Melbourne to obtain her State Registered Nursing Certificate. During this time she met her future husband Rex. In 1952, Bette nursed in London and visited Europe and after witnessing the Coronation of Queen Elizabeth II, returned home and married Rex in 1954. They have two remaining children and three grandchildren. Bette is a sixth generation Australian and is a staunch Republican. Bette and Rex (a retired radiologist) live in Camberwell, Melbourne.*

# Bad Dog

Donna Jackson

**I bought a T-shirt with the words 'Bad Dog'** on the front of it.

There was something about the title that gave me a lot of pleasure. Do I want to be a bad dog??

Why be a bad dog when I could be a nice human being — an intelligent successful, happy woman who could wear a T-shirt and brand myself — 'Home Renovator', 'Great Gardener', 'Home Hairdressing Heroine'.

When I first saw a bull terrier I was with my parents.

"Is that a lamb?"

It didn't have a proper dog-type head. It was definitely weird. Years later a lover pointed out to me that my Bull Terrier had no eyebrows. On closer inspection I realised he didn't have any eyelashes either.

A Bull Terrier is definitely not a person but I might like to be a Bull Terrier. When my girlfriend arrived from England she said, on introduction to Sump, "Oh golly that's the sort of dog the national front lads have. They're frightfully dangerous."

That secretly pleased me. Not the racism of the national front but the idea that my dog and maybe I was, by association — Dangerous.

We have a secret code — the Bull Terrier class. People either cross the road to get away as we walk down the street or they rush up to put their face into Sump's neck nuzzling him. They tell stories of how they once had a Bull Terrier who died, who looked exactly like Sump except smaller and with black ears and a limp.

"Diesel loved underwear. She was always appearing out of our bedroom with undies on her head. She used to chew them. She ate snail bait and, and . . ."

She staggers to her car to cry in private.

I became a lesbian, and eventually a lesbian dog owner, because I slept with a guy with a three-day growth. The morning after a wrestle with the hairy boy I looked in the mirror. I had a rash on my face that was starting to scab up. It was from him grinding away on top of me grating his whiskers into my face. I knew I didn't want to live like this. The women I had been involved with were so normal and mostly less prickly. A lot of them had dogs.

Before I bought the dog I was nervous. This was a real COMMITMENT. Not just a flirtation but FOREVER. Dog ownership loomed like MARRIAGE. But when I finally got the dog it was LOVE. What I hadn't been prepared for was the ménage à trois — him, me and the VET.

In our first encounter Ms Vet told me about alternative remedies for dogs as she ran her hands over Sump's muscular chest.

"Oh he's such a strong boy . . ."

"Some people reckon I look like him . . ."

"Yes I can see a resemblance."

Ms Vet has proved a very expensive flirtation. I could have bought her dinner six times over at Melbourne's best restaurant for the money swallowed by my dog in Bark Remedies.

I knew I was having withdrawals from the vet when I began to imagine symptoms in the dog no one else could see. I booked a consultation for the dog's depression. Well, he was depressed when he saw the needles for the acupuncture treatment. I felt her hot breath on my cheek as we pinned him to the table.

The dog later had a few stitches after an incident with a mad guide dog.

I realised the dog was also keen on the vet by his flirtatious puppy manner and the fact that he pulled his stitches out over night and had to be brought back for more treatment.

Sump saw his first beard on a Santa at the Newport shops. The Santa had black hair under a scruffy white wig with a real salt-and-pepper beard.

Santa approached, desperate for a punter. "Have you been a good girl this year?"

"I've been very, very naughty Santa."

"Well you get two sweets then!" He laughed.

Santa bent to pat Sump. As he did Santa's beard brushed Sump's eyes. Instantly Sump latched onto Santa's beard and wouldn't let go. Santa tried to stand but he had twenty-three kilos of dog hanging off his facial hair.

"Help! Heeeeeellllppp!"

People dashed out of shops. People appeared with small dogs and began to squeal.

"Pig dogs are evil!!"

Santa was going blue around the facial hair and whimpering.

I grabbed a stick and stuck it up Sump's bum.

Shocked Sump dropped his jaw. Santa staggered back crashing against the Newsagent's window whimpering and clutching his beard.

Sump and I crept away through the local shoppers.

One whispered, "That's the same dog! He's Bad. He started a fight with the blind guy's guide dog the other week!"

Some people cross the road when they see a Bull Terrier.

But I'm quite attracted to Bad Dogs.

There are a few beards I should have instinctively bitten in my youth.

The more time I spend with my dog the more I look like him.

*Donna Jackson is the founder of Melbourne's Women's Circus — a company of 120 women — whom Donna directed performing in sites such as disused warehouses, the National Gallery of Victoria and in a tour to Beijing. Donna has toured the country as the lead singer of cult glam rockers* The Sharons *and also with country cabaret band* Nice Girls Don't Spit. *She has written and performed her one woman show* Car Maintenance, Explosives and Love *around Australia and in the United Kingdom. Donna's hobbies are cars, home hairdressing and pyrotechnics.*

*Sump Jackson lives in Newport, Melbourne. He has been hit by a car, stolen twice, shot by the police and swallowed Ratsack. Hobbies: sunbaking and meditation.*

# For Holly

## Eloise Klein Healy

Holly look at that old dog it puts its gray face
under a hand and Holly I swear I am that dog.

Look at me wiggling here at your side your wise eyes
must know you are my friend and now here comes
my old gray face again and my nose nudges
all afternoon at your hand.

I would shed all over you Holly if it would mean
you would carry me around with you for a day wearing
the colors of my coat without concern for brushing
and plucking and cleaning away the hairs.

See I will uncurl here on the floor and sleep
on my side an old dog and faithful friend
who stays where you can reach me near your feet
and ready to move when you move.

This has to do with our lives Holly and not at all with our poems.

*Eloise Klein Healy is the founding
chair of the MFA in Creative Writing
Program at Antioch University, Los
Angeles. She is the author of four
books of poetry* (Artemis In Echo
Park *is available on CD) and a
chapbook,* Women's Studies
Chronicles *(The Inevitable
Press/Laguna Poets Series #99)
and the Associate Editor/Poetry
Editor of* The Lesbian Review of
Books. *Red Hen Press will publish
her next collection in early 2002.*

# My Dog 'Pluto'

Billie Hamilton Smith

**This is the story of my almost-human dog.**

I was in England when World War II broke out. My mother, sister and I evacuated from Warwickshire to a house my eldest brother owned in Weston-Super-Mare — a seaside resort. The house was opposite the beach, a very quiet area. Next to the house was a farm. We became friendly with the farmer and one day he said to me that he had a lovely litter of Great Dane pups and that I could have one. My immediate reaction was that I would be returning to Australia and didn't think it would be possible. However, seeing the pups, I fell in love with a gorgeous blonde one. I took him home to show my mother who also found it hard to resist him.

We managed to get him on a merchant ship which took about three to four months to reach Australia. Mother and I were on the last passenger ship to Australia — 1940. Pluto arrived in very good condition, he had evidently been very well looked after. He then had to go into quarantine. He was there for three months — I visited him each week. I then took him home to Elwood where we lived three doors from the beach. He was now quite a big dog. Although there was, of course, food rationing, my butcher was fond of my dog and was very kind in keeping him well fed.

My twin girlfriends and I all had bicycles and Pluto would run alongside us on the Elwood beach path. In the summer he would go into the sea — there was a small beach there — and I would take him out into the water and the children took it in turns to hold his tail and he would pull them in onto the sand.

I would take him in my car and if I kept him waiting long he would put his nose on the horn to let me know it was time to go. He would carry a basket or anything else that I wanted him to. One black mark against Pluto was in his exuberance he knocked over my future mother-in-law who was a very petite lady. She forgave him though — he was very popular — and friends and neighbours loved him.

We had a black-and-white cat named Petal and she and Pluto were great friends — they would even share each other's food. Petal would sleep between Pluto's paws and he would lick her. Pluto was great company for my mother as I was out a lot being with the USAAF Transport Division. Pluto was about six when tragedy struck. Petal came into the kitchen obviously in pain trying to tell us something was wrong — she just collapsed and died. I thought she might have been poisoned. The next day Pluto was not well; my immediate thought was they must have shared the bait. Unfortunately I took him to a vet twenty miles away who was not at all competent. I told him what had happened and his reply was, "You animal lovers always think your pets have been poisoned — he has gastroenteritis." He gave me some medication and after a couple of days Pluto was no better. I rang the vet and he said to increase the medicine. Pluto lived for quite a few days getting worse and eventually died. Too late I found a very kind local vet who performed an autopsy only to confirm my belief that Pluto had been poisoned. The vet said he probably could have saved him had he seen him at once. If only I had known about him earlier.

*I was born in England and came to Australia with my parents in 1934. I obtained honours in a business course. I went around the world in 1938 and returned from England to Australia six months after the war commenced. Early in the war I was honoured to be secretary to the late Sir Jack McEwan — he was later to be Prime Minister for a short while when the then-Prime Minister, Mr Holt, disappeared. I was not with Sir Jack then because during the war I joined the armed forces — American USAAF — as a transport driver and served to the end of the war. I was married in 1949 — my husband a wonderful man and dedicated physician — at the Cardinal Newman Oratory in Birmingham. We were blessed with three daughters.*

# 'Here's Looking at You, Babe'

Robyn Rowland

**We were so poor** that sometimes there was no money for food. University days were like that then. Jobs paid $1 an hour and I remember eating peanut butter for three days once because there wasn't anything else. The last thing we needed was a dog.

We lived in a communal house but ours was a large section with three rooms and we shared the kitchen and bathroom. Struggling for independence I came from the new middle-class rising from our gas works and bakery origins. Trevor was from a Broken Hill mining family with just the right dollop of contempt for the middle-class and a strong disregard for the rules. We lived 'in sin'. It was those kind of times.

Jessie came into our lives when she was three months old because Trevor found the guys in the other half of the house playing skittles with empty beer cans one night. Jess was the ball. He saved her and she adored him. We had to move then, because Jessie needed a yard and a bigger old house to be left in while we were at

Uni. She was really calm was Jess and we loved her.

We walked her every night around the streets of Wollongong. She was tall, the colour of peach sand, a cross between a Lab and a Kelpie. Really intelligent and with a touch of class.

When he saw her, he probably thought, "What a hot looking broad". He was that kind of dog; streetwise, decadent, tough and pumped full of testosterone. If dogs smoked, a cigar would've been hangin' out of the corner of his mouth. About four years old, he was a large long-haired terrier-cross with big floppy ears and silver silky fur over the brown beneath; full of seeds and smelling of the gutter. He had sherry eyes. Wow! What eyes. Melting moments. When he saw her, man, he wanted her. He came on in a big way.

We were furious. "Piss off you little bastard," Trevor threatened. "Grubby little prick. Stay away from my Jess." But nothing deterred him. He dogged our route. Nothing was going to lose him that dame. Trevor kept chasing him away until finally he threw a rock

at him and the dog ran onto the road. The car had been swerving everywhere but it managed to find its true straight in time to hit the dog. That thud; metal into soft life. Terrible. Stumbling from the car the drunk dragged him into the gutter and fled while we stood shouting abuse at the receding tail lights.

"You drunken bastard," I screamed, kneeling in the gutter. "He's dead," Trevor said. "Come on let's go." "I'm not leaving him." I felt into his fur, body still warm with hunger for the run. No heartbeat. I leaned close to hear his breath — none. I raised my eyes to the diamond sky praying for him to live; pouring all my energy into his body; hands over his ribs and his heart; willing him back to life. His dark fluid chocolate eyes beamed straight into mine; his mouth opened around a strange sort of clucking sound I thought meant his jaw was broken. He was laughing. He'd just agreed a bargain with me. And I didn't even know it.

The emergency vet said he thought his hip was smashed and that as we

didn't own him and he had no collar, if it was badly damaged he'd put him to sleep. If it wasn't we could have him back in the morning. Next day the vet was laughing: "His hip was shattered but I've pinned it all together. He'll always have a limp. I just couldn't bring myself to do anything else. Every time I went to give him the jab he just looked up at me and laughed his open-mouthed clucking laugh, like saying 'Hey, buddy, isn't life a buzz'."

We had no money. We didn't need another dog. And I had to ring and persuade my mother to pay the bill on the quiet. When we brought him home he had twenty-three stitches down his leg and was really bruised. He lay on the couch looking piercingly at Trevor. "He knows," he said. "He resents me because I threw that stone at him."

"He's a dog," I said.

We called him Byron, because of the limp. He looked at me like I was the love of his life and he was mine. He knew what had passed between us. He knew, and he never forgot. On that first day he shot through our front screen door after a male dog that had come sniffing around Jess, his crook leg held out like a sail. And he never stopped fighting off our demons for the ten years I knew him till the day he died. Jess loved him too, and he was a great foil for her. They looked so funny walking: the tall and the short of it; the light and the dark. Bogart and Bacall; Spencer Tracy and Katharine Hepburn.

Tension between the boys was high for a while. But about a week after he arrived, Trevor was cooking dinner

one night when he heard a tennis ball bounce behind him. Byron was up on his three legs bouncing the ball at Trevor's feet and backing off; wagging his stubby long-haired tail, itching for a game. "Come on mate. You're forgiven. Let's play ball."

Once he bailed up a semi-trailer out the front of our house. I heard a man yelling and cursing and hurried out to see this small grey dog in front of a huge truck and trailer, barking to stop him going down our road. "Don't be bringing your truck down here buddy. I might be small, but man, I'm a rogue. Really unpredictable, fearless; tenacious. Be afraid. Be really afraid!" I picked him up and brought him inside still barking. My Dad built us a chicken run and gave us his best bantams to lay eggs. Byron burrowed under the fence and finished them off. Carnage. The only thing left was a sad cock's comb and a couple of chicken's feet. Oh, he was difficult. He was lots of trouble.

When we moved to New Zealand in 1978, Byron and Jess came too. He got worse. One day I let him off the lead in the Rose Gardens by the river in Hamilton where we lived and he made a beeline for the first dog he saw. It was a big Labrador with pendulous balls just going over a hill. Straight up the hill Byron went, right between his legs and bullseye. His sharp teeth and snout gripped the lot like a vice. The dog let out a scream the like of which I've never heard since: long and high-pitched; a forever-changed timbre to it. The owner and I pried Byron's grip from around the dog's balls and profuse apologies did not stop the tears of both owner and dog. We made a break for it.

Not long after, by the river, Byron took exception to a German Shepherd three times his size who was growling at us. I thought there was no one around so had taken him off his lead. He shot past me, ignored my orders to heel (as always) and grabbed the dog around the throat. Trevor grabbed Byron by the back legs, but the tug-of-war only served to fling him into the air still attached to the bigger dog. The owner got hold of his dog and pulled from his end. There they were, stranger pulling his dog, Trevor pulling Byron and Byron holding on for grim death; a daisy chain of gnashing, snarling and yelling. Both men lost

their footing on the riverbank and all four of them fell into the Waikato River. Byron finally let go — he was not fond of water — and once again we were on the run. He clucked the whole way home and when we got there, snuggled up at my feet, his eyes shone like Tiger's Eye, and he laughed till he fell asleep on my feet. He was a very naughty dog. And he was real pleased with himself. "Hell yeah, what a great day." He was nerve-wracking.

He made an exception with female dogs though. He had a special prancing walk for them. His whole body went stiff and his tail stuck out horizontally and wagged in a vibrating sort of way. "Hey doll, I'm horny and I'm cool. Don't you just love a grubby scoundrel?" Frankly embarrassing, especially for a lecturer in women's studies.

He was getting pretty old when I left for seven months in England in 1983: still clucking fanatically his own rhythms; still fighting off any demons he imagined threatened those he held dear. He got thinner and thinner. They said it was cancer and he must have had it for a while. I reckon his life force energy was just too far away and he thought maybe I wasn't coming back. Trevor had to take him and have him put to sleep. He told me on the crackling international line: "I held him close Rob, while the light went out of him." Jess never really got over it and I've never had another dog since. No point really. You know what I mean. Once you've loved and been loved like that: I mean real mutual devotion

— of the one breath — unconditional — there's no point really in trying to find it again. My kids want a dog, really badly. But I can't do it. Really I can't. See, that was the one. That really was the one.

*Robyn Rowland is a writer and retired academic. In the last twenty years since Byron died, she has been Foundation Head of Social Inquiry at Deakin University, Director of the Australian Women's Research Centre and written seven books along the way. She had two children in 1990 and 1993, both boys, and feels that writing this piece might have led her into dangerous territory, because now, memory has her looking kindly on passing pups and fighting the desire to say 'yes' again.*

# Maxi and Me

Laurel Guymer

**"What you need is a dog,"** my friend said to me which I thought was the weirdest thing I'd heard for a long time. There I was, working full-time in Intensive Care, struggling to pay the mortgage with the rising interest rates, and had met my biological mother which resulted in a stream of strangers all wanting to tell me their version of the past events. And, as if life wasn't complicated enough, I had fallen in love with a woman who didn't have time for a relationship. My confidence was at an all-time-low; the last thing I needed was something else to care for, I thought.

But my friend convinced me to take a look. She took me to the Lost Dogs' Home in North Melbourne. We walked up and down the aisles; so many needy faces, all sizes, some barking, others wagging and then I saw him. Small enough to sit on my lap, all black, round as butter, with big eyes that said 'take me'.

And I did. I called him Maxwell.

A few weeks later my life changed drastically. I decided to leave Melbourne. Maxwell — only a few months old — and I set off on a trip of a lifetime. Within a fortnight I had quit my job at St Vincent's, sold my house in Clifton Hill and bought a sports car. Maxi and I took off in the Capri with the roof down and began the long journey up the north-east coast, stopping every two hours for him to have a wiz. We were so happy — both of us.

We arrived in Cairns at my brother's house in time for a tropical cyclone, one that kept us indoors for days without running water or electricity. Although I was petrified, we didn't complain, just listened to the hourly cyclone reports on the radio, powered by batteries, and waited. At the first opportunity, we thought we would drive out along the main street to see the damage. But before I had moved all the timber to get the car out from where it had been secured during the cyclone, my brother came in to tell me the bad news. His face was white, full of despair, speechless.

"It's Max . . . he's eaten a box of Ratsack."

My heart sank; the only thing I really cared for in the whole entire world was going to die. With Maxi on board I drove out along the main road scattered with palm trees and assorted debris, dodging powerlines to the local veterinarian. She put something in his eye that made him start vomiting immediately, and told me to go home.

"Leave Maxwell with me; I'll ring you later but I don't hold much hope."

The cyclone had passed, the sky was still and all I felt was the hot sun beating down on my head. My mind was spinning, the 'what if's' going around and around in my head. But all I could do was sit and wait . . . for hours. When the phone rang I was prepared for the worst. But she had good news. I could take Maxwell home at night as long as I brought him back during the day for ongoing treatment. As each day passed he got stronger and stronger until I had almost forgotten the whole ordeal.

Several days later I was woken by the sound of screams.

"Come quick Aunty Laurel, Maxwell is dead."

The Ratsack's secondary effects had taken hold and Maxwell was now bleeding internally. I felt numb, motionless, tears began to fall. This time I thought, he's really gone.

The veterinarian explained why Max had deteriorated and again attempted to prepare me for the worst. Ratsack has a double action. First it causes immediate bleeding and in case that hasn't done the job, it has a secondary delayed action. It meant more intravenous resuscitation and weeks of oral vitamin K costing vast sums of money. The vet even considered a blood transfusion. But I had hope, Maxwell had fought the first time and survived. So I paid and waited — a painfully long wait. Maxwell had become part of my life at a time when I felt the most vulnerable. Living without him now seemed unimaginable. He was all I had.

Ten years after the Ratsack drama Maxwell is still going strong despite the vet telling me three years ago that, "he won't see another Christmas". Against all odds — and back in Melbourne — Maxwell remains central to my life.

*Laurel Guymer grew up with dogs. She was just learning to walk when Penny arrived. After Penny was run over, her mother Bette and brother Steve adopted Prince. Once Prince had gone, it was only a matter of time before another dog joined Laurel's life. She is certain that Maxwell will not be the last either. Laurel is a contributor to* CyberFeminism: Connectivity, Critique and Creativity *and is currently completing her PhD on the sexual politics of contraception.*

# Bonnie Christine Morley

It was a hot summer's morning when she arrived
without warning. This beautiful German Shepherd

looking lost, lonely and neglected. I was a little hesitant
to approach her initially, But she seemed just to want

attention unconditionally. She would try and nestle
in under my arm. I was instantly enchanted

with her charm. I still have no idea where she
has come from, But I immediately had

a sense that she would belong. Despite this, we earnestly
searched, doorknocked and advertised for her owners.

No claims were made and I secretly thought,
what a bonus! Now all I had to do was convince

my family to let her stay. This was no easy task as she
stole the washing, dug holes and barked night and day.

But her playful energy and affection soon converted
the others. They love, value and nurture her,

even my mother. And how could they not with her
loyal nature, big brown eyes and

oversized feet? Dogs certainly do make our lives
complete. While I'll never know how Bonnie

seeking refuge at our home came to be,
I will be eternally grateful that she chose me.

Christine, and her best friend, Bonnie, are
practically inseparable. Christine has grown up
with a cat named Sam, who she also loves
dearly. She has lived in the Geelong region all
her life, but one day wants to move to
Queensland, where she visits regularly, because
of the gorgeous hot weather there. Christine has
a passion for travel, the beach, music and
Italian food. She is a social worker, with a
background of working as a counsellor/
advocate in the field of sexual assault, and
currently works as a lecturer in social work at
Deakin University.

# Toots Titi Chartay

**It was one of those iridescent mornings,** an indigo sky, a velvet consolation for the approaching heat of a Sydney summer sun. The woman I had shared most of my life with was still asleep; her hands curled like paws. I crept over to stare at the other woman beside her in our bed. Some tresses of her vibrant red hair were entangled in the black fur of my old friend. The red-head awoke and looked at me. She understood.

I was dying, and for this, I had to be alone. I needed peace and not the distress of that funny, devoted human I had traversed Australia with. This was my final conspiracy with the intelligent, sexy and political bi-ped my old friend had hooked up with. I was leaving her in good hands.

Creeping from the house, I shuffled my tired, arthritic body to the cool burrow under a weeping willow tree I had discovered on one of my peregrinations to the river. The view was gentle. I entered life alone and would leave life in solitary calm.

We had first met during a Melbourne autumn; already a teenager I needed a devoted human and some women knew that my human would never hurt me. Everyone had Patti Smith on their record player; it was the thin, black tie seventies. We experienced love at first pat. I went everywhere with her, meetings, parties, theatre, work, political demonstrations (I knew the annoyance of arrest), dances and different women's bedrooms. We were both young and active.

Not a big, butch dog, it was my alert terrier brain my human admired. She even tolerated, indulged my addiction — to sticks. I think it was my erudite dancing that would seduce her to yet another throw. We were true mates who didn't need the false camaraderie of war to maintain our affection through both happy and sad times. My short, Dutch woman and I were one of the most stable couples around.

I became mildly well known, a dog of trusted distinction. Once, over a Sydney radio station, an announcement uttered these magical words for a women's social event, "No dogs allowed, except Toots"! My human had missed this moment of media glamour and had to be told and convinced by others, but I basked in her amused pride and my own notoriety.

Our bond was almost psychic. Travelling back from Darwin after a women's festival through the glutinous, starry night of the desert I was almost stranded. My human was driving and I was snuggled with some new companions, the only dog among twenty-three women packed into a red-dust caked bus. We stopped for petrol and a piss break in a town that was nothing more than a closed pub, a few desultory houses and petrol pump. Everyone got out for a stretch and an amble including me.

Sniffing out any local gossip, I missed the bus. In a moment of sapient stupidity, my human didn't do a tail count as she clambered into her seat through the driver's door. Trust was one thing, double-checking another. Panic was beneath my canine dignity and assuming my best dog-on-a-tuckerbox pose, I sat next to the petrol bowser. And thought hard.

Later on my human would always tell the story with a slight gaze in her eyes, "It was amazing, I was driving along, completely focussed on the road and suddenly I get this flash of Toots. I turned on the interior lights and asked for her. She wasn't there! Freaking out a bit but also confident that Toots would be smart enough to stay put and not wander into the desert, I turned the bus around. Sure enough, fifty miles or so back to that tiny town and there she was sitting as cool as a cucumber." I was so overjoyed to see that bus lance through the darkness, however I uttered a couple of barks and with tail wagging, serenely jumped into the bus. That is how rumours that I was a wonderdog spread throughout Australia.

I had a nimble ear for human language. Though English remained my second language I did pick up a smattering of French, Arabic, German, Dutch and Japanese. Not all of this I learnt from my companion. With any good relationship there are moments when it's nice to spend time with others. Once taken anywhere I always knew the way, an inherited gift from my foremothers I suppose.

Occasionally I would stroll off by myself and visit people. Always welcome, I would sit around for a while, enjoy their company and then leave. A beanbag always held a narcotic thrill for me. Perhaps this is how the rumour that I was a spy started. If two meetings clashed, sometimes I would attend one, while my human, oblivious to my whereabouts, was embroiled in the tedium of another. My perky attention and prompt exits at the end of a meeting disconcerted some.

I enjoyed the fuss I made, but my favourite business foray was accompanying my human when she reviewed films. Welcome at every cinema, often with a sly handful of potato chips, I enjoyed the colours and the silly sounds. But fireworks, oh how I loved fireworks! In the Year of the Dog, Chinatown showered me with dim sum. For a brief, glorious moment I was the embodiment of good fortune.

The stealth of the sun is beginning to crackle the shadow of the willow tree and I am drowsy. I was never under-estimated and never anthropomorphised; if I wanted to stick my nose up some sexy she-dog's bum, my choice was respected. It's been a happy life and now I am just tired, the sandy river loam feels good. Just one last glimpse of the stick nestled under my paw and a final tongue-lolling pant. Is there a dog-friendly national park out there in the ether?

*Titi Chartay and her partner Caroline Dearing are currently the enraptured hostages of Frida the dog and Oscar the cat. Everyone is very happy with this arrangement.*

Section Four Dogs and Home Life

# Of Doggies,
# Mud and Housework

Lynda Birke and Consuelo Rivera-Fuentes

## Picture the scene . . .

The kitchen, a farmhouse in Wales:

Enter visitors, smiling: take offered wine, and greet the hosts.

Visitors — with smiles turning to bewilderment as they look around: "Oh, umm, it's, umm, nice, all the old beams and . . . umm . . ."

Hosts — momentarily fazed by the confusion: "Please sit d . . . d . . ." (voices fading as realisation dawns . . .)

Adjacent room, off kitchen (where everyone now looks):

Three Dogs, raising heads from all available sofas and chairs, vaguely wagging tails, but resolutely not giving up seats: chorus of "Nnnn".

*******

OK: let's rewrite the beginning: we forgot the important bit —

*Cast of characters*

Lisa: the Lurcher. Despite advancing age, she still loves to run. She particularly likes to sprawl on the sofa, scattering the cushions (does she think we'd like to use them to sit on the floor?).

Tam: the Sheepdog. Miss Jealousy herself. True to her breed, she likes to herd — mostly us, when we're swimming. She likes the comfy chair nearest the television; she also likes to bury her bones. Usually in the house. Usually under cushions. Luckily, people don't often get to sit there anyway.

Penny: the Dyke Dog (especially when Lisa is in heat . . .). She likes the other chair, from where she can guard her food bowl if she doesn't feel like eating immediately (although there is no manger nearby).

There are a few humans around, too, who very occasionally get to sit down. They play the bit parts, squealing when they sit on a bone.

We could write an alternative scenario, in the study of said farmhouse; there, the three dogs are equally at home, on soft chair and fluffy rugs. Occasionally, they glance up when one of their humans swears at the computer. If nothing more interesting is promised — a walk, or a biscuit,

for example — they return to the Very Important Task of sleeping. Sometimes, they have to ensure that their humans exercise; that requires dropping hints (Why are humans so obtuse? Why else would we point our noses first at the car and then at the dog-leads?). Finally, the stupid humans catch on, and dog-leads and dogs are piled into the car for an outing.

*******

Our three doggies are part of the family. Which means that visitors must put up with:

(a) seats occupied by dogs; (b) fluff on the floor (we avert our eyes; hoping that guests don't notice); (c) chew marks on furniture; (d) doors open even in winter, thanks to Tam, who is adept at opening them; (e) carpets resembling graveyards, littered with bones; (f) a car resembling a mudbath.

There is undoubtedly a difference between households who Live With Dogs, and those who don't. In one, we can feel at home, admiring the fluffballs in the corner. In the other, we wouldn't dare even to put our cup down in case it marked the furniture. Whoever claimed that women are innately good at housework obviously never lived with a dog. So maybe dogs are the ideal companions for rebellious women — we can't spend hours keeping the house spotlessly clean because of the fluff/muddy-paw-prints/bones/chew-marks — can we?

*******

*Memories; or what dogs mean to us*

Years ago, Consuelo was the queen of housework when she lived in Chile: tidy sofas, with neat throws, no hairs on clothes, no bones to trip over. Her mother would be horrified to see that she is no longer houseproud, and how dogs can lead the life our three lead. In Chile, dogs are dogs . . . and if they happen to be bitches . . . well, that is yet another story; even for dogs, gender determines who gets food first, who gets more exercise and the occasional visit to the unaffordable vets.

Dogs in South America live outside, banned from getting inside the house. Consuelo used to have a mongrel called Rasputin, who was allowed in the house only when people lit fireworks. The rest of the time, he lived and ran around in the patio and garden, delighted in barking at strangers passing. And the poor postman . . . after a while, he decided to just throw the letters over the fence, it was safer for him. But not for the mail which was never the same again.

Rasputin also liked to dig holes all over the patio to bury bones, bread or indeed anything which was worth saving for harder times. His little wooden house in the garden collapsed regularly because he'd been digging under it to bury his 'treasures'. He wasn't bothered though; he knew his humans would move his house to another part of the patio and that he was loved despite being told off.

Alongside our memories of love, there are inevitable moments of sadness: Lynda remembers several dogs who've shared and enriched her life — Susie, Ginnie, Tess, Kirie, Satan, Frodo, Lucy, Nick, Rosie. Like Rasputin, and his mother Duquesa, they all did their share of wrecking stuff — and more than their share of loving, too. But dogs' lives are short; eventually, there comes the time to say goodbye, the awful parting. Rasputin got distemper when he was ten years old; Consuelo's elder son had to put him down with a lethal injection. He said he'll never forget the way in which Rasputin just looked at him and licked his hand, almost thanking him for putting him to sleep forever. However many dogs you have, it is always awful. And let no one claim that it is only humans who find it so: Penny suffered when her friend, Ginnie (another Lurcher) was no longer there. She grieved, just as Lynda did. All of these dogs were our best friends; always there, always loving. And always in our hearts.

*******

If these memories are sad it's because, first and foremost, dogs mean boundless love for both of us. Who cares about muddy floors when we get so much love from our girls? We try to reciprocate, though we're sure they think they are the most long-suffering, unloved dogs in the canine universe whenever we leave with car keys and NO dog-leads. It doesn't matter how we try to disguise our intentions, they always know, long before we get to the door — just as they know, infallibly, when we are down and need a big lick.

Dogs mean inspiration, too — not only in our everyday lives, but also in our writing. How can anyone write if they don't have a dog — or some other non-human companion — in their life? Every so often, keyboards must be abandoned in order to pat one of the girls. Failure to do so means that your carefully crafted sentences are suddenly reduced to more gobbledygook than even the computer itself can manage, as your arm — along with mouse and keyboard — is butted by a canine head. Once the need to sleep or bark at the postman takes over from cuddles, we can resume our work with renewed vigour.

Our dogs also inspire *what* we write, since that is often about human relationships with non-human animals. If we get stuck, we can gaze at our doggie family (even if watching sleeping dogs is like watching paint dry). It's then, observing these intelligent beings, that we wonder: who fits into whose society? Do dogs adapt to living in human families, or is it that humans who like dogs learn something about canine expectations? Whatever our culture says about the 'inferior' intelligence of non-human animals (ha!), dogs at least have learned well how to live *in* our society, occasionally even obeying its rules: and they have done so far, far better than we have learned how to live in theirs.

It would, of course, be hard for an olfactorily-challenged human to learn canine social skills, such as the social niceties of sniffing bottoms. In this household, Tam and Penny have acquired the bi-cultural skills (or should it be bi-species?) to learn that sniffing bums is not acceptable practice with humans, yet Lisa carries on regardless: visitors beware! We, however, are functionally illiterate in doggie-speak; half the time we don't even notice when Tam gives Penny the evil eye and a growling match is about to start.

Our lives tend to revolve around animals, especially our dogs and our horses. So, doing things with these non-human friends, making sure they are all right, giving them food, are central parts of our lives; these activities structure our time. The downside of living with animals is that it is sometimes quite hard to just go somewhere — and even if you could find the time, you feel awfully guilty, as three pairs of eyes woefully follow your every move of packing, and three tails are shoved firmly down between hindlegs. But that is nothing compared to the sheer joy of living with them all. We wouldn't have it any other way. And what would we do with the time if we didn't have animals? Housework?

So we don't mind about mud, hairs all over the place, about getting bruised legs from Penny's insistent hard paws (and sharp nails) when she wants a cuddle — as we write, she's shredding a butter wrapper that Lisa managed to steal from the kitchen table. We don't care about Tam dragging our bathroom towels all over the floor (is it something about the wet towel/woman smell, we wonder?). Nor do we care if occasionally there is a suspiciously yellow liquid on the floor because one of them could not be bothered to go out the previous night: "get a life", they seem to say with their wide-open, bright eyes, "it was cold, rainy and miserable outside". They ignore our annoyance and go back to their daily routine of cleaning themselves. And we laugh, get a mop, and thank the goddesses for the bliss of these dogs' company.

Who cares about such trivial things as mud and puddles when we have these wonderful beings who have accepted us in their lives? We'd better stop now that the weather has improved, and go for a walk with them on the hills. *Come on girls . . . !* Oops, we shouldn't have said it out loud: now we *will* have to stop since the barking and leaping is unbearable — and writing is impossible . . .

*Lynda Birke (right on page 114) is a feminist biologist, with a passion for animals (both emotionally and intellectually), and has written extensively about feminism, biology, and animals. The various animals in her life (the dogs in the article, and the horses on the farm) are experts at manipulating her behaviour, making a mockery over her alleged expertise in animal behaviour. She lives with her life partner, Consuelo Rivera-Fuentes, who is a Chilean feminist writer interested in women's autobiographies and has written about animals in magic realist literature. She is not an expert in animal behaviour, but she too habitually falls into the tricks the dogs (and her horse Toby) play on her. Pictured (from left) Penny, Lisa, Tam.*

# Fun in the Tub

Pia Cameron-Szirom

**It was an ordinary Sunday afternoon** and my two cheeky little dogs, Timmy and Sheena, had got themselves filthy by jumping into a bucket of water and then rolling around in the dirt. All the mud had stuck to them.

When clean they actually look quite cute. Timmy is a King Charles Spaniel/Shih Ttsu cross — so he has long droopy ears, brown eye-brows, black-and-tan fur. Small and cuddly, he's a real lap-dog.

But on the other hand Sheena, there's a terror! She's a Lapsu/Maltese Terrier cross — white curly hair with big blotches of black. When you walk through the gate she will run up and jump on you, run away and come back, jump and run and return, as if playing 'hide and tag tiggy'. And when you try to eat your tea quietly in front of the television you'll hear whimpering and it's Sheena and Timmy at the gate wanting to get through, with Sheena jumping as high in the air as her little legs can jump, trying to get over the fence.

"I think it's time to give those dogs a bath," said my mum, matter-of-factly. That's when the fun began! Bath-time for Timmy and Sheena means bath-time for Pia too!

There was just one problem —

where were we going to put two unwilling dogs for a bath? Nowhere outside would fit them. We would have to put them in the bathroom — in my new gi-normous spa!

"Mum. Seeing it's one of the first baths that they have ever had, can I get in with them? Please, please, please, please?" I pleaded.

"Oh all right! But you'll have to have a shower afterwards or you will be stinking, smelly and disgusting — even worse than the dogs!"

So, I fill up the tub, which took a couple of hours it's so big! Took off my clothes, grabbed the dogs and locked the door. And in we got! Scratching, yelping and splashing, followed, in the next few minutes, with Timmy trying to clamber over my head and Sheena's wet tail whipping my face — not an easy situation to get out of! So I sat there, grabbed Timmy around the waist, plopped Sheena out of the bath I said, "I'm going to have to do this one at a time!"

So, I get Timmy, shivering as he is, as if he is paralysed, but I doubt that! I grab the puppy soap and start scrubbing — behind his ears, along his back, under his tummy and then a very yucky job, under his tail. Then I call, "Mum can you grab Timmy and dry him before I do Sheena?"

While Timmy is being dried I pick up Sheena and there's another big whack in the face with her big wet tail. "Sheena, if you're going to be like this I might as well just let fungi grow all over you!" I don't suppose she'd mind this but I doubt she'd be allowed in the house! I pick her up, shove her under my arm, start scrubbing her little head as hard as I can with the doggy shampoo, getting out all those yucky little bits, and as with Timmy, scrub her back, under her tummy and the most disgusting part of all, under her tail.

At last she's done — pop her out, wrap her in a towel and call, "Mum, if Timmy's done can you come and dry Sheena please."

So she's out, shivering under a wet towel and then it's time to do me! I have a shower, get out, dried and dressed. At last it is all over. Some times in life are good, some times in life are bad, but this one is a once-in-a-lifetime opportunity and I'm glad it is over.

*I am Pia Cameron-Szirom. I am eleven years old and have two mums, two dogs, two cats and three fish. I go to an all girls' school, and have lots of friends there. I enjoy dancing, singing and making things. When I grow up I would like to be a 'mad inventing singing scientist'.*

# Friends
Felicity Thyer

**This is Jepanka (left) and Holly** the last time they played together. Of course they couldn't have known at the time that they were soon to be separated for ever — never again to tempt each other across the road to indulge in a game of catch-and-sit-on or dribble-on-the-ball — never again to sit at the gate whining as the other one walked past — never again to sit and prick their ears at the opening of the other's front door.

Sadly, Jep was an army dog, who was by now getting used to making lifelong friendships, meaningful relationships and then moving on, so it was with a feeling of resignation that she accompanied her people, Dale and Kenny, on their trek northwards. That doesn't make it any easier, though. Holly still misses her friend who, though bigger than Holly, was a gentle giant. Holly, being a Kelpie, would stir up Jepanka, who would catch Holly, pin her to the ground and sit on her. Holly loved Jepanka! And Jepanka loved Holly!

But this story doesn't begin here — it starts long before Holly came to live with us. It does start with the name, though. Holly. I had to convince Doug that we did need another dog (Ruff was getting very old — eighteen years — and he wasn't really my dog anyway) and now that Mum and Dad had moved next door, we had back-ups who could feed and walk her when we were away. And I *knew* that they would love their first granddog — so far they only had four grandcats and two step-granddogs.

Part of the convincing-Doug process involved picking the name Holly (she was going to be Holly the Border Collie) and pretending that this dog existed. This meant calling her to heel when walking in public, making room for her on the sofa between us, and throwing sticks for her on the beach.

It didn't take long, though, before we were doing reccies of the GAWS (Geelong Animal Welfare Shelter) — GAWS dogs are the best! The first Holly applicant was a rangy looking Labrador-cross — pretty cute, but he had already gone when I rang back to enquire the next day. Then there was the cute little only-a-mother-could-love-her pooch who had already been reclaimed by her owner as an escapee. Then the Dingo — we were warned off her as a desperate escapee who wouldn't stay put — followed by the Heeler who was a bit of a loony, barking at any sound or movement, and who couldn't stand still for a moment.

We sort of knew, though, when we found the dog that I had been walking, talking to and teaching tricks to for the last few months. She was the *only* GAWS dog who would sit when asked, would listen to us, and didn't bark. The only sound she made was when we said good-bye on our third visit — and then only a whine. We had to wait a week in case she was claimed by her owner, as she had been found wandering, and visiting her during that week was quite stressful, in case she was re-claimed in the meantime.

Of course when we got her home, the butter-wouldn't-melt-in-my-mouth dog was replaced by the I-am-still-a-Kelpie-at-heart dog who would dig out under, or climb out over fences, and chase the cats. The digging under and climbing over has ceased — we have an agreement that involves one hour devoted *every* morning to a w-a-l-k — don't say the word aloud! The digging has since been modified to, "I will sometimes dig up your vegies and your flowers and look mortified when quizzed later" — still working on this one. The cat-chasing has also been modified to, "Oh shit — there's Scarey-puss — I'll just look at the ground and give her a wide berth". Eartha (a.k.a. Scarey-puss) rules the household, and has been known to leap on a dog's back and ride him, jockey-style, while he yelped his way out of her territory. Not Holly, though — she learnt a bit faster than the none-too-bright Siggy.

So much for Holly's enemies (well, enemy singular, really, although even Eartha is mellowing). Her Number One friend (except for us) is Grandma, who lives next door, and who Holly will always nick off to visit given half a chance.

Also Aunty Deb, who has dog-sat while we were away, can always be convinced to go for a w-a-l-k and over whom Holly will whip herself into a frenzy.

Then there are her friends at the Community Nursery. When these people meet Mum and Dad, and find out that they are my parents, they will firstly ask after Holly. She is a favourite at the nursery and usually out-ranks the occasional baby/grandchild visitor.

And of course as well as people-friends there are the special dog-friends — Rusty, Toffee, Mitch, Dougal, Cindy, Heidi, Keira, Poppy, Bonnie, Dolly, Molly and Stollie, as well as her first and best-friend — Jepanka.

The thing about my dog, you see, is she is *anyone* and *everyone's* best friend.

*Felicity Thyer has long been a cat lover but became a dog convert with the arrival of Holly. Her favourite pastimes are walking Holly on the beach and a bit of gardening (pooper scooping, filling in holes etc.). Holly's favourite pastimes are much the same, only in reverse!*

# Thank You to a Dog
Bronwyn Simmons

**A small, black-and-white furry thing,** big brown eyes, large white paws and a flag pole tail. A mix of Jack Russell and Silky Terrier I was told but who really knows. It's not very important. Billie, Dog, Chook, Hairy Hound, Buglet and other silly names, too many to mention and some long forgotten. And I still wonder why she doesn't come when I call her.

A great ball of wriggling legs and tongue when she leaps on to the bed in the morning. The morning shift: husband out of bed, dog on bed. A process of snufflings, scratching, rustling, chewing and finding the perfect spot on the wrinkled doona before settling for contented sleep. My nose peeping out to greet the rising sun is met by a shiny wet black nose. The dog and I get up together, my husband gets up alone to a quiet dark house. Dog races to the kitchen — maybe today is one of those days when a piece of old, tired cold meat is deemed no longer suitable for sandwiches. The dog bursts into the kitchen, greets my husband, "Is there any food for me?" No, just a pat and a friendly word. Dog is content and wanders off with tail wagging and settles in the bean bag.

Finish breakfast, coffee, a small bowl of milk left over from cereal for the dog, enthusiastic with anticipation. Wander out to say goodbye to husband as he rides his pushbike to work at 6.30 a.m. We kiss goodbye at the gate. The dog catches up on who or what has been past our front fence during the evening, nose down, tail up. We wander back to the house, the dog watches me closely. "Will we set off for a walk now, or will plants be watered and chooks fed first?" I begin to put on my boots in the back room, the dog jumps, leaps, squiggles about, eyes shining, it's the magic walking boots (a small joke the dog and I share which may be lost on anyone else). I reach for the lead and try to clip it on; an excited dog dances, circles around my hand in so much of a hurry that standing still is just not an option. We set off together in the quiet morning, pausing at the colour of the sky and wondering at the promise of the day to come. Which one of our walks today, the river, the beach or the cliffs? Sometimes I choose, sometimes the dog chooses.

We head to the river today, keeping the dog on the lead while on the road to reach the river. Snap of the lead and the dog leaps off, out of the starting gate. Sometimes we walk together, usually the dog dawdles behind sniffing and peering into the bush. Favourite smelling spots are a must stop, like a favourite coffee shop, these sites are to be savoured and thoroughly investigated, this is not a time for haste. I look for the swans I saw last week, the other birds and the new growth and flowers of the bushland. Both dog and I are content with each other's silent company, immersed in our own worlds.

We are back home, the dog stands quietly in the yard waiting to see what I will do. I am working from home today, we will have each other for company all day. I made a large wooden box for the dog one wet Saturday afternoon and this is the favourite bed. After snufflings, scratching, rustling, chewing, the dog settles in her wooden box, head resting on the old purple blanket and the morning sun falls on ruffled fur. Eyes closed, a happy dog.

Another perfect morning for a funny hairy little dog and I wonder how I could ever start the day without her. How can you say thank you to a dog? For all the hours of companionship, the many conversations, the absolute dogness and all the truly disgusting habits this entails at times, when I have been outsmarted and the sheer contentedness of a small curled-up dog nestled on my lap in the evening. Our morning routine is a start.

*I grew up in a very small country town and have always had a great love of animals and the natural world. Many hours of my childhood were spent exploring the native bushland and we always had animals at home, most of them at my insistence. Guinea pigs, rabbits, budgies, quails, calves, one horse, small dogs and cats. My parents often remark that in nearly every photo of me I am holding an animal. I had a very special cat who was born the same year as me and died in my arms when I was in my early teens, she showed me the remarkable bond that humans and animals can share. In my mid-twenties I lost my heart to a small black-and-white dog and she has been my loyal friend through many moves, country to city to coast, career changes and marriage.*

# Tipsy Kathryn Crofts

The day we got Tipsy was a complete surprise. Just that morning I had been sitting there, at the table, looking through the classifieds at the Pets section. That afternoon we were apparently going to a pot place called 'Pots Alive!' We got in the car with my brother clutching his money to buy a pot. We drove around for forty-five minutes until we reached this house. With my brother and I questioning that this really did not look like a pot place, we went inside. There we saw the most gorgeous little Sheltie puppy. He was mainly black with a white collar of fur around his neck, a white tip on his tail, tan around his muzzle and tan eyebrows. This little puppy was running around the house refusing to be caught. We were greeted with the pleasant news that this was to be our very own dog. I couldn't believe it! On the way home I kept asking, "Is he *really* ours?"

That night with one of our friends, Annalies, we were debating what to call him. Annalies came up with the name Tipsy. My father finished the name off by calling him Tipsy Wara the Famous. And it suited him down pat for several reasons. One reason was from when we first took him down to the foreshore. This woman had put down her glass of beer next to Tipsy. Tipsy then decided that he must have a taste of this liquid and so he did. When the woman saw what he had done she asked what his name was. We simply replied 'Tipsy'. To that this woman laughed.

Tipsy is one of the kindest dogs there is. He is always there for a cuddle, is most forgiving if you stand on his paw and is generally good company. Tipsy is one of the best friends someone could have.

*Name: Kathryn Crofts. Age: 14.*
*Lives: Newcastle.*
*Occupation: Year 8 student at Warners Bay High School.*
*History with Dogs: Tipsy is my first dog. My brother Andrew and I were begging for about seven years for a dog. In the end we finally wore our parents down and got Tipsy, a Shetland Sheepdog (Sheltie).*

# Connecting Family, Connecting Friends

Penny Crofts

**I still remember the day it happened.** The first hint that things weren't right was the early morning pooh hunt. In our household this is women's work and in particular my work. It's a job I find quite satisfying which is probably a measure of either my insanity, or more hopefully my affinity with our family dog — Tipsy. (More about the name later.)

The morning pooh hunt is a ritual. With scoop in hand I scour the yard looking for those neat little piles of pooh, strategically placed to ensure that unsuspecting family members will be reminded of the dog's presence in ways they don't appreciate. So pooper scooping is motivated by a protective instinct and flows as a natural consequence from the powerful bond formed through nurturing a puppy to an adult dog.

We wander the yard together enjoying the early morning sunlight on the glistening paddocks beyond the fence where horses graze close by in anticipation of feeding time. We revel in the peace before the household erupts into its usual morning chaos. Tipsy gives no clues as to where to scoop. He wanders purposefully around the plants inhaling scents that have meaning for him and about which I can only wonder. The predicability and absorption of his task fascinate me, and often distract me from my focus as I take time to enjoy his very presence. I find it hard to explain the meaning of his companionship — I only know what it would mean not to have it.

Which brings me back to that morning. The pooh hunt provided ample evidence that all was not right with Tipsy. On closer inspection it was clear that this morning he was different. He wasn't interested in a playful frolic with the ball as usual. Instead of the morning plant patrol, he was resting in the sandpit — but not comfortably. It was clear that instead of heading to work we were going to the vet.

The vet seemed unconcerned but felt it wise to keep him in for observation. So I headed off to work reassured that all would be well and looking forward to picking him up on my way home. My part-time work enabled me to call in at the vet's in the early afternoon, planning then to proceed with dog in tow to pick up my daughter from school. Her joy in his appearance at the schoolyard gate was a prospect to look forward to.

I was greeted at the vet's by very concerned staff who had been trying to reach me. They took me in to Tipsy who was hooked up to a drip and fighting for life. Despite this, at the sound of my voice he stoically but limply wagged his tail. This is the measure of a relationship with a dog — it is founded on unbridled loyalty and acceptance. Even in these circumstances he was still pleased to see me. I was overwhelmed by the realisation that he means the world to me and by the enormity of our potential loss should he not pull through.

Days went by without much progress. Finally we were referred to a specialist veterinary clinic in Sydney where pancreatitis was diagnosed. The two-hour car trip was a family affair. If Tipsy was to die then we would go through it together. This is the power of a dog's role in a family. So many family memories and connections are around Tipsy's antics. Testimony to his centrality in our lives were the ongoing calls from family members far and wide to hear of his progress.

At the specialist (read expensive!) clinic Tipsy was assessed and our last view as we left the 'hospital', a little reassured about his prognosis, was of him on a trolley bed hooked to a drip being wheeled off to the ward! The image is one we frequently return to with much mirth. A week later we returned to pick up a much revived dog. Again it was a family affair and this time filled with much relief and joy.

The experience was a powerful reminder of the significance of Tipsy's role in family life and in my life. He provides a focus, a source of joy. He accepts us all and relates to us all in different ways. It is difficult to imagine a future without him, but our lives have been immensely richer for his part in them. Even his name has a history — he was named Tipsy by a dog-mad friend who had lobbied for years for us to acquire a pup, much to the consternation of my mother who feels the name does nothing for his regal looks. In case you're wondering he is a tri-coloured Sheltie and a much-loved friend.

*Name: Penny Crofts. Age: 44 years. Lives: Newcastle. Occupation: Teaches Social Work at the Newcastle University.*
*History with Dogs: Penny had a variety of dogs as a child. As you do, she loved them all. Now Tipsy is her only dog.*

# My Granddog 'Tipsy'

## Barbara Mathews

**Some years ago** when my grandchildren excitedly told me they had a new addition to their family — a beautiful Shetland Collie puppy — a picture immediately sprang to my mind of a noble animal standing atop a green hillside, fur ruffled by the breeze and monarch of all he surveyed! Of course, he would have a distinguished name — perhaps Dougall, or Donald, or even just plain Mac — but "Oh no, Nan," said the children, "his name is Tipsy." Well, as time progressed and Tipsy and I became better acquainted, I found the children really were much wiser than I — his behaviour often did suggest he may have imbibed a dram or two o' the famous Highland tipple!

Anyway, over time Tipsy and I developed a firm friendship — I visited him quite often and he would sometimes spend a holiday with me when his family were away. They would arrive at my house laden with all the doggie paraphernalia, including his toys and special bed, but somehow he always managed to end up sleeping at the end of my bed, which I really didn't mind, except if I had to go to the bathroom during the night I would return to find him snoring gently in my nice warm spot, with his head nestled cosily on my pillow, and refusing to budge!

On most afternoons when he is visiting with me he takes me for a walk to the local park, where there is an area set aside for dogs, and he has a wonderful time romping and socialising with the local canines and exploring all the interesting nooks and crannies, not to mention the countless tree-trunk stops, after which he allows me to take him sedately home and we sit down together, with my cup of tea and his bowl of water, for a quiet chat. He always listens intently and agrees with my point of view, and never seems to mind if I repeat a story I have told him before, or if I happen to nod off in my chair for a few minutes in the middle of a sentence!

During his earlier visits to my house I would cook him a roast dinner as a special treat and when I had my lunch-time sandwich I would fix a tasty little snack for him. Sadly, though, a few years ago he had a very serious illness and had to go to hospital, after which he was put on a Very Restricted diet, so now his snack has to consist of a small plate of carrot slices, and although he doesn't complain, somehow my tasty sandwich doesn't seem quite so inviting when I look into those wistful eyes.

Last year, after having undergone shoulder surgery and having my right arm immobilised in a complicated sling for six weeks, I went to stay with my family for that time. My daughter was concerned that Tipsy might present a problem by jumping up at me in his usual exuberant greeting, but he instinctively seemed to understand the situation and would stay quietly at my side while the family were all at work or school. Every now and then we'd have some conversation together, or take a stroll around the garden, but wherever I went he was always close by my side to make sure I came to no harm.

So, that is the story of my Granddog Tipsy — my loyal part-time companion, my wonderful much-loved friend!

*Name: Barbara Mathews.*
*Age: 74 years.*
*Lives: Gosford.*
*History with Dogs: Barbara has had many dogs throughout her life. At one stage she was breeding Wire-haired Terriers.*

# Requiem

## Terry Wolverton

It is a sunny winter morning and I am struggling with you
to carry — up your steep hillside — the frozen body
of your dog.

Your first dog, Pencil, the good dog, the lady.
Who would sit with her front paws crossed, so dainty.
Who was often seen with a dog food can stuck on the end of her nose.
Who would press her face against your thigh and rest there
for as long as you let her.

Sunday she was playing with young girls in the laundromat.
Today she is dead and frozen like a popsicle and we are
trying to avoid your landlord as we trudge upward
with her stiff heavy carcass.

You tell me, "Pencil is still with me, but you are gone."
I don't feel gone, with this cold weight in my arms.
I have held you all night long, trying to make myself
more real to you than death. We have been failing
for a long time.

We at last reach the top, lower her body to the dirt.
You will spend the day digging. I advise you to let the other dogs
see her, so they will stop searching for her.

You disconnect your phone. Days pass. Though I hear you
screaming at me in my dreams, I do not return to your hillside
where Pencil lies deep in the earth.

*Terry Wolverton is the author of* Bailey's Beads, *a novel,
and two collections of poetry,* Black Slip *and* Mystery
Bruise. *A memoir,* Insurgent Muse, *is forthcoming from City
Lights in 2002. She says, "It's an odd thing to realise but I
have never had my photo taken with a canine. So the
pumpkin has to be a dog substitute."*

# The Canine Clown Julie Daws

**I've had some dogs who were really smart.** And I've had some dogs who were neurotic. But I've only ever had one dog who seemed to enjoy making people laugh.

Cerberus was an English Bull Terrier. White, with black ears and a spotty nose. A head like a football and a body like a white pig. When I first got her as a puppy not many people knew much about Bull Terriers. They had a fearsome reputation — even as a puppy some people were scared of her and refused to come near her. She would bite them they thought, and her jaws would lock and she would never let go. The little piggy eyes were full of malice — she was just waiting to get her fangs on them they said. Being named after the guardian of the gates of Hades probably didn't help that reputation, I guess.

Nor did one of our favourite games where I used to take her for walks and she would strain against the leash and I would pretend that she was trying to break loose in order to attack the innocent victim heading toward me. Some people looked truly horrified, most looked wary — some even crossed the road. Mind you getting her to walk on a leash

in the first place was a labour of Hercules. Bull Terriers are not only funny, they are also incredibly stubborn. Filled with dog-training enthusiasm, I clipped the brand new leash to her collar only to have her lie down and refuse to budge. Dragging her only caused gravel rash on the belly. I thought about it and bought some of those training collars — the ones designed to tighten and encourage the dog to follow the leash. She would prefer to vomit rather than do as she was asked. Eventually I did achieve a sort of training — she would come when she was called providing there was nowhere else more interesting she wanted to go to and she would happily allow anyone to take food away from her or anything else out of her mouth. I figured the last achievement was probably the most important with a Bull Terrier, anyway.

There was one time when she made the mistake of trying to grab a bone my father had removed from her mouth — the mistake was that she missed the bone and accidentally sank her fang into my father's thumb. Blood everywhere, screams, and one thumb chipped in to the bone. The look of horror and guilt on her face was comical — well, it was to us I guess. I have no doubt that my father saw nothing funny in the situation.

Nor did he see the funny side another time. Bull Terriers don't always seem to carry those massive heads very well. Cerberus was always bumping it and knocking it on things, like kids who grow too quickly seem to knock themselves. Sometimes the bumps and cuts would get infected and would result in a trip to the vet to have them drained and a course of antibiotics. After one particularly gruesome trip she had massive stitches, tubes hanging everywhere and was still recovering from surgery. I guess it wasn't the best time to be playing chasey round the house with her — she came bowling round a corner in that inimitable Bull Terrier style and ran crack into my father's leg. And crack was exactly the noise it made — howls and screams and blood everywhere once more — the howls and screams were my father's, the blood belonged to the dog. She never made a sound — simply turned and ran as fast as she could for cover, tubes and blood flying everywhere!

The stoicism of the Bull Terrier is legendary — I remember one trip to the vet being regaled with stories of bullies ripped open by wild boars and not making a sound while they were repaired. And Cerberus herself showed this a few times. Once my mother decided that the dogs should be given heartworm tablets because of a reported outbreak in the area. She took them along to be tested first — only to find that Cerberus was already infected. The cure was to insert a catheter into the vein and to inject enough arsenic to kill the worm but not the dog. After several unsuccessful attempts the vet decided that her veins were too rubbery to allow a catheter to be inserted — he would have to inject the arsenic directly. He warned my mother that this would be extremely painful and the dog would probably be in a lot of pain for quite a while and would need supervision as she would be very distressed. She took her along to work in order to keep an eye on her — two hours later she was forced to take her home because she had been driving the office staff mad by playing canine soccer with herself around the office and knocking people off their feet.

Another time she horrified us all by managing to find and eat an entire packet of Ratsack bait — box and all. It was really late at night on a public holiday — my mother rang the vet and he said to induce vomiting by filling her with salt water. We filled her so much that the water overflowed and still she didn't vomit — unusual because bullies seem to like bolting down their food then vomiting it up for a second taste. But this time was no-go. The vet promised to have something for her in the morning but by that time it was unnecessary — a trail of green diarrhoea up the driveway proved that the Ratsack was no longer a problem. Amazingly it seemed to do no other harm.

But bullies have the most amazing culinary habits. One time the cat had dragged a rat up to the back doorstep, as was her wont. My mother was naturally cheered by this sight first thing in the morning and stepped back inside for a moment to seek out a suitable receptacle. When she came out a few seconds later, dustpan in hand, the rat had vanished. Had it come back to life we wondered? Were we about to be haunted by the spectre of a zombie rat? A big white head suddenly peered around the corner — glancing down at the back doorstep it licked its lips — aha! Mystery solved! Bull Terriers do not eat their food — they inhale it.

They also tend to inhale other things. Cerberus had the ability to hold three tennis balls at once in her mouth. She loved nothing more than stealing balls from neighbourhood children who, of course, were too terrified to retrieve them. We were constantly plagued by requests to retrieve balls, and we would amaze people by simply wrenching open her mouth, putting our hands in and pulling them out. But balls weren't the only things she liked to steal — washing was also a prime favourite when I was trying to hang it on the line. Even better if it was wet and muddy and I was yelling and giving chase around the backyard. The aim of the game was to find the worst puddle and deposit the wet sheet or whatever. Bull terrier 1, kids 0.

But Cerberus always liked the last laugh. And even in her death she achieved this. My mother, who had been out, came driving up the driveway only to find my father staring at where her car was now parked and crying. All he could stutter out was that Cerberus had died and, for a few horrified moments, pandemonium ruled as my mother thought she had run over her while she had been basking in the sun on the driveway, as was her habit. But Cerberus had simply lain down to sunbathe and never woken up — she had died several hours earlier in the place where my mother was now parked and had been buried in the garden. But I'm almost positive a big white head was looking around the corner and laughing at all the fracas she had yet again managed to cause.

*I am thirty-six years old, have a Masters degree in Education, was brought up in Melbourne and lived for too long in the frozen wastes of central Victoria and am currently thawing out in Queensland. I share a house with a husband, two children, five cats and another dog with a heap of personality. And as I believe in reincarnation it wouldn't surprise me to have Cerberus come back to make my life interesting again one of these days.*

# Jim and Friends

Judy Barber

**Originally this story** was going to be exclusively about Jimmy, who came into our lives about six years ago. However on reflection I can see that his story is inextricably intertwined with that of Miss Pipi, our very beautiful and intelligent short-haired terrier-cross. Pipi with her sleek coat of brown velvet, and her little pointed face and ears that were never still as they expressed her never-ending curiosity. Another member of the crew was dear old Paddy, a black-and-white Border Collie-cross who had been raised by our children on a bottle when abandoned as a very small new-born puppy (not very bright, but full of love for us all), and then there was Mavvy, our very handsome ageing black Labrador and, last but not least, our newest arrival, Marie-Claire, our beautiful tan-and-cream Collie-cross-teenage girl-dog.

Jimmy, or Sir James to give him his official title, came into our lives about six years ago when he was rescued from the dog catcher by our daughter Sue. This little terrier, mostly black with a white blob at the end of his tail was found wandering the streets on a cold wet winter's day in a nearby country town. Huge, dark liquid eyes looked pleadingly up out of a shivering black bedraggled ball of fur, all spiky and wet, followed by a few pathetic rasping breaths, and Sue melted. He was wrapped in a towel, given some tinned food hastily procured from the local supermarket and settled down beside her desk for the rest of the day.

On arriving home that night he met Miss (Princess) Pipi, who disdainfully sniffed and then totally ignored him. Turning her back she began to eat her own specially prepared favourite chicken wings and, although usually a fussy eater, she then demolished the food set out for Jim also. With bulging tummy Miss Pipi, legs kicking frantically, was forcibly removed from the room to allow Jim to eat. This didn't worry Jim, who proceeded to devour a huge

meal, and after looking around some, decided he had had enough and walked off down the drive. He was brought back and introduced to his warm bed; but Jim was used to sleeping rough and for the next few nights, after partaking of a huge meal, he wandered off again, only to be intercepted and firmly brought back. After a time he decided that maybe he was on to a good thing and might stay a while!

Jim thus became another member of the family. He also fell in love — very much so — with Miss Pipi. Although initially he was tolerated at best, he was smitten; wherever Pipi went there was Jimmy right behind — he stayed behind because if ever he was presumptuous enough to walk beside Pipi he was quickly put in his place with a quick snap of her sharp little teeth. But this didn't deter Jim, he was content to worship from wherever he was allowed, and he *was* persistent. After many rebuffs, he was finally allowed to sit beside Pipi as she was reclining on someone's lap (quite a difficult fit sometimes, but they were small!). Jim was suitably grateful, and showed this by making himself as small as possible and not moving at all, because he knew if he did move another snap would remind him exactly where he was.

Jim, being a healthy young adult male, tried his best to woo Pipi, however he was doomed to failure and he was never rewarded for his efforts. At first we were fascinated with his little dance of love but, as it became more frequent, it was inevitable that our Jim had to have the big snip as the vet agreed that this was the best course of action for our little 'lover'. After this the situation cooled a bit, but Jim's devotion never waned; it didn't matter whether he was being patted or fed or cuddled, whenever Miss Pipi decided to go elsewhere, Jim hastily dropped whatever he was doing and followed close behind.

Pipi loved us all so; she would sense instinctively when any of her family needed comforting, inclining her head and looking at you with beautiful calm eyes, as though she was assessing your need, then she would jump up into a lap, sit quietly, perhaps licking a hand, sometimes licking a tear off a cheek, and just be there for you.

Similarly, when my husband was very ill some two years ago, Jim wouldn't leave his side and after a short while became very quiet and withdrawn, barely eating and rarely moving from his place beside Kevin's lounge chair. After a time Kevin began recovering and our attention was switched from him as Jim's behaviour and loss of weight suddenly became very noticeable. On consultation, the vet explained that Jim was severely depressed because of his empathy with Kevin's illness — it hadn't occurred to us that this was the reason for those big sad eyes. But happily, as Kevin continued to recover, so did Jim!

Our darlings touch each of us in different ways: for me personally it is the gladness I feel on returning home each night to the tangle of legs, wagging tails and joyous barks as they hurl themselves down the steps toward me, each trying to outdo the other in welcoming me home. No matter what my day has been like I know they all love me to bits and they are *so* glad I'm home! Watering the garden on a summer evening with Marie-Claire sitting quietly beside me as we enjoy the stillness and listen to the night sounds together; the peace of a winter fire with the rain falling outside, the soft sounds of dogs snoring contentedly around me as we drift off to sleep together. These are the special times for me that comfort, relax and restore.

When Miss Pipi was suddenly taken from us in a sad accident, Jim and Mavvy couldn't comprehend she was not coming back. They settled down in the drive to wait for her. For several days they sat quietly and waited — no amount of thrown balls or entreaties to come for a walk would move them. They only came in to eat (very poorly) and sleep. The whole family was grieving deeply and they were too. A friend gave Sue a beautiful pink rose in Pipi's memory, which we planted over her final resting place, and with a glass of champagne in celebration of her life, we talked of what our much loved Pipi had meant to each of us.

After a brief illness at the end of a long and happy life, Paddy left us also. Both have left gaps that will never be filled as each occupied a unique place in our lives. They are remembered by a special resting place in our garden, and a rosebush. Each year as the roses flower their beauty reminds us of their lives, of our love for these special members of our family, and the unconditional love they gave to us so freely.

*Married, with a grown-up family, I have been employed for some years as an administrative officer at Deakin University, and I enjoy beach walking, gardening and sewing. I am also trying to find the time to complete an Arts degree! Pets of all kinds have always been an important part of my life and at present we share our home and lives with four dogs.*

# Alice and Rupert and Dianne and Louise

Louise Allison

**Hello, my name is Alice** (left in picture). I am a seven-year-old Cavalier King Charles Spaniel and I would like to tell you about my family. I live with my brother, Rupert, a five-year-old Cavalier, Ruff the cat, rescued from the RSPCA, and my two mothers, Dianne (left) and Louise. We make a very fine family and I know that Rupert and I play a very important part in the lives of our mothers. Dianne bought us from the breeder at Bungendore and is therefore known as our mother. Louise joined the family a little later and is known as our 'other mother' or 'Other' for short.

Rupert likes to think he is responsible for creating our happy family as Louise, who previously had owned Winston, a Cavalier, for fourteen years, went for a coffee with Dianne and a mutual friend who was match-making, on the very day Dianne collected Rupert from Bungendore. This, of course, gave Louise, lover of Cavaliers, the excellent excuse to phone Dianne and ask how the puppy had settled, which gave Dianne the opening to say come and visit and meet him and the rest, as they say, is history!

We all live in a fine house in the Australian Capital Territory. Rupert and I sleep in our quarters in the garage with our nice beds and an electric blanket to fend off the chills of Canberra winter. A typical day starts with Other entering the garage about 6 a.m. and letting us out to do a wee then come inside and join the mothers under the doona. Rupert follows the Cavalier instinct and dives right under, curls up around one set of feet and falls asleep within seconds. After all we were bred to keep the aristocratic feet warm. I prefer the pillow and rest quite comfortably between the mothers, licking them happily until one or other growls — "Alice, settle" and I reluctantly do. We all sleep peacefully till around seven when Other arises and showers. She then dresses and takes Rupert and me out for our morning constitutional while Mother showers and dresses. Other very diligently carries a plastic bag and leaves behind no trace of our walk through the suburb.

We return home and report all the doings to Mother — like the number of cockatoos we've seen (Rupert's favourite) or the number of houses knocked down so that three more can take their place, or who has planted what in their garden. There's always something of interest happening. We then watch the mothers breakfast. If it's really cold we get porridge, too, or a nice bowl of warm tea. We're not spoilt. We deserve it all. Then it is off to work for some. We go out happily with an Outside Biscuit and they disappear for hours. Much later they return and we then settle in for the evening, with our dinner and a bit of telly. Rupert loves 'The Bill', 'Inspector Rex' and 'Harry's Practice'. Often I prefer the leather lounge, where there is more room to relax.

Sometimes we go in and out all night — to check out the stars and the cat next door — until Other growls again and we know that no matter how hard we scratch at the door she will be resolute and say, "You've been out six times and that's enough!" Sometimes Mother lets us out and forgets to get us back in and we run and bark and bark. We have fun but Other worries because our worst day was Boxing Day 1998 when a black envelope was delivered to our letter box with a death threat. Typed in large black letters on one sheet of paper was, "Keep your dog quiet or it dies". The mothers were very upset and bravely door-knocked all the neighbours to see who we were annoying. No one owned up and the mothers now try to keep us quiet — at least during evening hours. What we do all day, they'll never know.

What do our mothers mean to us? For me, they mean biscuits, cuddles, dinner, walks, treats (edible), company, bones and laps to sleep on. I asked Rupert and he said that to him they meant mutual love and a nostril or two to lick. I think we mean a lot to our mothers — as we are loyal, devoted and always pleased to see them no matter what time of day or night. We greet them warmly with wagging tails and smiling faces and always say, "Our day is better now cause you are home." If they are sad or lonely we pick up on this and sit on their knees and give them kisses. I know their friends think our mothers spoil us but we say no, they love us and we love them. We give them presents on their birthdays and at Christmas. Rupert tries his best to write on cards — last birthday he called Other 'Otter' by mistake, but she didn't mind. He did it with love and the best of intentions.

I have an answering machine that suits me well. When someone calls "Alice, Alice" they get a fine message: "You've reached Alice's answering machine. Please leave a message after the tone and I'll get back to you as soon as I feel like it, or if you have a biscuit!" Rupert and I can sit and wait at the kerb but I can't pretend we are well trained. What we lack in discipline we make up for in love. We are kind and affectionate and truly loyal family members.

Our day ends as Other lets us out for a last call of nature and puts us into bed with, joy oh joy, another biscuit. Rupert and I curl up contentedly. Not a bad life.

*Alice told her story to her other mother, Louise Allison, who lives with her partner, Dianne in Canberra. Louise is an ex-primary school teacher and mother of three adult children. For the last ten years she has been working in the equity and diversity field and is currently a Senior Human Resource Advisor. Louise and Dianne enjoy travel, reading, eating out and their home life with Alice, Ruff, and Rupert. Louise shares Rupert's passion for 'The Bill'.*

# A Suitable Girl Becomes a Suitable Boy

Pauline Meemeduma

**We set out for the big smoke** two hundred kilometres away to get a new dog. A Border Collie female puppy was the great plan. Border Collie puppies were difficult to get in our part of rural Western Australia. I suspect because sensibly the farmers wanted and kept them as working dogs. We had been lucky to get our first Border Collie puppy from a nearby farm. Two years had passed and Katie remained our only Border Collie.

We set out to get a girl. It wasn't just about getting a dog. It wasn't just about getting a beautiful black-and-white Border Collie. Gender was equally important. In a household of males (partner/sons) dogs had an important role in addressing gender imbalance. A ratio of 1:4 improved to 2:4 with the addition of Katie. With the new anticipated pup it would improve to 3:4. Indeed, if it wasn't for the local council regulations of two dogs per household, we could strive for gender equity and more in our house. Besides female dogs I 'knew' were just-that-much-more-wonderful than male dogs. Soft-shy-loving-reticent Katie represented all that is nice about being female; whether in a dog or a human. There was no debate, no doubt, a female the new dog would be.

We came home with Nelson (his new name) — a *boy*. When we got to the city the breeder said all the female Border Collie puppies had been sold and there were only two males left. "Not possible," I said, "has to be a female — their personalities are quieter and they are a lot easier to handle." "Na," said the breeder, "no difference between the genders in dogs — anyway just have a look, no obligation to buy."

There he was sitting with his brother, looking like an amalgam of a wharfie and brickie — square and solid and 'there'. Lovely-soft-shy-loving-reticent Nelson was not. He was neither a suitable girl nor even a suitable boy when the 'gender factor' is allowed for. When he licked your face he crashed into it. When he ran up to you he crashed on, in and over you. He was as solid as a two-by-two and as present as a ten-ton truck. He has got bigger but not much better. A wharfie-brickie with love I like to think of Nelson.

So why did I bring him home? He was so full of testosterone he was going to tip the gender ratio totally off the scale in our house. It is a 'thereness'. A very real here and now about his presence which is so different from Katie. Katie will quietly put her head on your lap and love and be loved. Nelson will put his head, body, legs, all on your lap — his notion of love is a oneness — a total symbiotic enmeshment with the object of his affection. He

doesn't do anything by halves, our Nelson. You have to love him because he is 'in your face', literally, about being loved. You have to admire him. Girls, i.e. Katie and I, need that kind of love so I reasoned. So I parted with the money and brought him home. He had the makings of a suitable boy for these two girls.

We would have to manage all this testosterone at home. Katie, with two years wisdom and feminine intuition, whipped him into the lower end of the hierarchical dog order very quickly — before he got too big. She quietly watches much of his hormone-driven frenzied antics in the garden from a shaded spot. My approach was more direct. Off to dog school for all that testosterone. Nelson was going to learn to be a suitable boy. We are still there, not learning a lot but having *fun*. Nelson approaches dog school the way he approaches life — one big over-the-top barrel of fun. He taught me dog school isn't about passing your exams to get to the next level — because he doesn't. It is about *fun* and laughs with other dogs and owners. It's about kind of learning 'heel' 'sit' 'stand' 'stay', enough so you don't totally humiliate yourself — he did get 66/100 in his exam (75/100 is a pass). Then dashing back next week for more fun. I think, based on our current attitudes, Nelson and I are going to be the longest dog school participants in the country.

I have begun to work out in the year Nelson has been with us he is the complimentary Yin and Yang of the female personality. He is the woman in purple — "here I am, hang what you all think". Neither of us gets left and right commands right at dog school — but what does it matter. He is the opposing balance to the behave yourself, worry about what others think, succeed world view of Katie and myself. He truly is a gal in purple. He truly is a suitable boy.

*Pauline has always considered dogs part of the wellbeing of herself and her family. She and her partner have three sons who have grown up with dogs as part of their family life. In her working life she is a social work academic and practitioner. In her home life she loves gardening (though spends a lot of time stopping the Collies digging holes and chasing through the flowers) and reading. Pauline lives in the south west of Western Australia next to the Indian Ocean with her two beautiful Border Collies. One of her greatest pleasures is her early morning walks on the beach with the dogs.*

# At the End of the Day…

Dai Le

**It was about five in the morning** July 1999. We could hear the scratching on the door separating our kitchen from the hallway. Our bedroom was at the front of our Federation house. I got up to see what was happening. Sheila, our Fox Terrier-cross dog, was panting. The newspapers we'd layed in her whelping box had been ripped and scattered everywhere. She obviously was in distress. I patted her and indicated for her to get back in her box, which she did obediently. I went back to bed, telling my husband that it was a false alarm.

About an hour-and-a-half later, we could hear some scuffling sound. I had that feeling and I was right. Sheila had produced a pup. I woke my husband up and excitedly pointed to a small grey-and-white pup. We then sat to monitor her next one. It was a white one (long hair). Then another grey-and-white (long hair), then a black and another white one (short hair). Sheila gave birth to five healthy pups.

It was a wonderful moment, witnessing such an amazing act, considering our Sheila was about sixty centimetres long and weighed about three kilos. The pups were huge!

So what were we to do with five pups? We've already had two dogs by this stage: Sheila, and our loyal and great watchdog, Bonnie! Well, we decided to keep the third pup, whom we named Brando. Yes, there are now three dogs in our household and, luckily, we still have a yard big enough for the three of them.

All three have their different personalities. Bonnie, a Bull Mastiff-cross-German Shepherd was our first dog. We inherited her from my mother. Mum wanted a 'black dog that would scare away the thieves'. But my mother was disappointed when, at three months old, Bonnie wouldn't

bark! She asked if Markus, my husband, and I would have her. I am a lover of dogs as far back as I can remember. Markus however didn't grow up with dogs so I was concerned when I asked him if we could take Bonnie home. To my surprise, he agreed. And I don't think he ever regretted it.

Bonnie has been a wonderful and loyal dog, as well as a great watchdog. She started barking at about nine months old. I remember one morning we were just waking up when we heard this bark. We looked at each other and thought, it couldn't possibly be. Bonnie, barking? We rushed to our backyard and looked at Bonnie. She stood there and just wagged her tail. We talked to her (as people often do, talk to their pets). She just stood there and didn't make a sound. We were wrong, we thought. But then as soon as we turned to walk back inside the house, she gave us a bark! It was such a lovely sound. It was as if you've just heard your child utter their first word. We were the excited parents.

Bonnie was an 'only child'. Until one day, my mother heaved onto us another abandoned dog: Sheila. She was rather ugly, a real mongrel. But we thought Bonnie needed company because we were often not home and would come home late from work. So we agreed to have Sheila. Again, I was so surprised at my husband's generosity to have one dog, let alone two dogs! As Sheila was small, we didn't think it would threaten Bonnie's territory. The two dogs got along very well. Bonnie, with her pleasant and accommodating nature, welcomed and made Sheila feel at home. They had never fought. I suppose, Sheila wouldn't dare pick a fight with Bonnie, or even try to steal her bones!

About ten months after her coming to live with us, Markus one day drew my attention to Sheila's bulging stomach. I confidently told him that she was just getting fat as she was now feeling more at home. He insisted that I look at the stomach more closely. I insisted she was fat. A couple of weeks later, her 'fat' stomach was growing unusually big. We were watching TV in the lounge room, sitting on the floor with both Bonnie and Sheila. Sheila came up to me and lay close to my legs as she would often do. I gently rubbed her stomach, and decided to squeeze her nipples too. Lo and behold, there was milk. Sheila was indeed pregnant! How could this have happened? We discovered that a dog named Mick who lives down the road from us was the culprit. He's a scruffy Maltese Terrier, whose owner lets him run loose in the area. Apparently our neighbour Victor, who loves taking our dogs for a walk, had momentarily left Sheila unattended. The next thing he saw was Mick doing his deed! Victor didn't pass on the news, for fear that we would get upset.

Sheila finally gave birth in July 1999. Markus insisted that we were not going to keep any of the pups. He felt two dogs were enough. I agreed with him. That was until I saw the pups. We nurtured and cared for the pups for six weeks.

It was so soothing and calming to come home from a long and hard day's work, and to have five pups running towards you. For six weeks, they were our greatest source of happiness. Even Markus, who is so conservative, allowed them to run inside the house on his polished floorboards and good rugs! Despite his strong stance about not keeping any, I knew he loved these pups as much as I did, and found it hard to part with them. We got them immunised and chipped, and then put an ad in the paper. My husband and I wanted to screen the buyers.

It was quite painful to see them go off one-by-one — Bully, Sleepyhead, Blackie, and Snow White. I pleaded with my husband not to sell Brando, the grey-and-white long-haired one, till the very last moment.

Bonnie, Sheila and Brando have not only protected our home, they have also brought smiles to our faces when we're down or depressed. They have comforted us and have given us company. Bonnie is ageing now, and we're dreading the day she's not around any more. She's suffering from arthritis and is getting infections in her ears. Despite her ailments, she still manages to bark with energy, and runs to us whenever we come through the gate. No matter how angry I am, how sad or how depressed I become, as soon as I see their faces peering through the gate as I approach it, my heart just lightens up.

Here's to our best friends!

*I came to Australia at the age of eleven with my mother and two sisters as refugees. After finishing high school, I worked as a cadet journalist for three years before freelancing. I now work as producer/journalist at ABC Radio National's Social History and Features Unit. My husband and I have just finished renovating our Federation house and I'm also caring for my ten-year-old sister Jaycie who's living with us. And, of course, our three lovely, wonderful and gorgeous dogs Bonnie, Sheila and Brando, who keep us entertained and are our source of happiness.*

# Her Father to a 'T'

Powhiri Rika-Heke

**"Your moko's outside."**

"Wie bitte?"

"Your moko, your granddaughter, dein Enkelkind."

Through the rain-streaked window in our back door, wet from head to toe, feet visibly filthy after her obviously mad dash through a Baltic rain storm, a hopeful look in sleepy eyes barely visible behind a scraggy fringe, stood 'our' moko, Nscho-Tschi. What a dogawful name. Named by her mother's people. Surely they weren't the type of German who played at being American Indians each summer, who actually believed that Karl May's *Winnetou* and his sister *Nscho-Tschi* were the real thing. What had they been thinking?

"Shall I let her in? Do you think she's run away again?"

"Yes, let her in. It's bucketing down and she could catch a chill in this weather."

*October had been a slow convert to autumn. Like me during the summer months, hesitant to take that first plunge into the lake to begin my early morning swims, Autumn was finding that October was like the unwilling bride also fearful of taking that first plunge.*

"But darling, you look absolutely marvellous in reds and oranges. So much more suitable to your personality."

*October had clung to the greenness of spring and summer. So, today, Autumn had fallen with a resounding crash, bringing all his determination to bear upon October. Time and Autumn's constant attention would see her submit.*

"Schatzmaus, don't forget to towel her down before you let her in. And please wash her feet."

Nscho-Tschi, although always keen to see her number one Oma, allowed me to wash and dry her feet before flinging herself out of my arms and running at speed through the kitchen to the living room where loving arms waited to hold her. No matter how many times we tried to encourage a more genteel behaviour, behaviour more in keeping with that of a 'lady', our efforts seemed for naught.

Grandmother and grandchild played with each other. Hide-and-seek amongst the big leather furnishings in the living room; catch-me-if-you-can between the upstairs rooms and then downstairs to the bedrooms. After the muffled sounds of squeals and yelps from downstairs, the sound of godde-knows-what falling from a bookshelf, both thundered back up the stairs until the older woman conceded defeat to endless energy and youth, finally collapsing onto the couch. The younger, wriggling onto a newly formed lap, snuggled in and relaxed.

Looking at the two, I could only sigh as I went through the rooms, straightening skewed rugs, righting toppled chairs, tidying strewn books I'd so carefully piled beside my desk earlier in the day. I couldn't be mad at them.

Nscho-Tschi and her mum were, apart from the albums of photographs taking up room on our bookshelves, the only tangible reminder of our son. Nscho-Tschi probably didn't remember her dad, she'd only been two when he died. Now, three years on, even though the ache was still there, we no longer cried for a precious lost son when our moko returned to her own home after one of her impromptu visits.

No doubt her mum would be on the doorstep soon, come for a daughter totally unrepentant about leaving their home in the pouring rain to steal a few moments with grandparents still grieving. Grieving for a son who had died too soon. Someone made a mistake. It shouldn't have been his time. So, for those precious moments, we could pretend/forget that our boy was gone because his daughter was such a joy. Her colouring she took from her mother, but her compact young body, her walk, even the way her fringe fell, that was her dad. But her personality, her way of being in the world was entirely her own. And

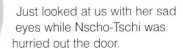

somehow, that made it easier for us when she had to go home. I think her mother would have let her stay, but those grandparents, no, they were strict. Nscho-Tschi had to learn to stay in her own home, sleep in her own bed.

The ringing doorbell was a clear signal that, not only had our son's widow arrived, but that she was also accompanied by her folks. They were lovely people but were probably anxious that their grandchild would want to stay with us. They really didn't know us. We would never try to seduce Nscho-Tschi into leaving her mother. Even now, Fifi preferred to remain alone. Shunning any advances made by the local studs, our son's widow seemed content to live with his memories. She had been such a good companion to our boy. Their love and their friendship for each other was always apparent. Yes, they had been lovers and good friends. Totally besotted with each other and loyal. No wonder our moko was such a beautiful child. She'd inherited good genes.

"Come in, come in. Don't worry about taking off your shoes. It's only water."

"Oh thanks. But really, we only came to collect Nscho-Tschi. Come on Nscho. Hurry up." This from the grandparents. Fifi said nothing.

Just looked at us with her sad eyes while Nscho-Tschi was hurried out the door.

There she stood. Her young body quivering with excitement, or was it impatience, while we and the other grandparents made polite conversation. Fifi, actually Madame Fifi Wackelschwanz (Madame Fifi Wagging Tail) — what was it about these people and the names they gave their children and their grandchildren — turned to join her daughter. They schmoozled each other, Nscho-Tschi pushing against her mum, her mum gently and playfully pushing back and then, at some signal only known to the two, Nscho-Tschi was off, hightailing it around the side of the house, tearing through the garden between the shrubs and trees, leaping over the rockery . . . of course, it had to end.

"Nscho! Komm hierher!"

Such a hang-dog look. Pulling against the lead, this action was her father to a 'T'.

*Author's Note:* This is a work of fiction in that Fifi and Nscho-Tschi's 'folks' would never put their dogs on a lead and they are most loving, friendly and kind, both to us and their four-legged children and grandchildren. 🐾

*Born in the back-blocks of Aotearoa/New Zealand's winterless north, Powhiri has recently returned to her homeland to work at the University of Canterbury in Christchurch after having lived in the ice-age-formed landscape of Germany's far north for most of the last decade of the last millennium. She writes and gets published but does not consider herself a writer.*

# Bunny the Stringybark Farm Dog

Barbara Palmer and Kay Graham

**Bunny was a small dog.** Her mother, Christie, a Sydney Silkie, her father, Laddie, a Chihuahua. When we chose her you could hold her in the palm of your hand. We called her Bunny, after the many rabbits on the farm. When she was little and I was working on the computer she sat on my lap or curled up on the desk, keeping track of me.

She was always a great walker. Over the years we have had Kelpies and Cattle Dogs, or so-called working dogs, on the farm. Bunny always kept up with them except when they took off after kangaroos. One day, late afternoon I went for a walk up towards the back of the farm (it's 530 acres). Bunny, Maggie the Kelpie, and Ginger the Cattle Dog were with me. Under the gum trees they spotted a group of kangaroos — and off went the dogs. I could hear the barking and howls of excitement in the distance but, of course, no risk of any of the dogs catching a 'roo. Well, Ginger and Maggie eventually came back to me, but no Bunny. I walked up through the bush calling and whistling, but no reply. Back I went to the house to pick up the little Suzuki truck. Bunny loved the truck and I thought if she heard it she'd appear. I drove around until dark, tooting the horn and calling. No Bunny. Back to the house for a good cry. My partner was on duty at the hospital and, at 11.30 p.m., back out we went, calling and calling with no reply. At day-break I went outside calling and across the paddock she came. She'd survived a night in the bush with foxes and whatever else, and made her way back through electric fences, gates, bush, tall grass and things that go bump in the night. We still went for long walks but she never disappeared again.

Kangaroos were her greatest love but chasing rabbits came a close second. And she could catch them, or at

Bunny Graham-Palmer 1983–1999

least the smaller ones. One day she caught one when we were out collecting wood with the Suzuki truck. The door was open and on to the front seat she jumped, the rabbit in her mouth. No amount of coaxing, threats, grabs at the rabbit would get her off the seat. She growled and snarled at us (which was unlike her) so we finally had to drive back to the house and leave her to it. She ate everything except the tail, which she always left. Sometimes after she'd caught a rabbit she'd try to bring it into the house to eat away from the other dogs. However they always had a healthy respect for Bunny despite being more than twice her size. I think they knew she was top dog.

She was great with the rounding-up of the goats. We'd say, "Bark-up, Bunny", and off she'd go. Sometimes they would turn and lower their heads at her or stamp their feet but nothing scared her. She stood her ground. When we marked the boy goats and removed their balls we'd throw them on the floor of the shearing shed. Farmers call these delicacies 'bush oysters'. Bunny loved them. She'd wait patiently for them and gobble them up before the Kelpies who, on the whole, stood back for her. At shearing time she'd be down in the shed, helping to round up and keep the goats in their pens, sort out the kids from the adults, and the bucks from all the others.

She was a great swimmer, and the ducks on the dams were a challenge for her. One day, out on a walk, we came across some baby ducks on one of the dams. They had not learned to fly and were swimming with the adults who flew away. In Bunny went, to catch a duckling. Round and round she went. As soon as she got within striking distance they'd dive and swim away under water. No way would one be caught. This went on for half-an-hour or more while we called and cajoled her to come out. We eventually walked away and she finally followed us across the paddock.

As she got older her eyesight started to fade but she still went for walks with us when she felt like it. She guarded the farm house very well. Her bark was intimidating, although she never bit anyone. She knew when there was a snake about. Her bark changed and became loud and insistent.

Reminders of her are all over the place. Bones from the butcher that she buried are still turning up in the oddest places. She seems to be in every photograph we took at the farm. She was a champion and we miss her very much. She's buried in the home paddock close to where she lived for sixteen years.

*Barbara Palmer (left), bookseller, and Kay Graham, nurse, partners at Stringybark Farm for twenty years, sometime collectively, sometime singly, farmers, goat breeders, builders, farm holiday owners, bird-watchers, gardeners, travellers, activists and feminists, and lovers of dogs.*

# In Bed With the Animals

Kristin Headlam

**Like many people,** I can't help thinking that animals are like people, but better. I'm not quite sure why better. There must be some good reason.

As a child I always had cats. When I was four, I was promised a dog for my sixth birthday, but it never happened. But in the absence of siblings I was fairly happy with cats, and devised for each one a complicated psychology which was certainly satisfying enough for me, while the cats just got on with being themselves.

At a fairly late stage in my life I decided that I needed a dog, after all. It started as a going-for-walks thing. I began to picture a dog accompanying me on my walks around Princes Park and Royal Park in Melbourne. All sorts of dogs were imagined — spotted Dalmatians, silky Weimeraners, darting Whippets and eager little Jack Russells, but in the end it was a five-month-old Kelpie/Bull Terrier-cross who sat on my lap for the return trip from the Lost Dogs' Home. I have the suspicion that it was her choice more than mine for it seemed to me that she looked at me in such a way that I could not possibly have left without her, despite her rather homely looks. However, I soon believed that she was the prettiest of dogs, and that no other dog quite matched her.

I called her Dora, which was a name I liked at the time. But at some stage during her first week with us, the word 'pamphlet' came up and I decided that she should have a surname as well. It had a nice ring to it, Dora Pamphlet, a sort of vox pop version of the more aristocratic Doria Pamphyli: with good Freudian overtones, of course. Mostly these days she's just called Pamphlet, which she seems to accept.

What I discovered that is pleasing about my own dog is that she regards me as her own human. No matter who else is there, she knows who butters her bread. Perhaps at the time when I felt I needed a canine companion on my walks I was really looking for someone who attached to me in, let's face it, a pretty unconditional way. I always had a problem with the idea of children though I'd heard some of my friends talking about the unconditional thing with babies, and that was why it was nice to have them.

Well, OK, it probably is unconditional for a while, but pretty soon conditions are most definitely attached, as far as the children are concerned anyway. The idea, therefore, of a dog being a child substitute never really washed with me. In fact, it often seemed the other way around. All those friends having children were just really looking for a dog substitute, I thought.

Pamphlet can do a lot of the good things children can do and not so many of the bad. She is a wonderful companion, not only on walks, but in the studio and around the house generally. We communicate wonderfully. Some of the time I think she wonders what on earth I am talking to her about, but she seems to put a favourable complexion on most of it. Her patience and forbearance can outlast that of most humans, particularly the young ones. Day in, day out she comes with me to the studio, lies there under the table, occasionally sighing wistful sighs as she waits for dog hour, which is wondrous walk time, quality time, dog time.

Sighing in the studio, observing the evolution of art, however, is infinitely preferable to being left at home, waiting, waiting, with only a bone for company, while I go out skipping and playing, or bringing home the bacon.

Anything is better than that and, as far as I can tell, any activity that is done with me is better than any other. However, even though I know this, I still leave her for hours on end without wondering too much if it is stunting her emotional development forever.

As she loves me, I do reciprocate in my inadequate way. It's not as equal as it could be, but I do my best. The cats, on the other hand, do not attempt to do so. When Pamphlet arrived they were outraged, and showed their displeasure in various antisocial and distasteful ways. Pamphlet's tail-wagging efforts to be friends were rebuffed with disdain, and eventually she gave up. In due course they were able to cohabit civilly enough and my bed became the arena for settling territorial disputes. As it stands now, the end of the bed belongs to Pamphlet, and from there she keeps watch like an old sailor; the cosy bit between my hip and forearm is the domain of Hercules, the sluggish, thuggish brown Burmese. Nimble Oscar, the black one, only stays long enough to see who's there.

As a testament to this peaceful arrangement, I decided to paint us all there together, just like that.

*Kristin Headlam is an artist. She was born in Tasmania in 1953, but now lives in Melbourne. In 2000 she won the Doug Moran National Portrait Prize for her painting, 'Self-portrait: In bed with the animals', which drew her attention to the large part her dog Dora Pamphlet plays in her life. She divides her time between her studio and teaching painting at Monash University's Caulfield campus. She has work in public and private collections across Australia.*

# Section Five Dogs Who Make a Difference

# My Hairy Little Saviour

Belinda Morris

**Sitting here looking at Bessie,** I realise how much she has changed my life. For one thing, all these walks are putting a severe dent in the laziness I've always been rather proud of! But the greatest impact Bessie has had on me, is helping me to feel again. To feel love, happiness — even light-hearted. For a long time, I didn't feel any of those things. Most of the feelings that broke through the numbness were pain, anger, disappointment and frustration.

A little over a year ago I had a miscarriage. The pregnancy wasn't planned and definitely wasn't wanted, and I would not have continued with it. So, in the scheme of things, a miscarriage was the best result, bringing with it great relief. But it also brought the hormones. I knew to expect hormonal fluctuations and therefore mood swings, and tried to circumvent this by taking herbal anti-depressants from early on. But the ironic thing about anti-depressants is that they make you think you're okay, so you stop taking them, only to find out you're really not, and going on and off various anti-depressant remedies just served to exacerbate the hormonal depression. I had very supportive friends and a partner who did as much as they could to help, but there's only so much anyone can do, and none of them really knew the extent of my depression — in retrospect, I don't think I really understood it myself. I frequently thought it was all over, that I was finally better, and then I'd come crashing back down and have trouble dragging myself out of bed in the morning (or the afternoon!). A lot of people assumed I was upset about 'losing the baby', but this was really never even an issue. I have never wanted a baby, and don't regret the pregnancy ending (although I certainly regret getting pregnant in the first place).

On the other hand, I have always wanted a dog. In fact, I recall telling my partner, through a blur of the various drugs I'd taken for the pain, that if it had been a puppy I would have wanted to keep it! Dogs have always been an important part of my life. When I was growing up and feeling completely alone in the world, my dogs were the ones who helped me get through everything. When I felt like no one at home wanted me around, my dogs were the ones who cared. They were the ones who showed me love and affection, and often a well placed lick.

So in the throes of my hormonal misery, when I felt like I was struggling just to survive (and of course, trying not to let on to anyone that I wasn't coping), I was walking to work one day with tears rolling down my face, and all I could think about was how much I wanted to hold and pat and play with a little dog. I hadn't had a dog of my own for years, as I'd been in rental properties, but I'd never stopped longing for one. A few months after the miscarriage I moved house, and when I later met the owners, they agreed to let me have a dog. I was so excited I could barely speak properly!

Regardless of what many people said to me (and no doubt many more thought to themselves), Bessie is not a substitute for a baby, and I am not playing out my maternal instincts with her. It amazes me the ideas people will come up with, to not have to accept the fact that not every woman desperately wants to reproduce. It seems it's easier to believe that I really must have these innate, biological urges that I'm just denying, or transferring! Yes, the miscarriage affected me profoundly

— I suffered from depression for many months afterwards and to this day I am still feeling the ramifications. But not because I'd failed in my role as a woman. I was miserable, angry and frustrated because this had happened to me, and I had no control over it — over my own body.

People talk about women's right to choose an abortion — what about the choice of whether to be pregnant or not in the first place: now *that* would be an actual choice. I was careful, but with the options available to me even today, that wasn't enough. And as a woman, I was the one who had to bear the consequences. My partner could have as much or as little involvement as he wanted, but I had no such choice. So on top of my hormones running rampant, I was also trying to deal with my frustration and despair at the situation. I also had to contend with horrendous doctors (but also one very wonderful one), and not being able to explain myself to those who thought that since I hadn't wanted to be pregnant and would have aborted, I had no reason or right to be upset about it, that I should simply have cruised happily through the miscarriage and been grateful for it.

Of those that knew what had happened, only a couple of friends and Bessie didn't question me at some point, or get tired of listening to me (not that she let on, anyway), or get impatient with me for not having 'gotten over it already'. Bess was always there, whenever I needed comfort and she gave me unconditional love (plus licks). She always wanted to be with me, and didn't need explanations for why I was crying or being irrational — she simply loved me as I was.

By being one of those wonderful little creatures that dogs are, Bessie has changed my life, probably even saved it. She has reminded me what it's like to feel okay and to smile again — even to laugh. I still have my down days sometimes, but no matter what the problem is, Bess can always make me feel better. Curling up with her on the couch (or in the bed, when she's snuck in); watching her rolling around on her back in the sun, snorting, little legs waving about; seeing the expressions on her face and her excitement when I come home — everything she does brings a smile to my face, even the naughty things.

I love the noises she makes when she's trying to tell me something, though I feel guilty about my ignorance, and the frustration it causes her — she's made the effort to learn some of my language, and yet I still fail to comprehend what she's telling me. In my defence though, I have managed to decipher some of the more basic commands, like "take me outside please", "I'm still waiting" and "excuse me, but *now* would be my preference". I have also come to understand that a short bark from the couch, followed by a glance at the toy on the floor means, "I'd like you to pick that up and bring it to me so I don't have to bother jumping down and then back up again, thanks very much" (dog language is much more succinct than ours!). Bessie loves to play ball, but just to be fair she takes her turn at throwing — usually from the couch. She gets quite exasperated though when I don't fetch quickly enough, particularly when it takes several barks for me to move into action.

It's been said on occasion that Bessie is somewhat spoiled (rotten), but I prefer to think that she is just very very loved. And as much as I adore and dote on her, I will never be able to repay what she has done for me. She has shown me how to be happy again. I don't feel alone anymore, and I can't imagine my life without her. Bessie gives me a reason to get up in the mornings (or the afternoons), even if it is because she's scratching at the door, or jumping on my face!

*Bessie is supposedly a mini Fox Terrier, who looks suspiciously like a Jack Russell. Her interests include barking at everyone, hiding things under the couch, and looking sweet and innocent. She also enjoys licking herself and anyone else who gets close enough. Belinda is a twenty-nine-year-old woman who looks suspiciously like a slave to the doggess. Her interests now include stretching under the couch, buying and picking up toys, and sitting very still in uncomfortable positions, so as not to wake the snoozing Bess on her lap. She occasionally studies and works in Women's Studies, but most of her time there is spent talking about Bessie to anyone who'll listen (and many who don't).*

# Love Me, Love My Dog!

Barbara Heinzius and Martina

## Martina's story

**She was the first** to answer my ad, and I was very curious to get to know the woman who was such in a hurry to meet and who had such fine handwriting and an erotic voice on the phone.

For our first meeting we chose my hometown — mainly because of my dog Arco. Arco was a vivid reminder of my last relationship and due to his size, more a hindrance than a help for my aching back. But he is a real friend and my constant protector.

I was very nervous the day of our first date. I ran around the rooms in my house trying to clean them and put them in some sort of order — you know, just in case . . .

Arco was quickly infected by my excitement and followed me at every turn, leaving his hair all over the place, and meaning I had to start tidying all over again.

Finally I started fixing myself up, I wanted to take extra care to look and smell good for my date. I knew I smelt good when Arco sneezed three times, as I walked out of the bathroom.

Just as I was about to jump in my car and head to the station to meet her, leaving the dog to mind the fort, Arco decided to whine pathetically

and show me he urgently needed to go out. I had no alternative but to resentfully go for a short walk with him, even though I had no time to spare.

I couldn't believe it . . . I would be late!! I would be late for our first meeting because of my dog's bladder, I swore at my poor dog with each step of the walk.

Finally in the car and on the road, I stepped on the gas to make up for lost time and hoped I wouldn't be too late meeting her.

Once at the station, I ran as fast as I could to the platform, hoping she would like me and wouldn't hold my being late, against my dog.

Then suddenly I saw her . . . it had to be her! She was just as I imagined from the voice on the phone. She looked so nice standing by the railings . . . but a little annoyed too. The train she had arrived in, had long since left the station.

My heart was in my throat as I approached her. I apologised for being so late and explained how Arco needed to go for a walk at the last moment. She just smiled and said, "I don't mind, I am just glad to finally meet you."

So we started to walk around the city, we walked and talked the whole day, stopping for occasional breaks in a café and Biergarten and finally settling for something to eat in a lovely Thai restaurant.

I must admit, I rarely thought or spoke about Arco the whole time we were together. I was totally captivated by the woman in my company.

As the end of the day turned into evening, I didn't know what to say or do. I didn't want the date to end.

Once more I swallowed my nervousness and explained that I had to go home soon, that Arco would need to go out and that he couldn't spend so much time locked up in the house. "Would you like to come home with me?" I asked. I was kind of glad to have him for an excuse. She agreed immediately.

On the way home, I prepared her for Arco, my protector. She told me that she was only used to cats — even though she had nothing against dogs.

When I opened the door, Arco surprised me: he just wagged his tail and welcomed her like an old friend.

It proved to be a good sign — dogs evidently have got the sixth sense.

# Barbara's story

**She was the one** who put the 'Lonely Hearts' ad in the paper, and I was the one who responded. So I answered it and I gave her my phone number to call.

When she did, I thought she sounded nice. We both had had bad experiences, and we both wanted a new relationship.

"I have a dog," she said. "I don't have anything against dogs," I answered. To be honest, I wasn't interested in the dog at all, I only wanted to get to know her.

On our first date she was late showing up, but she looked very good. "Sorry," she said, "I had to take the dog for a walk before I left."

"I don't mind," I answered, but I was slightly annoyed — I didn't know much about dogs back then.

On that first date, she showed me her town. As we walked through the picturesque medieval city centre she told me that her dog had had bad experiences too. She had got him from an animal shelter.

After the walk we went to eat something. I already really liked her. It was a warm summer night and we sat and talked in the garden of a Thai restaurant. It was only our first rendezvous, but I didn't want to go home and finish our date just yet. As if reading my mind, she said, "I have to go now. I can't leave the dog alone for the whole night. Do you want to come with me?"

It was the first time I liked the dog.

Before we arrived at her house she warned me, "The dog might growl at you because he doesn't know you." But the dog didn't growl at all. He wagged his tail and welcomed me. Perhaps he sensed the love I already felt for his owner.

As we were sitting on her couch, I wondered if she brought me home to get to know her or the dog. The dog was lying beneath a window, watching us, apparently asking himself the same question. When I finally reached over and touched her, I knew why she had brought me to her home.

The dog looked content.

"Usually the dog sleeps on the couch," she said.

"So let's leave him to it," I answered.

For a short time I thought, "Dog, you're my friend."

However he didn't sleep on the couch that night. He came into the bedroom to see what his mistress was doing. "It's only a dog," I thought, trying not to be too paranoid, but somehow at that moment I knew from now on not only this girl, but this dog too, would be part of my life.

*Martina, born 1956, studied pedagogy and computer linguistics. She works as a teacher at an elementary school in Bavaria.*

*Barbara Heinzius, born 1961, studied Italian literature, German literature and sociology. She works as an editor at Goldmann Verlag (Random House Germany), Munich.*

# The Adoration of the Dog's Eye

Sandy Jeffs

*Sandy Jeffs lives in a household that has a passion for Australian Cattle Dogs and Burmese cats. She had the privilege of living with Bluey, with whom she shared her madness and tennis, for many years. Jessie, a feisty character, also shared her colourful life with Sandy and her friends, until recently. Sandy has had four books of poetry published, two of which won prizes. She lives on the outskirts of Melbourne with her friends and new puppy, Ruby.*

*Taken from* Confessions of a Midweek Lady. *(Poems by Sandy Jeffs, drawings by Veronica Holland)*

*In memory of Bluey*

I'm not the greatest tennis player
to have graced the dusty, red court —
hit and miss forehand
pathetic backhand
thundering serve that never goes in
hot one moment, cold the next —
a nightmare for my partners
who look skyward and sigh
frustrated by their misfortune
at having to play with me.

Bluey was aware of my
misunderstood genius though.
Sitting court-side, close to the action,
only she appreciated my unrealised potential
understood my fragile temperament
applauded my occasional winners
shared the gutsy wins and dreadful losses.
She didn't give a damn about my mediocre game
or my hairy legs, daggy clothes and cheap racquet.
Together we took on the world as
her big brown eyes swallowed me and
made me feel as though *I* was the greatest!
Martina Navratilova stepped onto sacred ground
every Wednesday morning
and played the game of her life
dedicating each triumph to Bluey
out of whose eye the sun shone.

# Lyn and Ralphie

Lyn Zboril

I didn't ever intend getting a dog. I've always liked dogs but have never been 'crazy' about them like some people are. In fact, when people raved on about their dogs, I used to think that they must be lacking in some area of their lives — to be so crazy about their canines — I just couldn't understand it. All that was about to change on 14 July 2000.

On that particular day I had arranged to have breakfast with some friends. During the conversation, we discussed dogs and I casually mentioned how, now that I had a backyard, I wouldn't mind getting one — one day. I was nonchalant enough to go to the RSPCA 'just for a look'. I emphasized that I was not yet ready for the full commitment of dog ownership. When we got there however, something happened within me. There were so many beautiful animals desperate for attention, desperate for love and a home. As my friend and I walked through a maze of cages, we saw him. A little bundle of dirty white fluff, so scared and frightened that when we put a lead on him for a test walk, he pulled back in fear. The most gorgeous dog I've ever seen. I fell in love.

I named him Ralphie. Ralphie is a Maltese-Bichone Frise-terrier cross and he was a stray, so I know nothing about him. I know now that he has come from a good home because he is very happy and comfortable around people. His age was estimated to be eighteen months. I've had him now for four months and in that time he has completely transformed my life.

I am forty-one, single and have a hectic lifestyle. I have my own hairdressing salon employing four people. I have a wonderful family and have lots of fantastic friends. I had always thought that I was doing okay, but Ralphie brought out something that I hadn't thought existed within me. A love and nurturing so deep that it sometimes frightens me.

To receive back such unconditional love is even more scary. He has done for me what no human has ever come close to doing yet — he is bringing down my defences!

I make a point of walking Ralphie around the neighbourhood every morning and night. I'm very glad that I do. One Sunday I had taken him as usual for his walk, came home and bathed him. I then had some friends over and we decided to go out for lunch. It was raining so I decided not to take Ralphie and he wasn't very happy about it (he always manages to break my heart when I leave without him — he looks at me with his big, black eyes and looks so sad!) We all left and returned within two hours. As soon as I walked inside, I knew he was gone. With horror I realized that I hadn't put his identification collar back on after his bath! I was distraught. I sobbed uncontrollably and was useless to my friends who immediately sprang into action. They rang all the dogs' homes, police, council and anyone else that they could think of. They photocopied photographs of him and made posters with 'Reward' written all over them. They went on a neighbourhood search (in the rain!). Meanwhile I was blubbering miserably, totally incapable of doing anything except to berate myself for not putting on his collar and taking him with me. I decided that I could at least hang the posters. Still unashamedly weeping I hung them in supermarkets, laundromats, streetlights — anywhere I could. A leaflet dropper was looking out for him, a dog walker was doing the same. A friend I met with along the way was comforting me while helping me look. I was shattered. My lunchtime companions had done all they could so said goodbye. All of this happened within one hour of our return from lunch!

I went to the local café for a coffee and to contemplate my life without Ralphie. While sitting there with tears still streaming, coffee going cold, staring into space, my mobile phone rang. It was my neighbour excitedly shouting that he was back home! Home! Ralphie's home? I sprinted back and there he was, happily gnawing his bone, his tail wagging and totally unaware of the grief he had innocently caused me. When I burst into yet another pool of tears, he walked up to me, looked at me and then gave me a big doggy kiss. He had escaped through a tiny gap between the house and fence and had returned the same way.

Ralphie had gone looking for me and found his way back home by 'sniffing' his own markings and familiar trail!

This incident, more than any (and there have been a few) drove home to me how much love I have for this little dog. When he was on his walkabout and I was crying in my coffee, images of him played upon my mind. I saw him skip when he was happy, but slink slowly toward me, head down, eyes up, when he was in trouble. I saw him sitting with his face screwed up waiting for the dreaded face washer to clean his mouth and nose after burying his bones. I saw him trotting around at my gym, jumping onto my stomach and sitting there while I did my abdominal workout. And I realized how much he loved me and how much I loved him.

I wondered how I was going to cope without him because I never fully realized how deep the bond was that we had formed. I truly believed that all joy would now be gone in my life and I prayed that he was safe.

It was during that reflection that it hit me. I realized then that all those dog crazy and loopy people had been right all along. They were not lacking in *their* lives, but I was. They already knew what had taken me forty-one years to discover, which was that a dog can and will deeply enrich a person's life. The impact of having Ralphie in my life has been overwhelming. He is a dear little thing. He makes me so happy and brings so much joy and fun into my life that I am forever grateful to whatever force was involved in somehow bringing us together when all I did was to go for breakfast with friends.

*Since I've had Ralphie, I've been on a journey of learning a lot about myself and my relationships. This has been an exciting experience for me — fancy a little dog leading me to a published piece of work! At the time of writing we reside happily in Elwood, Victoria, but if anyone would like to catch up with us, come and say hello at Kyzan Hairdressing in North Carlton, in Melbourne.*

# My Poet
## Emily Ballou

**She came to me as a gift of Fate.** She came to me because somebody said, "this girl, this workaholic writer with no pets and no lover needs a dog." It is the work of mystery and love, coincidence and bravery that brings two such beings together. I had never had a dog. I had a fish that as a child I trained to answer to Pavlov's bell but that is another story. I had nothing to prepare me for the responsibility a dog would bring, but neither did I have any precedent for the love that would grow between us, for what I would feel. I lived alone in a small one-bedroom house in the inner city and devoted my world to my own private machinations. It was my first act in my new art of bravery to accept responsibility for the life of a six-week-old runt Kelpie puppy who had only just managed to escape drowning in a river with her siblings and had lived all of her short life on a farm.

I named her after my favourite American poet H.D. (Hilda Doolittle), in homage to both the past and the poet herself, though my dog will always be a Hilda, and never an H.D. I have sat her on my lap as I typed poetry on my 1940s Underwood Portable and I like to think that when she hears the sound of me jack-hammering the keys, it reminds her fondly of her childhood. She has worked in a bookshop next to me, dropping her red ball to each patient customer who might play with her, their books cracked open in their hands, reminding everybody that play is just as important as reading. I have caught her staring at moonbeams and howling along to The Cranberries. I have watched her watching the sky, still as a statue, nose in the air, in dawn's light.

We have walked the span and length of the world and I have tried to inspire in her a contemplative spirit as together we climbed mountains, crossed beaches and fields, watched birds without eating them, sat for hours on the tops of cliffs, overlooking the sea and swam in slow rock pools. We lay on long piers while night fell around us and watched the spilling of green water in the light, like a show put on just for us two. I have seen things I wouldn't have otherwise seen without her, forced as I was to brave state-of-emergency weather to walk her. Pouring rain and winter nights when the wind cut holes in my skin, I found new midnight stars among the constellations and wrote poems in my head dedicated to her shadow dashing through the surf.

Hilda takes me deep into the night and she shows me how to see in that darkness. Wherever I walk, we leave double footprints in the sand.

We inhabit desert places, underwater places, we explore the sea, and we shuttle through deep space in white suits, headed for the Moon. We go to Italy, Europe's answer to dog heaven, with dogs conversing under tables while their owners swallow espressos. We go to Greece and roam the streets with the wild dogs, learning haphazard Greek and chasing cats over the cobblestones.

I have been accused of investing my relationship to my dog with too much symbolic meaning. But her presence in my life has healed me: helped me to love and be loved, to have relationships, to grow up, to give, to take responsibility, to care, to come home early from clubs, to get up when I wanted to sleep in (her cold nose nudging mine from the toss of dreams), to concoct all sorts of ridiculous arrangements so she would not be alone or lonely or hungry or scared.

She has taught me that you can throw yourself into love with abandon, no fear and deep faith. She has taught me that you can get back much more than love in the process.

She is a stick-obsessed, self-pleasuring, over-talking, hard-working, sensitive, elusive and strange girl. She twirls in circles, jumping down the street, whacking into everybody she passes. She rounds up the waves at the beach when she can't get a hold of chickens. She would round me up every minute too, if she could, and herd me out for a walk. Yet if she is left outside the café while I partake in some caffeination and company, she will sit still for hours, calm and watching as the world pulses past, a portrait in brown fur with a salt-licked bleached blonde tail.

After all, she knows the afternoon is still possible. She knows there are blue cliffs out there with our names on them.

Hilda and I live in Tamarama.
Together we make up the entity known as 'writer'.
She is the Muse and I am the slave.

# The Zorya

Kiersten Coulter

**I think the love of dogs is inherited.** It's in the genes. My inheritance and my passion for dogs came from my mother. She was someone who, as a child in the depression and war years, would sneak her precious dinner into napkins in her lap, and with great skill, escape to the back lanes in her suburb of Cottesloe in Western Australia. There she would feed the motley crew of stray dogs and cats gathered eagerly in waiting. As a result of her malnourished state she suffered scarlet fever and many other serious conditions. Over the years she has adopted a string of animals and birds, all fiercely loyal to her. Whilst I do not profess her brilliance, my dog has always played a prominent role in my life.

When my red-and-white Siberian Husky found her way into my life as a ten-week-old bundle of blue-eyed fluff, the decision to call her Zorya, as one of three female pups in the litter, was met with a dubious, "Zorya!! What about Ruby?" My cat-identified partner Di was far less enthusiastic about my new charge. The Zorya, in Slavonic mythology, were three sisters. They were the protectors of the universe. Each had a distinct role to play or part of the universe to watch over. Little did we both know in early 1997 that Zorya was to play a crucial role as my 'protector' in a long and painful journey through life-threatening illness.

Not that Zorya has been an angel. She has grown particularly large and fills the entire back seat of our car. One of her blue eyes has changed to a half-blue, half-gold party eye. My party girl has enjoyed herself, often disappearing in a flash on one of our twice-daily bush walks and, on one occasion, ending up in the local pound. She gaily greeted me with a grin that stretched her whole length, as I parted with the necessary hundreds to have her freedom reinstated. She is a gentle giant, turning to a wagging, goofy, licking mush of joy around children of any age and delights in play with any other dog who has the same joyous sense of romp and fun. She is an intelligent dog and, despite the fact that Huskies are reported 'to do only those things which they can see a point in', she has learnt some hard lessons and learnt them well.

In June 1998, when Zorya was barely eighteen months old, I was diagnosed with acute lymphoblastic leukemia. On the last walk I took with her before being diagnosed and hospitalised, the pressure of her lead pulling against my thumb had caused a haematoma, major swelling and bruising. I knew something was seriously wrong. By day two, the diagnosis was confirmed, the Hickman's central line inserted into the heart arteries and chemotherapy had begun. My immune system was about to change dramatically. Being around Zorya was not recommended. Whilst we all dealt with the shock and changes of those first few weeks, Zorya was placed in a trusted kennel, but I clung to thoughts of being reunited with her, of seeing her fully mature and romping with her in the bush again. She became my motivator, a role she willingly adopted and expanded, as required.

While we dealt with diagnoses, drugs, dehydration, side effects, blood counts, lumbar punctures and shock, Zorya was busy acclimatising to the dramatic change in her circumstances. She clearly decided early on that she had best make the most of it and set about endearing herself to the kennel staff. After some hesitation about taking a Husky at all, Zorya became their favourite charge. The frequent trips back and forth to the kennel over the ensuing two years, one stay lasting nearly three months, ensured the continuation of this valuable relationship.

After two weeks I was released from hospital. The two-year chemotherapy regime started with a series of three drugs, one to be administered daily, seven days a week. We were determined to keep me from hospitalisation and made the one-hour journey in to the hospital and then back again. It was very hard going and at times I was unable to shower myself and walk the small distances to and from the car. Nonetheless I asked for Zorya to be brought home. I had a vision one day of just how easy it would be to give up and die. It frightened me into fighting harder to live. Zorya was part of that.

Neighbours and friends stepped in and walked her daily. She adapted to the loneliness and long hours on her own adjusting to one, not two walks a day. She lived in her pen now, excluded from the house on health grounds, and when I finally made the trip up the stairs to see her she was being held away from me. We had been warned that one jump for joy could rip my Hickman's line from my right breast. It had happened before we were told. I couldn't touch her without gloves and wore a facemask. I was not to feel her soft fur for nearly eighteen months. She was overjoyed to see me. It was mutual. From our bedroom window I could see her sitting at the fence staring down the hill. She knew I was different. She knew everything was different. From a dog that would howl if I was ten minutes late for her walk, she became, almost overnight, a patient soul, who just waited and waited. As the weeks rolled on, I tried to keep up my strength by walking, even if it was only for five minutes.

Di had to walk with us and hold Zorya; her strength, if she decided to pull, far beyond mine. She had been taught to heel but if something interesting caught her eye she suddenly forgot it all. At thirty-three kilos she weighed only thirteen kilos less than me. There was realistic concern that I may collapse on these walks or not be able to get myself home again, so on all counts I needed Di's support. The most amazing thing about Zorya through this time was the profound changes that took place. She became absolutely gentle and careful when I was around. She sat patiently and waited when I needed to rest, her blue eyes often staring deeply into mine. Only weeks before, if I had stalled during a walk, she would have grabbed the lead between her teeth and tugged impatiently. Intuitively her behaviour changed.

Complete lack of freedom was another big change for her. There was no chance of letting her off the lead. If she decided to do one of her bunks I had no strength or energy to retrieve her. Occasionally, if I felt well enough I would take her lead. During this critical time she never pulled me around. She was so careful. For me it was like having a tiny piece of my liberty, dignity and independence returned. I'd lost the majority of each through the treatment process. Just having her lead in my hand gave me a rush of excitement and heralded possibilities. It was some semblance of normality and life before illness.

Within three weeks of the initial diagnosis we faced further bad news. I had the Philadelphia Chromosome, which significantly upgraded the seriousness of my condition. Chemotherapy was unlikely to have anything other than a temporary effect on my cancer. The only hope for a 'cure' was a bone marrow transplant. With this treatment I had about a thirty to forty per cent chance of surviving two years. Siblings make the best, if only occasional, matches. I won the lottery. I have only one brother Peter, who was seriously brain injured in an accident at fourteen (but that's another story). He was a perfect match.

After five weeks of chemotherapy, another bone marrow biopsy showed I was in remission. The perfect time to transplant. While they waited for me to heal from a wisdom tooth removal and a fissure in my anus, all potential infection sites during the dangerous process of transplantation, I was given three weeks reprieve from treatment. During this time my tasks were to get fitter, stronger and gain weight. Quite quickly I began to feel much better. Zorya and I with family in tow, headed off for some longer walks in the bush. I felt exhausted, as if I had no strength. But there seemed to be a muscle memory. A memory of being able to walk these hills that drove me around, motivated by the sheer joy in Zorya's body at being out there again and having me close by her side. Thanks to my four-legged protector I entered the transplant phase fit and well.

To maintain my fitness while I was confined in isolation for nearly three months we hired a walking machine. I had a large enough room for the machine to be placed by the window. Di found a beautiful picture of Zorya and me walking in the bush and stuck it to the front of the machine. I could stare into it and transport myself away from the industrial concrete wasteland that existed outside my ever-closed window. A large photograph of Zorya sat above my bed, the talking point of doctors and nurses. I stepped onto my walking machine for all but two days of those weeks in isolation. I took my pole, stacked with pumps and tubes pumping drugs and nutrition into my body to keep me alive, and walked with Zorya in my imagination. Some days it was only five minutes. On several occasions, prior to imminent transfusions, my platelet count was dangerously low and my nose bled profusely all over the machine. Still I walked. I was going to run with Zorya again. I was going to survive.

After I was released, 'outpatient' maintenance took us back into the hospital at least three days a week and sometimes many more. In addition to these regular requirements of transplant patients, I kept spiking temperatures, which meant a rush to the hospital, a series of tests and at least four days hospitalisation on intravenous antibiotic. Again, I wanted Zorya home. Again neighbours and friends stepped into the fray and made it possible for Zorya and me to snatch a few moments together here and there. I tried to start walking again.

There are many profound changes that occur through this process. 'Cure' no matter what the final outcome, is a nebulous word. You imagine you'll be the same and do the same things. But nothing is the same. You look like someone else, you think like someone else and you feel like someone else. Some of this abates over time, but many of the differences remain. There are constant repercussions from treatment that topple into your living space like molten rock, shocking not just you but your partner, friends and family. Over the ensuing two years we faced a procession of these, which included regular flares of Graft versus Host disease where the graft was rejecting my body, infections, instant menopause, threatened onset of osteoporosis and others. Zorya adapted to chaotic daily changes and lack of routine.

The most immediate and profound effect of the transplant process is absolute exhaustion. It's not like anything ever experienced before. Just lifting the cup in your hand at times takes a supreme effort. Getting up, showering and dressing can occupy your whole day. Ongoing fatigue is the bane of all bone marrow transplantees. The motivation to move is minimal. Getting fit and building muscle again is crucial. Zorya took on the role of my personal fitness trainer. Within four months of my transplant we were walking up to an hour a day. She became more demanding as circumstances improved. No matter how bad or unmotivated or exhausted I felt, she was there, needing to be walked. She returned to howling if I was not pulling my weight.

As I grew stronger we started walking twice a day again, going bush and being given the freedom to take off together alone. I was able to let her off for a run. We started playing games together and developed a boisterous version of t'ai kwando. I have to try and touch her underbelly with my hand and she has to stop me. Although she makes a lot of noise, she has never hurt me or grabbed my arm in her teeth. She just mouths me gently and when I say 'enough', 'gentle', she stops the game immediately and grins from mouth to tail.

We have had one terrible scare together. It rained for forty-eight hours and our local creek rose some twenty feet. I was curious and Zorya and I went down to the footbridge we walk across every day. The bridge was nearly covered in water. Before I knew what had happened Zorya had slipped in to the rushing water and was washed back into the bridge, her leg getting trapped between the wooden slats in the fast running water. I couldn't free her. My protector was in real trouble. I thought her back or legs would snap at any moment. She was screaming in pain. I yelled and screamed at the top of my voice for help but no one came. Finally I shoved the top of her body back into the water knowing she would either be freed or drown. Her leg jerked free, I grabbed her; my Akubra went down river but we were both high and dry. Zorya was on three legs and as I bent down to have a look, blood trickled and flowed down my arm. In her panic when she was trapped, she had bitten my arm, her canine tooth piercing deep into the flesh, a site for serious infection. However, Zorya and I

both recovered within days. "Your immune system must be doing something," the doctor said to me, amazed. "It's all the walking," I grinned back.

As I write this, my latest bone density scan shows I am making, not losing bone and am almost back to the bottom-end of the normal range. This can only be attributed to my personal four-legged trainer getting me out there walking the hills. It is now two-and-one-half years since my transplant and life is beginning to look half way 'normal' again. I am about to finish my thesis and begin a PhD, and in a few months I will step back into work. I have a lot of people to thank for my life and the extent to which I have recovered, especially Di and my family. But to those who made it possible for me to remain connected with my dog, I owe a tremendous debt. Zorya has motivated, assisted and trained me back to health. My dream of seeing her mature is realised. We romp regularly in the bush. At four years of age, she has the best years ahead of her. With her help, I believe I will see her through this time, into her twilight years and beyond and beyond. And Di, who you may recall at the beginning, was not so enamoured with my doggy mate? As we were falling asleep the other night, she said, "You know I think someone should train up Huskies as fitness training companions for people with cancer. I think it would be a great idea!" So do I.

At the recent gay and lesbian picnic-cum-dog show for Midsumma, Zorya attracted crowds of admirers. She is so beautiful. "I think I should get a dog," our cat-identified single companion quipped. Not just any dog I thought. I smiled to think not one of them fawning all over her has any idea of just how special and how beautiful she is. She's been a 'quality-of-life saver'.

*Kiersten is a criminologist, animal lover and bush baby. Her passion for social justice and human rights, especially those of women and Indigenous Australians, drives her work. Her dog helps drive her zest for life in recovery from life-threatening illness.*

# Finn and Me

Libby Hotchin

**Finn arrived,** a boisterous, happy, loving scruff, not long after the Ash Wednesday bushfires. I was working and living with hurt and angry young people. My first puppy had been run over after escaping through a hole two of the boys had made in the fence. They loved her as much as I did and were devastated, threatening retribution against the driver. I never told them how their destructiveness contributed to her death.

I don't think I realised what an act of faith it was to share another puppy with them. It was a great gift, and one that empowered Finn and me to continue giving to people in crisis. Finn came to the turmoil that was a residential unit for young people. We took him to our hearts. And he remained a heart-dog, gifted for our journey.

He lived with me for seventeen years — a typical Border Collie — lively, loving, intelligent and just a bit crazy.

Finn died two days before Easter. Plain wore out. After a couple of tough last days, a long commune with my Border Collie family by full moonlight, and chats with some special friends, I decided that life was not much fun for Finn any more. I loaded him into the car with a couple of blankets Mum had made, and requisite tennis balls, and took him to our vet. I held his dear old head and patted him while Narelle administered the injection, and gave him good-dog cuddles whilst he died. My friend Sue and I dug him an extra good hole and buried him with blankets, tennis balls and sticks, and planted a lovely champagne rose over him. Rain drizzled at the end of another drought, watering-in the rose.

The end of a great old dog's great old life.

Finn was the very best dog friend I could have asked for — through residential work around the inner urban area; living in Blackburn, Richmond, Eltham and on the Surf Coast; in our early pre-car years travelling all over town and the countryside together by train; holidays from Port Augusta and the Flinders Ranges, via Adelaide, Victor Harbor, Port Fairy (including seven Folk Music Festivals), Apollo Bay, Mildura, the Gariwerd Grampians, Eildon, Bairnsdale, Mallacoota, Canberra, the Snowy Mountains, Pambula and the Blue Mountains; dog's-body surfing on some of our best beaches; sea-gull and swallow chasing anywhere he could find them; swimming for miles down the Yarra (Yarra Junction, Millgrove, Eltham, Warrandyte, Templestowe, Collingwood, Kew, Richmond) and in the Murray, the Torrens, the Wimmera, the irrigation channels around Bamawm and Coleambally. World's best walks and bike rides.

Somewhere amongst all that, we did lots of training together, and in spite of the fact that I had almost no idea what I was doing, he got a novice obedience title in four out of four trials in five weeks with two consecutive scores of 194 out of 200. In partnership with Finn, I developed an enduring love of dog sports and of the people and dogs who participate.

Best of all, Finn had the most splendid of people-orientated natures — a truly perfect people dog. Present and loving and accepting and patient. Just gave *everyone* (the hurt and sad and damaged children I worked with, and the regular ones who were and are my friends, my nieces, my grown-up friends and family, and me) unstinting time, comfort, joy and entertainment. Never threatened anyone, never hurt anyone, never frightened anyone. Reliable, safe and so much fun.

It's hard to choose my best memories, but curled up in the tent camping, with Finn snuggled in against my knees would have to be pretty close to perfect for plain nice times.

Some of his achievements as a therapy dog with children were just outstanding.

Finn gave me love, companionship, security and independence. Shared in wonderful adventures. Lent me the confidence (both physically and emotionally) to make some crucial moves in my life. Shared in my initial involvement in many activities that remain at the heart of my life today — long walks in wild and remote places, dog sports, camping holidays, animal assisted therapies. Enabled me to sustain my work with damaged and dangerous people in ways that would have been unsafe otherwise.

Finn had a fantastic life, as full and wonderful as any dog could have. He was a sensational companion for me and Taryn and Sorcha (left), and managed commendable patience with Django (right) and the 'puppy-nuisance' brothers and sisters. In spite of his sworn enmity for cats, he was a very special buddy for our 'kitty', Tasi. He possibly overdid the friendship thing when he dug up our dead canary, Enrico. As we buried Finn, Sue and I promised him that there were no giant canaries waiting to take their revenge!

His spirit continues to contribute to my life every day. The experience of his companionship is an enduring gift. 🐾

*Libby lives on the beautiful surfcoast in south western Victoria, Australia, with her equally beautiful Border Collie family — Taryn, 15, Sorcha, 5, Django, 18 months and Sorcha's ten baby puppies! Django and Sorcha are active partners in the Animal Assisted Therapy programs that she incorporates in her work as a psychologist within school communities. Libby also uses and promotes positive training methods in preparing for and participating in a range of dog sports, and in instructing others to train their dogs to be happy, loving, well adjusted family and community members.*

# The Story of Buffy: A Small Dog

Elizabeth Diane (Judy) Kelly

**'If only'** may be an unorthodox introduction to a story — nevertheless that is the way I start this story, the reason being that, if only my dear sister were still alive, she could, far better than I, tell the tale of a little toy French Poodle named Buffy.

Buffy became a member of our family in 1966 when she was two months old and her owner Jenny, our daughter, was six. Buffy was a 'reward' to Jenny for being an excellently behaved hospital patient, following a fall from her bicycle. To say that Buffy was pint-sized would be a great understatement — she was in fact tiny, yet in other ways she was very big — intelligence, affection and fun were attributes she possessed in plenty. We all loved her and she returned our love in full.

Home was an irrigation property in the southern Riverina district of New South Wales and consisted of six hundred and forty acres where the crops of wheat, sorghum and sunflower were grown and sheep and cattle were grazed. During the ensuing years, many working dogs came (and went) sheep dogs and cattle dogs. Buffy, however, was not a working dog and chose to keep herself quite aloof from the other dogs.

We had four children — two girls and two boys. It was a busy life, particularly at harvesting and shearing time. I can recall many occasions when I was busy with 'home duties' when I would suddenly realise that I had not seen or heard a child for some time. Invariably my efforts to locate them would be rewarded by the sight of a small black bundle sitting on the banks of one of the channels or dams 'minding' the children as they swam and played. The two boys, being older than the girls, were excellent swimmers which was just as well, considering Buffy's lack of lifesaving expertise. I am happy to remember that the childhood days of the children and Buffy were happy, carefree days.

Jenny and her young sister Fran (pictured on p. 167) took great delight in dressing Buffy in baby clothes complete with sun bonnet and taking her for walks in a doll's pram or a basket on the handlebars of a bike. Buffy was a willing participant in these activities.

Things were to change quite dramatically in the seventies. Due to a downturn in the farming business, we were forced to sell the farm and move to Melbourne in the hope of gaining employment. Not one of us wanted to leave the farm and make the big change from country to city living — from self employment to a job in the paid workforce. However, economic circumstances made it inevitable.

We were to move to a rented flat in Melbourne and one of the many disadvantages of this plan was that no pets were allowed. At this time I felt everything was all too much and worried incessantly about the big change to our lifestyle and environment. Added to a long list of worries was the question, "what was to become of Buffy?" We had no volunteers to 'adopt' a mildly spoilt, non-working little dog used to luxuries in life such as her regular clipping and grooming.

My sister and her husband, although not dog lovers, were appalled to hear that given no option, euthanasia was being considered. With many misgivings they offered a home with them for our little dog.

Thus began a new and important chapter in Buffy's life, as indeed in the lives of all of us. As a family, we relocated to the city where, most fortunately, my husband and I both found employment. My brother-in-law Cyril suffered a

terminal illness and had become very despondent and anti-social, a condition which made it extremely difficult for my sister to continue her school teaching profession. With Buffy's arrival at their household, Cyril became a changed man. He now had a purpose and a routine to follow daily. Each day he and Buffy would drive Joan to school and then return home to prepare for a walk to the park. Cyril made many new friends, thanks to Buffy. Many elderly people would take their dogs to exercise in the park and thus conversation would be exchanged and new friendships begin. The change in the sick man was incredible. He had never owned a dog and now he loved one. Later in the day the two of them would collect my sister from school and she would be regaled with stories of "what Buffy and I did today".

My sister's life also changed for the better — it was a big load off her mind that Cyril was no longer alone during school hours and no longer so depressed and miserable. Buffy settled in to the scheme quite wonderfully. I feel that perhaps in some uncanny way she realised these were the two people to whom she owed her life and she was going to repay them with her utmost devotion. Whilst she was very happy to see Jenny or any of us who visited, she seemed to have decided that this new home was to be hers indefinitely — it seemed she had found her raison d'être.

Whenever we Kellys tried to express our gratitude to the Clancys for their acceptance of and kindness to Buffy, they would smile and say how grateful they were for the gift of Buffy. Several years later, Buffy became subject to arthritis, heart trouble and many of the attendant ailments of old age. Sadly, the veterinary surgeon thought it best to end her days in the kindest way he knew. She was sorely missed and Cyril died soon afterwards.

If only my dear sister had thought to write a story about Buffy, I know it would have been a glowing tribute to her.

I have no illusions or fantasies regarding this being a *big* story, but then Buffy was only a *small* dog.

*Elizabeth Diane (Judy) Kelly was born in 1929 in Bendigo, Australia and educated at the Sisters of Sion convent in Sale, Gippsland. Judy married in 1952 and lived on rural properties in Victoria and the southern Riverina district of NSW where she assisted in running the properties and household as well as raising four children. In the seventies, forced to sell the family farm due to economic pressures, Judy started her second career as a caterer for big companies. She is now retired and lives with her husband in Nagambie, where she is involved in volunteer work for her local community.*

# smile forms in the place of scars

Delanie Woodlock

eyes barely open
hit again
bruise on my arm
worthless
empty

i am
nothing

my friend curls up in my arms
sleeps in the small of my back
smile forms in the place of scars
i start to see the me reflected
in this little dog's eyes

words
language
tools of another power

unfiltered love
pure
unconstructed love
for me this is only possible
from sam

panicphobiadepression
isolation
oppression at its cause
trapped between my walls

where am i
driving in my car
screaming
how do i drive again

small
chunky
ball of fluff
jump to me

i fall back into myself
sam brings me home

i serve others' needs
make bargains that have limited
my already locked-up life
'no woman is required to build the world by destroying herself'
isn't that selfish

i watch sam
while he loves others
he loves himself more
sustaining and nourishing himself
my friend teaches me about survival

not controlled by guilt
constricted by fear
overwhelmed by violence

sam inspires my fight
gives me a glimpse of my capabilities
of our potentials

sam is who i want to be
unruly
wild
wilful

free

*Sam is a ten-year-old Maltese Terrier who still looks and acts like a puppy. His main hobbies include looking innocent and sweet to strangers — then terrorising them, eating and playing with socks. He also brings out compassion in humans and inspired Delanie to become a vegan, assisting her in seeing the connection between women's oppression and animal cruelty. When Delanie isn't occupied with Sam's demanding lifestyle she sometimes fits in studying Women's Studies at Deakin University, radical feminist activism, web design, art and writing.*

# Branka

Ursula Blattmann

**When our Laika,** an adorable bitzer, passed away, we decided that a 'dog break' would be in order. I had high hopes that my husband Rolf would recover from his massive liver operation and beat the cancer and that we would again be able to live life to the fullest. However, without Laika, our house in the Swiss countryside near Zurich was shockingly empty; my son and I missed her terribly and Rolf too suffered her loss. So often Laika and I had gone together to the hospital to visit him, and her exuberance, when she raced ahead to greet him, gave him great joy in that time of pain and sorrow.

Soon we had to give up hope for a new joint life. The cancer was already too advanced. Rolf's pain increased, the chemotherapy which drained all his strength did not work. He became weaker and weaker and we were deeply saddened. One day Rolf commented, "When I'm no longer with you, you should have another dog, but I really would like to get to know this dog too." Urs, our son who was then seventeen, looked at me with tears in his eyes. It was clear that we could not afford to wait long. So out came the magazine *Dogs* and the search for breeders and breeds began.

Of course, in our heart of hearts, Urs and I agreed that what we really wanted was a Doberman. Our first dog had been a beautiful male Doberman. But we were worried to even mention this to Rolf since we all knew how much time, training and strength was needed for this particular type of dog. So we pretended to talk about all kinds of dogs but in the end we mentioned the word 'Doberman'. As we had expected Rolf was not happy about this idea. However, in the end, we convinced him that what we really needed was a good guard dog. We contacted a Doberman breeder and Urs and I drove there quickly to discover five tiny 'Dobi' puppies with colourful collars. And then, for the first time, we saw what would become our Branka: a beautiful female

pup. We also met her parents and were impressed by how well behaved they were.

A few days later, on 2 June 1989, Urs and I collected our cute little Doberman bundle. When we got home we put Branka down at the door and she ran through the whole house — straight into Rolf's bedroom. We put her on his bed and watched the joy in his face. Action was about to start.

Rolf's state of health deteriorated rapidly and the worry and care for him almost crushed me. I simply did not have the energy to be cheerful and play with little Branka — something she needed very much. So she would wait longingly for the moment when Urs came home from school. At long last, playtime was about to start. After a short time all I needed to say was, "Urs is coming" and Branka raced down the stairs to meet him and, when he finally came in, greeted him with total happiness and enthusiasm.

By that time Rolf was almost totally confined to bed and nurses and the GP came to our house. Branka wanted always to be part of it. She quickly raced into the bedroom through a gap in the door and it was obvious that she was delighted to have tricked the nurses. They, on the other hand, were less than impressed and sternly insisted that the dog was to remain outside. The GP was more tolerant. And indeed, when he let Branka in, she was on her best behaviour and lay down quietly. On those occasions when she was refused entry, she vented her annoyance on anything she could get hold of. She jumped up to knock down clothes as well as the brass hooks from the wardrobe and tore them to pieces. Books, shoes — everything was chewed up. One day when I came out of the bedroom she had my brand new glasses in her bed and chewed them with obvious delight. When I indignantly showed Rolf the ruined glasses he laughed and said, "just get a new pair." Of course all these events were signs that she was bored

because she didn't get enough attention. When she was alone with Rolf she lay silently in front of his bed and didn't move. She knew how sick he was.

The day arrived when Urs departed for France to begin his exchange year. Rolf insisted on coming to the train station, although he really did not have the strength. So Rolf, I and Branka went with Urs to the station. Urs and Rolf knew that it was the final goodbye. Sad, without any words, we drove home. After this day Rolf rarely left his bed. Branka missed Urs incredibly much. Time and time she went to his bedroom, laid herself down on his big teddybear and gently chewed and licked it.

My routine became even more hectic. In the morning I first looked after Rolf. We had breakfast in the bedroom, next came the nursing care. After he was settled and asleep it was Branka's turn. We did our rounds and Branka challenged me frequently by racing after a car, a cat, a crow. I was too exhausted and lacked the patience for obedience training; something I'd been good at with our previous dogs.

Rolf was getting closer to the end and we talked about the future when he would no longer be with us. His advice was that upon his death I should immediately take Branka and travel to Sylt at the North Sea — the region I had grown up in. He then asked for the priest which upset me terribly as I did not yet want to accept that the end had come.

During the night of Monday 25 September Rolf's condition had gotten much worse. There was no time for a walk with Branka, so I just let her out into the garden. I wanted to spend the last hours with Rolf. I sat on his bed, held his hand and read to him from the bible. He fell asleep, peacefully, and at 3 p.m. he left us for ever. Although I had been prepared for this moment for a long time, I could not believe it. When I left the bedroom Branka was curled up in her bed, stayed there, and her big eyes gave me a sad look. "You and I are on our own now," I said, "Rolf has left, he's been released from his pain." She understood and licked the tears from my face.

My friend Rita came to take Branka for a walk so I could be alone with Rolf before the GP and the nurse arrived. But within minutes she had come back and was howling dreadfully in front of the door. After a short time on their walk she had turned back and ran home. What was I to do with her? After some thinking, I took her to the garage and opened the car door. Immediately she jumped in and lay down on the seat. Branka never looked for Rolf nor did she ever go back to the bedroom.

Urs came home and Branka and I went to the airport to collect him. She saw him coming before me, broke loose and raced towards him leaping straight into his arms. She barely tolerated me hugging him! After the funeral he returned to France. Branka and I were alone together.

We escaped from the empty house as often as we could and were on the road most of the day. We walked for miles through fields and woods which were turning on their autumn colours. Only in the evenings we would return. At night I often lay awake and thought everything had just been a bad dream. Finally, in the morning, I fell asleep and would have stayed in bed if Branka hadn't come in, nudged me and put her head on the cover. "Come on," she seemed to say, "I need to go out and it'll be good for you as well." So I got up and we did our rounds. We often met other women with their dogs and the talks with them helped me in my grief.

Branka demanded my full energy and attention. She was a passionate hunter and there was not a dull moment on our walks. I was always on full alert and tense. After two months I decided to join the Doberman Club in order to train her. This was a big challenge for both of us. But when we came home after the training I was exhausted and Branka was quiet and content. The Club activities helped me to temporarily forget my sad thoughts and I made new friends. In the evenings at home, Branka sat near me, or on my lap, and looked at me with her gorgeous brown eyes. How could I ever have made it through this time without Branka?

She was a quick learner and I too regained confidence, strength and skills. Soon we passed the test for company dogs and after that the one for guard dogs. We were both very proud. In between the training we went for trips to the North Sea in Germany where Branka could run herself ragged for hours on the beach. Chasing seagulls was the best play of all. We both had a great time. Unfortunately our time together was also far too short. Branka only lived to five years of age. As my diary entry for yet another time of sorrow reads:

"5 August 1994. Today we had to put Branka to sleep. A cancerous stomach ulcer was the cause. What a sad day. Everything happened quietly and Dr Rohner was very good about it. An impetuous dog life has come to an end as has a demanding but beautiful togetherness. Good bye and thanks, my dearest Branka, and have a wonderful time in dog heaven."

What Branka and I shared together was much more than a friendship. She was my companion in the saddest time of my life and gave me the strength to keep going. The urn with her ashes is buried in our garden and at Christmas I always light a candle on the grave.

My life did not remain dogless though. In 1995, my Inka, another Doberman female pup, joined me. And in 1997 cheeky Dwarf Pinscher Tiny came to us. The dogs love each other and enjoy lots of romps. The three of us are happy.

Translated by Renate Klein

*Ursula Blattman was born in Hamburg, Germany but has lived near Zurich in Switzerland since 1956. After the death of her husband she became very involved in dog sports and is an active member of the local Doberman Club.*

# Home Comforts

Sandi Hall

**Just before mobile phones** kept us connected, I returned to Auckland from a time of sorrow abroad. Below the plane, I saw at last the eagerly awaited trail of green islands that points to Aotearoa. My mind checked my heart for quivers of known joy. But numbness held me.

Soon after my return, I moved into Ring Terrace, a marvellous house curved into one of the shallow hillsides above Auckland's inner harbour. All its north-facing windows look out over the water, where little boats seem to dodge between squat storage tanks, and Rangitoto backdrops every moment with its low-slung blue volcanic cone.

It was there that I fell in love with Millie, an elegantly attractive standard Poodle with black nappy curls covering a well-muscled body. She was as dykely beautiful as her Special Friend, Pen. Ring Terrace was their home, and I felt relief and pride to be a 'paying guest' (the Edwardian term for flatting) in that spacious house.

It was new to me to share my city life with a dog. In my girlhood, I lived on a cattle farm which had several working dogs. How smart and proud they were, doing their daily work! Their shining eyes said that they knew they had an important place in the life of the farm. Because of that, I was troubled to see large dogs in the city, where they had no function, and no free places to run. From the first day I moved in, I offered to take Millie for runs on the beach and Pen, with a swift, knowing glance replied, "Sure. She'd like that."

Pen's family bought Ring Terrace in the late '60s from the estate of its owner, whose ghost, when I arrived, was still restless in the inner sitting room. I noticed Millie often looked at the deep armchair with her ears pricked. But I also knew my sensibilities were stretched almost to breaking point, so I asked Pen about the male presence who seemed to resent my sitting in a certain place in that

room. "Yep, he's always been there," she affirmed, "but he's harmless. Don't worry about him."

But I did. Death and the transitions to that boundless state had been my university over the past months. I thought of that old man's spirit, unable to leave a place that he had perhaps loved; I recalled that Maori wisdom regards the wavy-armed pohutakawa tree as the bridge between this world and the mystery beyond it.

I said to Pen that I would like to bring a branch of pohutakawa into the house to release the old man's spirit. "Good idea," said Pen, who knows about these things. Then, after a pause, "Be sure you get permission. Take Millie, if you want." By now, Millie and I were friends, and I was finding a great deal of comfort in her constancy. Often, when silent, razor-edged tears were slitting my throat, she'd come to me, look up at me briefly, and settle herself against my leg with a throaty grunt.

At the local bay, the pohutakawas had not long finished their blooming: drifts of their dark red needle-flowers crusted the rumpled flesh-coloured sand. Millie was a speck in the distance, a dancing knot against the dazzle of the sea as I walked beneath the trees, feeling my way. How should I approach the trees? How would I know what to do?

Millie dashed up to me, eyes brilliant with pleasure, ears like Piglet's in a high wind. She was so eager, I involuntarily laughed. She gave a little dancing jump, and rushed off again.

Slowly, I felt drawn to a particular pohutakawa. I stood in front of it and spoke silently of the old man's spirit. Pen's reminder about permission came into my mind. "May I have one of your branches to help his spirit, please?" I said aloud. The small branch near me seemed warm under my hand, and needed almost no pressure to take from the tree.

I put the branch in the corner of the room. Millie sat and looked at it, ears forward, eyes watching something. I wondered what she could see. The room was warmer than it had been, and over the weeks, Pen and I agreed that the old man's spirit had gone.

Millie and Pen and I lived together for nearly two years, after which I had enough money to put a deposit on a small house; but it was quite far away. I knew I would miss them both, but I didn't realise I would miss Millie as much as Pen, who had become a good friend. Of course I missed Millie's bright-eyed beauty and the way in which her running was an earthbound form of flight. But most of all I missed her graceful, gentle spirit that, once friendship had been established, connected to mine with a steady and loving warmth.

Last week I had a call from Pen, to tell me Millie had died. I felt that stab to the heart that you do when you hear a beloved has gone. Today, under the pohutakawas, I held a branch, and spoke to her: "Millie darling, I feel like Isak Dinesen talking to Saabu,* and I am Saabu, of course. I hope that the beaches are long and wide where you are, and that some Time, we will once again dance on them together."

* Isak Dinesen was the Danish writer whose life story is told in the film 'Out of Africa'. Saabu was her servant.

*Sharing in the affinity between dykes and dogs, Sandi Hall is a New Zealand writer, but not dog owner. However, she is 'auntie' to Bella, a chubby Scotch Terrier, Sasha, a sleek Alsatian, and Susie, the cutest miniature Fox Terrier in the world!*

# Memories of Love Honoured

Shannon-Caroline Taylor

**From my earliest memories** animals have been intrinsic to my life, and a life-blood of my soul. That I have remained on this earth has much to do with animals. Much of my will to live, my philosophy and thoughts have been inspired by my life with animals. I have always afforded them the greatest respect and love, just as they have to me. All animals, all creatures.

One December day a girl was born and grew into a little girl and then a young girl and then a young woman. Each of these stages was marked by what one judge described, when sentencing the perpetrator, as a hideous history of every kind of abuse. I recall the day that I got 'Kimmy'. (That's her pictured on the left.) I was approximately four years old when Kimmy was handed to me from the pet shop cage to carry home. She was a little 'bitzer' as adults called her, but to me she was the most perfect dog. She only grew to about 35cm in height and was black with a tail that coiled over her back and was white underneath.

When the abuse began, Kimmy was the one creature that I could trust. At that time in my life we lived in poverty, and my life was made even more complicated with numerous moves around the country with strange living spaces and later, numerous schools. I would hug and stroke Kimmy's soft coat and kiss her and whisper my sorrow to her. I knew she understood. When I would hide from my abuser and tormentor, Kimmy never gave away my hiding place. My pleas for help went unaided and the resulting punishment I endured for seeking help crushed my sense of self and forced me into years of silence. Like others victimised from childhood I suffered emotional abuse along with the sexual and physical violations. I believed that I was the most worthless, most ugly and most unlovable person on this earth — but I believed that animals saw me differently. Among my animal friends Kimmy was the love of my life because I *knew* that she loved me in the most holistic sense possible for a child to understand.

As the abuse grew worse Kimmy was never far from me, but I was not able to take her to bed with me. My vulnerability at night was suffered in darkness and in solitude. I told Kimmy everything — not always in words, sometimes just in a flood of tears. But I know, in the deepest part of my heart, that Kimmy knew. I told Kimmy things no human being had ever heard, and that I could not dare tell a human out of fear and a belief that I was worthless. In the latter part of my teens, Kimmy died. It was a wintry day in June and I went to give Kimmy her dinner. She wasn't in her usual place and when I found her I knew that she was gravely ill. With no way of getting any veterinary aid, I felt helpless as I carried Kimmy to my room and cradled her. As my tears fell upon her, I prayed aloud that Kimmy would be all right and would remain with me because I loved her so dearly and it was often Kimmy who helped get me through each day. My tears came from a well of despair so deep that I thought I might also die at that moment. Suddenly Kimmy lifted her head and looked at me and, for the briefest moment, I thought that she was going to recover. I looked into her eyes and connected with the inner-most of her being. She leaned her head forward to lick my hands which were bathed in my own tears. Her head fell forward. She was dead.

I remember letting out a scream. I felt a sense of grief and aloneness, a degree of loss and devastation that caused physical, not just emotional pain. When I buried her, I felt that part of me went into her grave also. I made a cross to mark her grave, but the emptiness I felt remained.

A number of years went by before I 'adopted' a male Chihuahua I called 'Jabberwocky'. Like Kimmy, he quickly sensed the sadness in my life and often witnessed some of the incidents that made this so. When I cried he would look at me with an expression of deep concern and love and he would make little crying sounds too — just as Kimmy had done. I still mourned Kimmy, but loved Jabberwocky with the same degree of wholeness. Jabberwocky did sleep with me and I realised that he sensed my fear of night time, knowing that my bed offered no protection against abuse. Jabberwocky developed a similar sort of hyper-vigilance, as though he understood and connected with my own fear.

One of the most profound and significant moments of my life was the escape from the years of abuse. Though Jabberwocky was one of the few possessions I fled with, he was violently stolen from me a short time later. The absence of my dog and other animals (I also had a favoured horse) was heart-breaking. I had no family whatsoever and few, if any, friends in my post-escape world. Soon after the police became involved I discovered that Jabberwocky was dead. To this day I have no firm details about his death and I do not know where he is buried or if he was buried. Grief leaves an indelible mark.

A couple of years later, a policewoman involved with the case bought me a dog — in fact I was able to choose the puppy, a female Chihuahua, from the litter. I called her 'Loki,' after the Norwegian god of mischief. Like Kimmy and Jabberwocky, Loki came into the life of a person who seemed to exude sadness — even though I was trying hard to create a sense of peace and a new life. I noticed that Loki also sensed when I was feeling sad, even before I shed a tear. It was like a sixth sense and at these times she would seek to be especially close to me. Whenever I cried,

Loki would insist on licking my tears away. In addition to Loki, I now have another dog that was in need of a home, a Scotch Collie I called 'Sheppy'.

The unconditional love that these dogs and other animals gave — and continue to give — were gifts that no human was ever able to offer for a large part of my life. Their sense of decency, of respect, of compassion and empathy influenced my character development in the absence of human love and human decency. I 'survived' all my life pre-escape and much of my post-escape life because animals enriched my very sense of being. The burgeoning sense of identity that I developed, but was not fully aware of for a long time, resulted from the love that animals gave me. Despite a continuing sense of wounding that is often times painfully conscious and ever-present to myself, my animals held alive something inside me which no human could ever destroy. I now realise more than ever before that there was a part of me that no human could destroy — a part of me that was nurtured by animals.

Animals taught me the purity of true love, of unselfishness and of giving without reserve, of loving without expecting in return. From them I know that a noble and true life is filled with these things and I have seen the essence of spiritual wholeness reflected in my animals. My animals taught me courage and I now realise that I have been courageous all my life, even when I thought I was weak.

I unashamedly seek the qualities I found in my animals in my human friends. I am fortunate for I have found a most beautiful man who loves me as my animals did and still do, and lucky for me I have also found two-legged friends who are worthy in character like my animals. I continue to grieve over my animals who died or were murdered when I escaped the abuse. Of Kimmy, all I have is one blurred photo, and the few I have of Jabberwocky I guard close to me. I have come to realise something quite significant about the four dogs that have been in my life. Despite the love I willingly gave Kimmy and Jabberwocky — and despite the abundant love they bestowed upon me in childhood and young adulthood — in the few photos I have of them, they look as sad as I did in the few photos taken of me. Although I gave them hugs and kisses and preferred their company to that of humans, I believe they shared something of the emotional experience of my terror and distress and sadness as a result of the abuse they too sometimes witnessed. Their sharing of empathy was profound and, as my new life has developed and I have gained some sense of healing, I have noted how Loki's demeanour has changed markedly. Loki and Sheppy have travelled with me on some exciting adventures and now live on a tranquil property with other happy animals where they are free to roam, free to play and to dance to the tune of their soul — just as I finally have those same freedoms.

Though I mourn my animals still in a way that haunts me, someone said, "If your animals could speak to you they would tell you that you were worth dying for and that they gladly gave their lives if it meant that you could be set free." That Jabberwocky lost his life not long after I escaped the abuse, and that his life and death is significantly intertwined with my escaping is not lost on me — nor has this loss and its impact diminished over time. I often feel a deep sense of sadness that Kimmy and Jabberwocky in particular never saw me 'free' and that they are not here to share in my new life. But I have no doubt that they are nearby in spirit. It is with deepest gratitude and love that I hug their memories and honour them for making my life worthwhile. And I think they would be proud that the little girl with the tear-stained face and frightened demeanour, who was given heartfelt moments of relief and love by her animals, is now alive. 🐾

*Shannon-Caroline Taylor, with Loki on lap and Sheppy, lives with her partner and a menagerie of animals on a property in Victoria. Since escaping her abuse she has rebuilt her life; changing part of her name and subsequently attending university. Shannon-Caroline is passionate about animals and social justice for others, particularly children. Her interests include travelling, horse-riding, photography, writing poetry, bushwalking and hosting dinner parties for friends. She is an academic and has published in journals and books nationally and internationally, and is a frequent public speaker on issues related to her work and research. She has recently completed a PhD.*

*Kimmy is left and Jabberwocky right on page 176.*

Section Six The Dogs of Our Lives

# Good Dogs, Heaven and Me

Moira Rayner

**When I was about six** my Dad brought home a floppy-eared, curly-coated, black-and-white Water-Spaniel-cross called Smutty (after my Dad's jokes). She and I would 'talk' for hours. Dad used her as a hunting dog. "Ducks!" he would say, and she would leap barking into the boot of his big old green Humber, off to the lake. Mum was not as keen, yelling, "Off my garden!" and banning Smut from the house when I broke my leg and the plaster evidenced too much hair.

Smut was family. She 'wrote' a daily diary — a commentary on the family's events — forged by my father, for years (I still have these treasures). She was a glutton — one winter day she snuck into the kitchen and pinched the roast from the stove. We came home to Smut, *in flagrante delicto*, tossing the hot leg of lamb onto the snowy lawn. The spoilsports took it away, and we had baked beans.

As she got older, Smut became very fat — she squeezed, audibly, into her kennel — and very placid. I can now see how absent-mindedly cruel we were, to deny a normal lifespan to her by simply feeding her too much, exercising her too little, and excluding her from our company. She may have been lonely. She was certainly invisible.

It is still exquisitely painful for me to recall that, when Dad confessed over tea one night that he had "taken Smut to the gasworks" because our neighbour said she had snapped at my baby sister, we had not noticed her absence over nearly two days (I still called him a murderer). How could we have failed to 'notice' the absence of the dog we had loved so much? Perhaps it was the distraction of our new baby sister. We had relegated the dog to a separate and solitary life. That's why I have never consigned my companion animals to the apartheid of yard and kennel. Why have a dog, if not as part of the family? But really, we had simply become adolescent narcissists.

My next dog, Flossie, came more than thirteen years later. She was a big, black adolescent herself, part Doberman, inherited from a friend who had, in turn, rescued her from a life tied to a clothes line. Flossie and I bonded, because she came into my life a few weeks after I had thrown my husband out of it.

There is no companion like a sympathetic dog. Once, driving past the local cemetery, I lifted up my voice and wept aloud and was astounded when Floss lifted her own and howled in sympathy. She would travel with her head in my lap, sleep on my bed, and gently forgive the lack of regular walks in our first few years together.

Flossie generously shared her home. We formed a pack of people, cats and other dogs. Timbo, an apricot-coloured hyperactive and asthmatic Pug, was rescued from my boyfriend because his idea of helping him overcome his fear of water was to throw him, shrieking, into the surf. Timbo was baby-like. I would never have chosen a pedigree or a pug, but came to adore him. He died of a broken heart, I think, six weeks and two days after I had taken up a job in another state, intending to bring him over when I had a house. Pongo, a Kelpie crossed with some curly-legged mongrel, a classically plain but very smart pup, came in the arms of a teenager who wanted something of her own to love, then left her behind. For two

years my sister's German Shepherd, Golda lived with us, too. By this time my Dad and I would take the three of them, each morning, either to the glorious beach, with an ice-cream container for the dog poo, or walking around the golf course, or the park. They were very happy times.

Flossie had a bump on the top of her lovely head, and a habit of slipping silently behind you and introducing her muzzle into your hand, and leaning affectionately. She survived many illnesses and accidents: run over (shock, abrasions, neurosis); skin lesions (flea allergies); battle wounds (a friend's psychotic German Shepherd); diabetes (I would take urine samples, morning and evening, with a jam jar at the end of a long stick. It looked absurd, because Flossie would be too embarrassed to pee); arthritis (gold injections!); and epilepsy (medication). Then she was unwell one Wednesday; diagnosed with stomach cancer; and in such agony, three days later, that I called our vet. Flossie's last act was to wag her tail for Dad. Her heart seemed to beat long after she stopped breathing. She and Timbo are buried together by the back gate. I can never sell that house.

For two years after first Flossie, then Timbo, died I could not bear to have another dog. But I could hear a puppy whimpering each night, from a house in the same street. We met at the front gate of this house of young sharers, one morning: a pup remarkably like Flossie: brown, not black; flat-footed, not elegant; male, but adorable. Weeks later Olly/Folly walked in my front door off the street. I left a message at the house, which provoked an offer from the kid who was bored with his ex-puppy, to take him. I did.

We hit it off. Folly ("When lovely woman stoops to . . .") was a Hound From Hell (very badly behaved) but also my companion of dawn walks through Fitzroy Gardens, where we met foxes, possums, cruisers and cops. I would take him to the long beaches of the peninsula where he ran, and ran, and smiled. At his first Equal Opportunity Commission picnic, on the river, Folly chased a passing cyclist for a couple of kilometres (Flossie once chased a man in a wheelchair to the end of the street, while I was incapacitated by horrified hysterics). Folly lived noisily and cheerfully through the burglary. ("Just as well he's no watchdog," said the police. "The last job, they rammed a screwdriver through the dog's head.") I shuddered and rejoiced in Folly's frolics.

Folly accepted the domination of cats, looked wounded when Justin (a cat) bit him, fled Amazing Grace like a gazelle, and was my best friend when I was worried. We walked together for many dark hours.

But Folly blossomed when the neighbour's puppy joined the home. It was obvious that the pup was energetic, and not well matched to her owner. Their mutual anguish was audible and distressing. We suggested our neighbour relinquish the dog to us. That Saturday when Murphy was carried in, she shook. Within an hour she was rollicking up and down the stairs, puddling and canoodling with an ecstatic Folly. They became and have remained a couple. Our relationship took longer to set.

It arose from disaster. Just before Christmas Eve in 1994 Murphy slipped past me at the front gate onto peak hour Hoddle Street. She played with me and six lanes of heavy traffic for ten, nightmare minutes, as I flagged down cars and trucks and buses and ran and pleaded and called her to the safety of the footpath. Then a four-wheel drive mowed her down in front of my eyes.

Murphy survived. Her shattered back legs healed slowly and she required daily nursing for several months. I worked from home and did what I could. We talked. She became a mature and reflective companion.

I have gained much from my relationships with dogs. I have walked Folly and Murphy most mornings through darkened parks and gardens, Now, I am relatively fit — and my diabetes is well-controlled — because I was responsible for their health and happiness. I miss them, but as part of a household they do not seem to miss me. I have never had a 'one-woman' dog. I could not bear the responsibility.

I have learned an enormous amount from dogs: what unconditional love is; how dependency relationships are ethically complex; that making a dog dependent on a human is a responsibility. From Flossie, I learned that you always die alone. No one can accompany you.

If it is true that dogs have no soul, I would not want a place in heaven.

*Moira Rayner is the Director of the Office of London Children's Rights Commissioner and lives in a studio in Belsize Park where she misses her beloved dogs who are in Melbourne for now. She is a lawyer and human rights activist and a social commentator as well as author:* Rooting Democracy – Growing the Society We Want *(with Jenny Lee 1997), and (with Joan Kirner)* The Women's Power Handbook *(1999). Folly (back), Murphy (front).*

# A Tale of Two Dogs

Rose Zwi

**I was about six** years old when my father brought Ruby home. He had found the whimpering pup in the lane behind his shop, starving, rheumy-eyed. Before my mother could say dog's mess, I had installed him in the laundry, on my doll's blanket. The stiff, expressionless kewpie doll was no competition for the warm, brown-eyed pup who looked at me with trusting, soulful eyes.

Ruby had the long body and short, bowed legs of a Dachshund, and the head of a Beagle. As a puppy he tripped over his own ears. Stupid dog, was the family verdict. I knew better. When the lights went out, and everyone was asleep, Ruby crept quietly into my room, and slept at my feet till dawn.

We were inseparable. He ran with me through the veld; sat on the pavement while I skipped with my friends; waited at the gate for my return from school. After my brother was born and I lost my place at the heart of the family, I clung to Ruby more fiercely than ever. He too had been abandoned, and thrust into a cruel, uncaring world.

Dogs are dirty, my mother said as she brushed Ruby's hair off the couch or carpet; the baby will get asthma or ringworm. I haven't got asthma or ringworm, I argued. And he sleeps on

my bed every night, I whispered to myself. Babies are different, my mother said. I became aware of whispered conversations, during which Ruby's name was mentioned. But I did not suspect treachery, not even when I saw my mother talking earnestly to the man who sold live chickens in wire mesh cages from the back of his cart.

One afternoon, on my way from school, about a block from home, I recognised Ruby's agitated bark. My heart iced over and I began to run. As I turned the corner, the chicken man pulled away from our house, all his cages empty. Except one.

I was inconsolable. Promises of another dog drew fresh floods of tears. I don't remember how long my grief lasted, nor indeed whether I fully regained my trust in people. For a long time I remained wary of giving unconditional love again. Until I got

Spike, and he wasn't even 'my' dog.

After our children were born, we had a succession of much loved cats and dogs, some of whom lived to a reasonable age. Others were lost to traffic or disease. After the death of Satan, a gentle Alsatian who had been a reject from a school for guard dogs, I said, no more dogs. He had lived for fourteen years, but in his declining years, he had suffered from a degenerative hip disease which almost crippled him.

Satan hadn't been dead two months, when my daughter requested a dog for her birthday. An Alsatian, she specified, like Satan. Only if you all take responsibility for walking, bathing and feeding him, I said. All three children promised, and they probably meant it at the time.

We found an advertisement in the newspaper for four Alsatian pups with an impressive pedigree, but no guarantee against hip disease. Our choice was unanimous: the cheeky pup with floppy ears who approached us boldly, grabbed my handbag, and ran off with it. A robber baron. To deflate pretensions to canine aristocracy, we called him Spike.

He was a most egalitarian dog. His best friend was our domestic help's baby, Michael, who was born a few months earlier. Spike and Michael crawled and ran all over the house, squealing and yapping with delight in one another's company. Spike even allowed Michael to eat dog biscuits out of his dish, the equivalent, perhaps, of breaking bread with friends. When they were older, they followed Michael's mother, Joyce, to the shops. Don't worry, Michael would tell black people who associate Alsatians with the police, Spike's a good dog. He doesn't bite black people.

All this happened in South Africa, during the worst years of the apartheid era. Because schools in the cities were closed to black children, Michael went to a church school in the country, where the dormitories smelled of urine, and meals were served out of aluminium tubs. He lost his English accent — chech, he said, not church — was badly taught, and consequently did not do well at school. He spent every holiday at our house with his mother, and maintained his friendship with Spike.

While Michael was away at school, Spike accompanied me to my study every morning. He lay down near the desk, resting his chin between his paws. Spike, I would say occasionally, what's a better word for . . . ? He'd flick his tail, indicating in no uncertain terms that I should stop fooling around and get on with my work. Sometimes we'd sing. I'd do a melodious howl, he'd repeat something very near it, and soon we'd be harmonising. At other times I'd say, don't look so

solemn — he had slanted markings above his eyes which gave him a whimsical look — smile! He'd roll on to his back, and open his mouth in a wide grin. He was a loving, much loved dog.

Spike died when he was twelve years old. Like Satan, he suffered from that painful hip disease. He grew weaker and weaker, and eventually could not climb down the stairs to my study. When Michael came home during school holidays at the end of the year, Spike greeted him joyously, but could no longer follow him across the field to the shop. Early one morning, several days after his return, Michael found him stretched out on his blanket in the laundry, dead. He wept inconsolably as we buried Spike under a deodar at the far end of the garden.

Seven years later it was we who wept at Michael's funeral. He had been arrested by the police one night for an unspecified 'crime' by the police. They beat him up, locked him into the boot of the police car, and he was dead on arrival at the police station.

*Rose Zwi was born in Mexico, lived in London and Israel but spent most of her life in South Africa. She has lived in Australia since 1988. Author of five novels, she has won several prizes for her work, including the 1994 Human Rights Award for her novel* Safe Houses *and the 1982 Olive Schreiner Award for* Another Year in Africa.

# Watch Out for Falling Apples in the Garden

Cathie Dunsford

**"Watch out for falling apples in the garden,"** Mum reads, "the weight of an apple falling from a tree could kill a Chihuahua."

I look down into the eyes of Tiny, the baby Chihuahua nestled between my breasts. I'm a mother substitute and she's so vulnerable.

"Hang a net under all fruit trees. Oranges, tangelos, nashi, persimmon, mangoes, papaya. They can crush such a small dog," Mum reads from the Chihuahua manual.

Tiny squeaks from between my breasts as I bend. "Are we ready for such a huge responsibility, Mum? It's like having babies. You have to watch them constantly in case the wind blows anything larger than a kiwi fruit their way."

Mum smiles. She knows I've never been much of a one for babies. Except for turtles. And they can swim on their own.

The falling apple day was just a rehearsal. Some time later, Basil came into our lives. Yes — Basil. We inherited the name from the owners from whom he was rescued. He had AIDS, no hair on his body and the farmer had treated him — like all their animals, with lysol. "They'll either survive, or die. That's nature," he said. Basil survived. Just. He was ugly. And frightened. He cowered. He sulked. Not at all like my beloved Sheba (pictured above), whom I'd shared my entire life with. But like Sheba, Basil became one of the family. He survived falling fruit from the heavens and fell in love with my cat Pele. When she was a kitten, she'd lie in wait on the couch and jump on his back and hang on tight with her claws for a ride around the room. Basil didn't seem to mind. He'd had far worst in his past. He soon learned to hide in the bush behind Mohala and throw out his paws to grab Pele as she passed. They romped and played and rolled about lusciously under the treeferns together.

Basil wasn't a real Chihuahua. He had Foxy and Jack Russell in him too — probably why he survived the falling apples. But he could smell dinner from the end of the beach and would be licking your toes by the time you came to serve it. His magic worked on you until you came to love him totally and forever. He came from a long line of magicians. His mother Pipi could sing a tune and levitate in the air — no kidding. My dad saw her do it — and he never lies.

I often wished he could have met my first dog Sheba. My music teacher called her 'an animated dishmop'. She was Australian Terrier and long-haired Dachschund and shared the autumnal colours of her mother Rusty. She became so distressed when we went away one year, she found her way through the maze of about twenty kilometres of city streets to be back on the doorstep when we returned. Sheba was loyal. So loyal that when I competed in the Lake Pupuke Annual Sailing Regatta in my small P-class boat, Sheba decided to jump in and swim beside me for the last leg of the race. I was one of the few girls in yachting at that stage and you can imagine the response from the boys. But Sheba made it with me — and I hugged her all night for that. I liked her far better than the boys anyway!

I often think of them in Doggy Heaven:

S: "She'd sail out on that log with a towel over her head and expect me not to get worried."

B: "Yeah — she'd dive into waves, knowing I was afraid of the sea."

S: "I loved the ocean — ya couldn't keep me away. She'd take me surfing and swimming and I'd bark like hell when she was flying behind the boat on those thin planks of wood."

B: "Thank Pele I missed that phase."

S: "You survived the falling apples though, eh?"

B: "Did she try out that routine on you too?"

S: "Na. I wrote the book. Never much liked chihuahuas. Until I met you, that is."

B: "I'm a mongrel anyway. So why did ya warn the No-Tails about the apples?"

S: "They're into apple-in-the-garden stories. Besides, I knew they'd take no notice."

This is a true story. I even have pikkies to prove it. They are both now in Doggy Heaven. I miss them terribly and remember them daily. Falling apples, mangoes, boats, beaches, water, swimming, preparing food and feeling a wet tongue over my ankle. What is it that stays with us so deeply, even after they've gone? Something rare. Loyalty. Trust. Absolute Joy in the moment of being — whether chasing a stick or licking an ankle. The look of pleasure in their eyes after retrieving the driftwood and you say, "Tau mahi ra, e te iti kahurangi — Well done, you little beauty!"

Aroha mai, aroha atu: love received asks for love returned.

*Cathie Dunsford is Director of Dunsford Publishing Consultants, publishing women's and Pacific texts globally: <dunsford@voyager.co.nz>. Spinifex Press has published her first four tnovels in the* Cowrie *novel series:* Cowrie; The Journey Home; Heart Warrior; *and* Song of the Selkies. *The first two novels were translated and published in Germany as* Kia Kaha Cowrie.

# Dogs I Have Loved

Alison McMichael

**Barney was about thirteen** when he was accidentally sprayed with water from a garden hose. He walked off and never returned. We never said goodbye, after all those years of friendship — we had grown up together. I used to imagine that he had found a safe spot somewhere and just lay down to die. I hope his death was a painless one, after all the pleasure he gave me as a child.

Barney, an Australian Terrier, was mostly black with some tan as I recall. He was definitely 'an outside dog', an early rule set down by my father. But he was always there, ready to join in any of the games we devised. When I was alone, without my brothers, I sometimes dressed Barney up in ribbons and pretended he was my doll. He was such an even tempered dog who would let me play with him while he patiently endured my pretend games. I don't think my brothers ever found out.

Some of the best times were at the seaside, at my grandmother's house. We would take him to the beach where he would guard our clothes while we swam. Then, we would invite him in — actually we would pick him up and carry him into the water. As we carried him out, his little legs would start paddling in the air and when we finally plunged him in, he would turn for shore still paddling until he reached safety! This gave us endless hours of simple pleasure.

The only times I remember him coming inside the house were when there was a thunderstorm. Then, my father relented and Barney crept in to sit on a piece of newspaper until the storm had passed. I am sure he relished those moments — I did!

Barney was part of the family, and a great companion for a girl in a house of boys. When he just disappeared, there was a great gap, which I sought to fill with another dog. Bruno arrived, but he disappeared quickly — he apparently followed me to the bus stop and that was the last we saw of him. He was followed by Pedro, a Fox Terrier, who became my firm friend.

Pedro was definitely 'an inside dog'! He did sleep outside, but in the mornings, my mother would open the back door and Pedro would thunder up the back hall, arrive at my bedroom door and leap from the door to my bed, no mean feat! (My father must have mellowed.) I was not the sort to tease a dog, but my brothers were. A favourite trick was to hang Pedro's towel up on the Hills Hoist and make him jump for it, which he did with panache.

Pedro came into my life as I was flexing my wings and not around as much. But he was a dog with great spirit and a risk-taker — something I have always treasured.

It was many years before I once again had a dog of my own, but the happy experience of those early years of Barney and then Pedro led me to share my life once again with a dog. This time I chose a female, Tammy, a Skye Terrier. She is not only 'an inside dog' but sleeps in the bedroom with me, often on the bed. (I don't ask my father what he thinks of this).

This dog has long, ground-length white hair, which also covers her eyes. When I first took her, at ten months, she looked like a Greek Flokati rug; it was totally impractical to walk with such a coat. So (don't tell the breeders) I have her clipped regularly which actually makes her look younger. When she is difficult — rarely — I tell her that the next dog I get will have short black hair, which doesn't seem to faze her at all.

If I hadn't had the experience of loving a dog as a child, and feeling safe and special with Barney, I may not have sought to share my later life with Tammy. As it is, I could not imagine life without a dog now. The welcome every night when I return from work is priceless. No matter what I feel, she is there to comfort and protect. She is good for my health, as we need to walk every day. She talks to me — yes, she does — and I talk back — yes, I do. No one can hear us — just as well.

I guess I learnt to respect and love animals through having Barney all those years ago. Despite our different views on where dogs should be, I have to thank my father for including dogs in our lives, as it is a dimension which is now most fulfilling.

*Alison McMichael (pictured with Tammy) grew up in Adelaide where she completed a first degree in social work. She moved to Melbourne with her daughter and has worked as a social worker in clinical and academic work, which included an MSW. She continues to teach social work students in the field. She also reads tertiary text books to blind university students.*

Cassis, Kirstie (left) and Rye live together in an inner city suburb of Melbourne. If you wondered, Cassis is part chow chow and part standard poodle and she has a purple tongue. Other members of the household include Greta, the whippet (a recent addition) and two Burmese foster cats.

# Haikus for Cassis

Kirstie Murdoch and Rye Senjen

*Longing*

Wind and hail
as night falls
Torment of longing

Torment of longing
your furry cheeks
bring calm

*Heartbreak*

Numbed by heartbreak
your furry cheeks
a refuge

Deep in heartbreak
your furry cheeks
a refuge

# Dog Spirits

Anne Coombs

**July:** It is no accident that Dog is God spelt backwards. They are gods, at our place anyway. All three of them.

They are credited with special powers, able to divine the truth from a person's scent, to judge a character good or bad. I trust my dog's assessment ahead of my own. As gods, offerings are made to them. Small treats laid before them each evening after dinner. And we spend quality time with each of them, a time for mutual devotion; because if they are our gods, we also are theirs. When it's their turn for quality time, each comes into our cathedral and prostrates him or herself on the floor, writhing blissfully.

When you have three of them you soon learn their strengths and weaknesses. None of our three had the best start in life. All were neglected puppies. Scruffy had probably been dumped, thrown from a car, before he found his way to my place; he can still affect the creeping, nervous gait, the sidelong glance. But he has learnt that it is the way to insinuate himself — into one's heart or in through a doorway. Craftiness is Scruffy's special skill. He has a way of sitting with his back half-turned to you, then twisting his neck and gazing up at you with a flirtatious grin. I call it his Marilyn Monroe look. No one can resist it. He's the smallest but the oldest; it's nearly fourteen years since he first fell into my arms.

Boy belonged to neighbours and was so ignored and badly fed that he responded with joy when we paid him some attention. A tiny, dirty ball of delight. He's big now, the biggest of the three, but his eyes still light up with that same joy when he hears his name. 'Boy'. Not much of a name, but better than 'Oy!' which was all his former owners ever called him. He's bright, Boy. Never has to be taught the same lesson twice. But curious and full of life, so much so that he's always getting into trouble for something.

Jacko was meant to be a boy but turned out to be a girl. But she's a real Aussie mutt so the name stuck. A bit podgy, going prematurely stiff, but the sweetest nature. Her only misdemeanour is to eat the cat food. She does it every day — she never learns! Not big in the brains department is Jacko, but the kindest heart. When she first arrived she couldn't take her eyes off Scruffy. She'd been taken from her mother too young and was desperate for an adult dog to cuddle up to. For the first year she ignored us; Scruffy was her only god.

The three of them together are a bit of a handful. Boy's goodness and intelligence is undermined by Scruffy's cunning and Jacko's blockheadedness. They get on together remarkably well, but they're like an unruly clutch of children.

But they're sensitive, too. They can sense my state of mind even when they are not the cause of it. They often offer sympathy — a nose against the knee, a proffered paw — but the problems I might have are not for them to solve. I like that. It is enough to have their steady gaze and loyal presence, a cool wet nose or warm dry paw. What other relationship offers such uncomplicated love?

**August:** Scruffy has died. Three weeks ago, only days after I wrote this. A dreadful accident, sudden and unexpected. It only happened because he was getting old and slow and a bit vague — 'Alzheimerish'.

Even though he died so suddenly I think part of me had been expecting it. For months, watching him getting slower and less sure of himself, I'd been unconsciously

# Women and Their Dogs

Susan Varga

preparing myself for the loss of this most loyal of friends. Scruffy was not one for a slow, lingering death. His life was littered with dramatic incident.

The thing I miss most is his ever-present sympathy, the liquid brown eyes, wise under their shaggy brows. The way he would silently come to my side when I needed comforting.

When Scruffy ran into my arms that day nearly fourteen years ago, he put his trust in me. My side of the deal was not to betray that trust. A trust that was offered wholeheartedly, till death us do part. When you think about it, it is an awesome thing.

We can give them commands, play with them, berate them, but these are surface things. The relationship between dog and human is visceral. They are flesh and blood as we are, their beating heart is in our hands. It is a sacred thing, caring for this warm, live creature who adores us. Physically they are at our mercy, and it so often goes badly wrong for a dog. Their relationship with humans can slip easily between sacred and profane.

Physically, Scruffy is no longer with me but he was a forceful little character and I sometimes think that death is just the latest challenge to his spirit. I feel him with me constantly, something I have never before experienced after an animal has died. I see him trotting along the drive with his jaunty little step, or feel him following me up the hallway. The other night, half-asleep, I thought I heard him pad into the bedroom. Comforting, this.

And it's not just me. My partner Susan, his second mother, loved him equally. She says that when she goes to visit his grave he is not under the earth but standing by her side. So close he's almost touching.

**A dog lover may lose many dogs** in a lifetime, might suffer more than once that intense, unalloyed grief — a grief purer perhaps than what one feels for a human's death.

I lost a dog called Scruffy barely three weeks ago. In the first few days of shock and tears I said to a friend, "I hate to admit this, but I feel worse about my dogs dying than about people. Why is that?"

She said, "Because you love them more. Simple."

Well, not quite so simple. I'm no misogynist. I don't really prefer animals to people. But after my partner and my parents, who shares more of life and love with me than my dogs?

Scruffy was not really 'my' dog. He came into my life eleven-and-a-half years ago as part of a package. A couple of months after Anne and I met, she and Scruffy moved in with me. I already had Jed, my innocent, superbly good looking German Shepherd. He and Scruffy hit it off immediately. Scruffy was no great shakes in the looks department. People he'd never met would stop him in the street and croon, "Aren't you a scruffy dog?" He was picture-book scruffy; cute, hangdog, and as cunning as a shithouse rat. Within weeks, if you'd asked me to choose between Scruffy and my adored Jed, I would have been in trouble.

Scruffy was the witness and adjunct to my growing relationship with Anne. At age forty-five I was moving, in a scared, confused fashion, out of heterosexuality and into the first truly loving and rewarding relationship of my adult years. I loved Anne for having Scruffy, and I loved the ways she dealt with him. A bit the way she dealt with me, really. On the one hand matter of fact, sensibly, on the other with a depth of unshowy love that impressed me deeply. She was very physical with her animals, handling them with great confidence. Easy to do with a dog, but she was just as hands-on with Nat the Cat — throwing him about, having play-fights with him. I, who was just learning to be a cat person, was bemused. There was such trust and honesty between Anne and her animals that anything was permissible. And so I began, timidly, to see that I, too, could venture further with this woman than I had dared with anyone else.

Scruffy lived in the city with us for three years. He was a dog full of sly ingratiating devotion and also a dog of fierce and adventurous spirit. He would scramble over our six-foot garden fence where Jed the German Shepherd couldn't, and he'd bring home treats from his midnight jaunts to the shops — Kentucky Fried chicken bones mostly — which he shared with Jed. He was once rescued from the middle of the Sydney Harbour Bridge by a kindly policeman. We had his balls cut off to render him less ferocious towards much larger dogs — Pit Bulls were his avowed enemies — but it didn't work.

When we took him with us for a quieter life in the country, he just exchanged the feverish delights of the city for twenty-four-hour orgies of wombat chasing with Jed. We all suffered through Jed's death. Scruffy pined for months before he grudgingly formed an avuncular relationship with young Jacko, who was acquired mainly to divert him from his grief.

Now Scruffy himself is dead. He was old, but he died unexpectedly and with a flair for drama that was his trademark. He has been with me throughout the most transforming years of my life — the years when I finally found my vocation as a writer and have lived in happiness with Anne. And in the bad times — there are always bad

times — Scruffy was an empathetic friend. He did a great deal of standing close, sympathetic gazing and long, slow licks. He was both immensely loving and totally independent. Tough, scurrilous, obstinate. Unique.

So what does a dog mean to us? Each is different, so different! But my life is viewed through the stage each represents, and the life-lessons I've learned from them all. With my first Sydney Silky, a birthday present at age eight, I found refuge when the human world proved difficult and treacherous. And I learned my first lesson in death; the huge pain of accepting its permanence.

With my first German Shepherd, Tess, I learned about patience and endurance and trying hard — and that it sometimes isn't enough. Tess comforted me for years through a hopeless relationship. A month or two after she died, I finally moved out. Tess was the last threadbare link of love between two struggling humans. But it took her death to show me that.

And now Scruffy. Every time I visit his grave he tells me firmly, as he dogs my heels, that there's no point in grieving, or making sentimental visits to a piece of earth. I'll never forget him. Anyone — person or dog — who has so much guts and heart never dies for those who love them.

*Anne Coombs' (left) books include* Sex and Anarchy: The Life and Death of the Sydney Push *and* Broometime, *co-authored with her partner Susan Varga.* Broometime *explores contemporary life in the remote town of Broome. Anne and Susan's home is in the Southern Highlands of NSW where they have a menagerie of horses, cows, chooks, a cat and — now — two dogs.*

*Susan Varga was born in Hungary but came to Australia as a child, an experience explored in her first book* Heddy and Me. *Her novel,* Happy Families, *published in 1999 won both Braille Book of the Year and Audio Book of the Year. Susan is also a published poet. Pictured on p. 197 is Scruffy (left) and Boy (right).*

# Terrier Woman
Diana Mummé

as a woman who lives alone
they are my everything
friends family
yes
but it's not the same
coming home at night

body contact loosens
the lonely tightness
in my tum

spinning my own life
in the dappled garden sun
nurtures me mostly
even on cold nights

with them
when I'm good
I am very, very good
and when I'm bad
I am horrid

I demand obedience
like a raging bull

goddess I adore them

in the morning we sit together
and at night
we sleep as one

they are my shadows
we pace one another
and keep each other safe

my old cairn Ben
was with me for 18 years
senseless in the end
sight
sound
smell all gone but
praised on his condition

only when Duncan came
could I let my darling go

Duncan is a cairn too
rescued from a very
uncertain future

even though I buried Ben
beside the pergola
He is Duncan
I am sure

Polly is a Boston
with Bostons you either
love them or loathe them
I think Polly was a prototype for ET

she is the gentlest creature alive

last year my two friends went away
and my old animal family all died
one dog
two cats

Carman was with me
when I had Ben put down
and we got my pups before she went

I worried so that I was a bad mother
but the vet said if you
have a dog for 18 years
you must be doing something right

and it's taken me a while to take that in

the old family died
and now the menagerie is here
two dogs
two cats

with the new century
it's new blood
and I can feel it racing inside

my dogs bring closeness
to every day life
and we speak a language
all our own

*Diana Mummé is a fifty-three-year-old, single woman living in Somers on the Mornington Peninsula in Victoria where she entertains her friends in local restaurants, wineries, galleries and craft markets. She loves living by the sea. She has two cats and two dogs and is a very keen gardener. Diana works full time as the site manager and counsellor at the Rosebud Base of Peninsula Community Health Service. Her background is in social work. She is interested in myth, ritual and seasonal festivals.*

# Monkey and Other Sherron Dunbar

**Once upon a time,** in 1946, there was a plump black dog; he was no thoroughbred but he loved my mother Sheila, way out in western Queensland in Hughenden where I was born. And he was my lonely mother's friend; my father was a young constable there and was away a lot; my mother had left her family and old nursing friends, and was waiting for me to arrive; she had no idea then that she would give birth to another five children. But she loved Butch, and he loved her and together they walked for miles across that hot flat dusty place and along the hot dry dusty river-bed. She mourned having to leave him behind when in 1948 we set out on the journey south to Brisbane. He is still there, in the photos of me and my mother and father and their lovingly enmeshed memories, all that long time ago on the road between Mt Isa and Townsville.

Years and years of being afraid of dogs passed by, filled with strangers, and friends, and dogs, in different places in Australia, England and Germany.

Then came Josie; sweet Josie; slight, black messy-haired Josie. She loved our walks in Melbourne, in the Clifton Hill Park and along Collingwood streets, crossing Easey Street with me remembering the two Sues — the Easey Street murder victims, whom I had never met but felt I knew in their terror. She sat with me behind the factory on the Merri Creek and knew I could not see the point of living anymore, as her father and I had separated, in spite of the birth of our dear red-head daughter. I survived, and she and my dear daughter began to spend time with me sometimes and my daughter's father at other times; so I drove round picking up and delivering children and Josie the small scraggy black dog.

Then she ran in front of a tram and my daughter drew a sad picture of herself, her Turkish-born and then violently orphaned foster brother, her father and Josie. The crèche displayed it and let my daughter tell the sad story to her little friends.

Into our ordinary lives came Scruffy, by name and nature. He turned up in my daughter's father's backyard a few days after Josie died, and refused to leave. He weathered our odd but predictable relationships and routines, then when we could no longer work out who should have him most of the time, he went to a dog's blissful haven with eccentric, generous friend 'K'. She owned one of Melbourne's unofficial dog and cat sanctuary networks behind Rye's back beach, and there he died years later, having a heart attack as he sat up one evening, an old dog, watching television.

Years passed and into our lives came Zyber, a beautiful black Greyhound-cross. He was tall and lean and true to my daughter and her friend in their drug worlds in Melbourne and Brisbane. And he knew the mean, sad night streets of Fitzroy and Collingwood and West Melbourne down by the rail yards and the Remand Centre; he knew my car and my sadness and my fears, and he looked after my daughter and her friend no matter what. But cancer and the illicit-drug chaotic world of Kangaroo Point on the Brisbane River killed him; and we really mourned; he was a protector, a knower of much, and a friend. He travelled thousands of kilometres with my daughter and her friend up to Alice Springs and back and up again, to and from Brisbane, up the New South Wales north coast. A small, tattered black-and-white photo of him still hangs on a kitchen wall in Melbourne where my daughter now lives.

Now there is another black dog, and his name is Monkey. He is no thoroughbred, but he loves my daughter, and her father and me. He lives almost exclusively with my daughter sharing her house and much loved garden, as she struggles with a great deal of determination to get the Other Giant Monkey off her back.

But at this moment he is lying at my feet as I write this homage to the dogs in my life of fifty-five years; he has just been subjected to the indignity of an oatmeal and aloe vera shampoo bath, and his black coat shines in the hot sunlight. He has no idea or image of the other dogs in our lives — Mum's, mine, my daughter's life; neither does he need to have. But, like the others, he gives his companionship and dog understanding and loads of dog love.

*Sherron Dunbar was born in 1946 in Hughenden in Queensland, then spent her childhood, teenage years and young adult years in south-east Queensland. Seeking broader horizons she went to the UK and taught for a few years, then to Germany. She returned to Australia in 1976 and studied social work in Melbourne, which remains her home of definite choice.*

# Angel

## Barbie Burton

**She was a Scotch Collie,** one of those 'Lassie' dogs. My brother got her when I was away so I'm not sure about how or why. Nor am I sure if I actually saw her when she was little or whether I just remember the stories about the soft, gorgeous goldenness of her. I know she came home hidden in his leather jacket with only her brown eyes peeking out. I've always suspected 'Angel' was my mother's choice — just the sentimental sort of name she would have liked — but now, remembering my brother's bikie connections, I begin to wonder.

If people ask, I always say, "Of course I like them, but I'm not really a dog-person." Then I add, "I've never had a dog." I realise that I say this because I've never thought of Angel as an animal at all, let alone as mine. Certainly she was part of my family — in many ways its most stable element — and everyone's best friend.

My father pretended he didn't like her but I wasn't fooled because he pretended he didn't like anyone. He complained about the cost of feeding her and ranted about "that silly bloody dog", especially when she was nearly run over. But I know how much he really loved her because I'd hear him talking to her. "Ah, you bullet-headed bastard," he'd say, looking into her eyes and stroking her long nose tenderly, "I should part your hair for you, part it right down the middle — with my tomahawk."

But he was all talk, for talk was about all he could do since his accident. Increasingly, he sat in his chair watching television with Angel at his side. Those days when he couldn't even get up, she was there, by the bed. He'd talk to her for hours about 'Bastard Bolte' and 'Pig-Iron Bob'. Once I said, "Dad, can I have this last chocolate?" and he said, "No, I'm saving it for someone." Who for? Surely not for mum? "It's for the dog, if you must know," he said haughtily, ending the conversation.

I don't know that anyone ever walked her but she didn't seem to mind; she grew into a gentle, comfortable, lay-about sort of dog. I'm not sure why she was out in the garden on the day my dad died, but she was. He was standing, talking, in the doorway between the kitchen and the diningroom when he had a massive heart-attack and dropped down, dead. I was sent for and we did the sort of things people do when someone dies on the kitchen floor and no one much thought about the dog. Not till after they'd taken him away. When Angel came in she walked very slowly across the room, right up to the spot where he'd been and she stopped. She whined a bit, lay down and stayed there. I like to believe that she never again crossed through that doorway, always going round the long way, but maybe she did eventually.

After that she became my mother's dog, watching with her through the empty nights. She was given scrambled eggs for breakfast and barley broth for tea. If I stayed there Mum would say, "Don't go to sleep until Angel comes to kiss you goodnight," and I'd sigh and wait and she'd trot in and give me a kiss, just like I'd kiss the nieces, and trot off again.

After Mum moved away, Angel went to live with my brother and his family. She was very good with babies and sat with Marg, my sister-in-law, through the long hours of breast-feeding. She was patient with the kids and endured their pullings and pokings with fortitude. If we were sitting talking, she'd pad up and snuggle into the group, sometimes listening, sometimes just being there. She particularly liked to settle quietly on the floor right behind the feet of anyone standing talking, and gave only the smallest yelp of disappointment if, unaware of her presence, they stepped backwards onto her — as quite frequently happened.

One day it was decided that the kids should call me, and Marg's sister, 'Auntie', not just Barbie and Helen. But it never worked and instead, somehow, Angel became Auntie Angel, shortened with time to Auntie. The name suited her well for she'd grown quite matronly; her walk was almost regal, slow and dignified with her bustle-bum swaying behind her, her bullet-head held high. She was referred to as 'the Auntie'. The answer to such questions as "what'll we do with this old stew" and "who put white hair over the couch" was always 'the Auntie'. And I don't think my brother minded one bit if people thought I was the Auntie referred to.

But she got old and frail and one day they asked if I could sit with my niece Suzannah while they took Auntie to the vet (Suze was only little and they thought she'd be upset if she knew what was happening). One of my saddest, most precious memories is of Marg, kneeling beside Angel, brushing her honey-coloured coat for the last time, getting her ready for her journey.

But it turned out that Suzie wanted to go with them. She wouldn't stay in the waiting room but went into the surgery and up to the table where Angel lay. She stroked her head and this is what she said. She said, "It's all right Angel, you can go to sleep now and when you wake up, you'll be a lovely new puppy." No one told her this; she just thought it out herself. And she wasn't a bit upset (though the other kids were when they found out). Which all goes to show how loving things can help you through the bad times.

*Barbie Burton has had several dogs over the years, though they've always lived with other people. Today she has a Golden Labrador called Pip who was born in Oxford and lives in Kew with a family from Singapore.*

# The Dogs of My Life

Jan Fook

**I am going to come straight to the point.**

People are all very well in their own way, but they are not dogs. Therefore I will write of dogs.

This is a somewhat abbreviated version of the beginning of a favourite book of mine, written by 'Elizabeth' and entitled *All the Dogs of My Life*. Dogs, she says, are free from the fluctuations of human relationships. "Once dogs love," she claims, "they love steadfastly, unchangingly, till their last breath. That is how I like to be loved. Therefore I shall write of dogs."

I do not really know why I write of dogs, but I do know that I love and have loved each of my dogs — not perhaps steadily, or unchangingly, but certainly till their last breath. And in my dogs, I perhaps see the story of my own life, with its fluctuations, its unsteadiness and changes, its losses and its lessons. Therefore I will write of all the dogs of my life.

Frisky was a literal answer to prayer. I was raised in a seriously religious, church-going family. We were taught to eschew many of the material comforts of life, but somehow I couldn't forgo the idea of a dog. By age seven, I had been praying for a dog for some years. Frisky, a black, white-star-chested Kelpie, turned up, from out of nowhere, on the doorstep of our Sydney home, a 1950s suburban brick veneer. It was a dark and stormy night. It was almost as if God had sent her in a flash of lightning, a shivering mutt to warm the life of a too earnest child. My father, who could never quite manage to cloak his innate kindness in religious rigidity, dug some well chewed (by us) bones from the garbage for her to eat, and cleared a place in his overflowing garage, for her to sleep. I remember marvelling at this rare glimpse of his generosity. He even decided to leave the garage door slightly ajar, risking valued security, so she could relieve herself during the night.

In some ways Frisky became an important symbol for my own secretly guarded independence, in a household with too little privacy of thought or action. She lasted a good sixteen years. She died the same year Elvis died, which was also the final year of my social work study. My friends from this time understood my love for dogs. One in particular, Penny, did something about it. She bought me Peanuts, the gawky, gangly Old English Sheepdog-cross, who looked like an Afghan Hound. Peanuts' life spanned the fraught period of my young adulthood. She came with me to set up home in a neighbouring city, Newcastle, where I had been driven further afield in the quest for employment. During her thirteen-year life with me, she inhabited nine different properties, in four different cities. She uprooted with us, as we struggled to find a career footing in the academy, in times not so conducive to the employment of younger people. Peanuts was not the ideal dog for this period of my life, but in some ways I grieved most for her. Her patience and affection I had often taken for granted in a life which was largely uncertain, sliding sporadically between dreams and disappointments. She represented all that was constant about those years, a reminder that home life could always be depended upon, even if career could not.

Although her life might have been generally unfulfilled, Peanuts had one spot of unadulterated joy. This was Chelsea, who to this day I also remember as my unadulterated joy. She came to us in a period of sacrifice and experiment, when my partner, Al, and I, disrupted our cosy home life so he could take up employment in a town six hours away. The joy of Chelsea ended more than twenty years ago, yet the vision of her feisty face and ebony eyes is as clear to me now, as the fine fur of my beloved Minty who lies beside me as I write these words. The young Wire-haired Fox Terrier pup Chelsea was one of those souls who was born already knowing its own place and its own value. Peanuts, Al, and I were smitten from the earliest moment. It was lucky she died young. I can only tell you that I cannot imagine the grief that the loss of a full dog life of attachment to Chelsea would have brought. Nor do I want to imagine it. The grief at the loss of five months of Chelsea life was almost overwhelming. The day after she was run over, a good friend of ours phoned with the news he had won $142,000 in the lottery. I would have given back a million lottery prizes then, and today, if I could have had my bright girl back.

Peanuts and Chelsea both taught me about different kinds of loss, one about the grief of the slow and inevitable passing of life, and the other about the wrenching anguish when life is ripped out of your hands and heart. So with Zoe, I thought I would learn how to manage grief. I set out to find a replacement for Chelsea who was not really a replacement. She was to be like her, yet not. Accordingly I chose the runt of the first Wire-haired Fox Terrier litter I could locate. She was small, dainty and doe-like, where Chelsea had been robust, rambunctious and devilish. Zoe turned out to be the biggest mistake of my dog life. Smelly, anti-social, and hard of hearing, Zoe seemed only to use her considerable brain power when scheming how to avoid toileting herself on command. Her specialty was soiling the house immediately after she had been taken outside for this very purpose. Once she managed to soil every room in our five-bedroomed Edwardian country home, in one evening. It was as if she couldn't decide exactly which spot would be the most exasperating so was hedging her bets! Zoe was the oddest little dog character I have ever known, yet when she died, I think I learnt more about attachment than any of my other more attractive dog family members had ever taught me. I understood then, I thought, something of the paradox of human existence, how the most fraught of relationships can still inspire love and care. She caused me such angst, but she was mine, for better or worse.

Bob was intended to be a radical departure from the trials and tribulations of Zoe. He was a male dog — our first ever. In many ways Bob was a victim of his gender. He began life as sweet tempered as you could imagine, a dog of children's story books and fairy tales. He was also as handsome a Wire-haired Fox Terrier as you could imagine. Straight of leg, direct of eye, he brought to mind an artist's model. Many pictures of Wire-haired Fox Terriers I have seen, look exactly like my Bob. But over the years, despite his looks, his hormones ruined him. He evolved into a bad tempered, highly strung, handsome monster, with separation anxiety. He developed the ability to climb rose bushes (Cecile Brunner) in order to follow his loved ones over the fence and to work. It was about this point in time we hatched the completely inspired plan of acquiring a companion for Bob, a submissive girl dog who would not challenge his authority, but would ease the anxiety of his day time loneliness. So Nellie snuck onto the scene.

The story of Nellie is the fairy story of gender relations gone right. Submissive and companionable she was. Non-challenging she also was. But somehow, within about two weeks, Nellie became top dog, although I don't think Bob was aware of this, even on the day of his death, six years later, from bowel cancer. The neat little Sheltie-Scottie cross had the street-wise brains I have always wished I was born with. I think it is true to say that with Nellie, both Al and I experienced what dog companionship was always made out to be in the books. My first major trip overseas to Europe, at the ripe age of thirty-seven, was marred only by my mind's constant image of her pointed little mouse face, her clear amber eyes scanning for direct contact with my soul. I had to seek regular 'dog contact' overseas, in order to stave off feelings of homesickness. Now, whenever one of us leaves on a too frequent trip, the dreaded suitcase in hand, little Nellie hangs back, the anticipated pain of "good-bye, be a good girl" overcoming her staunch temperament. Her loyalty inspires the same. She is a major reason I do not want to leave the house during the day, and cut dinner engagements short at night.

The other major reason for this new found delight in domesticity is Minty, the pure-bred Shetland Sheepdog who has adopted me as his shepherd. The delicate yet stately creature has the looks of a prince and the soul of a baby. He is never much more than a metre from my side. If I inadvertently shut him out of the bathroom when I am inside, he will lie right outside the door, his little black hairs poking underneath to reassure me of his presence. His gentle being calms and sustains me. The way he runs to me, and presses into my body, or sits quivering on my feet at the least frightening sound, kindles in me the most satisfying protective instincts. There is a huge responsibility inherent in being adopted by a trusting animal. It is a responsibility which I hope brings out a better side of me. Minty in my life has brought a warm contentedness, a delight and comfort in things small and ordinary. At the same time, he frees me up to be me. He has given me new vistas, opened up possibilities of new creative pursuits, of living with, and writing about, more dogs.

Maybe it is with Nellie and Minty, that the dogs of my life will become my life.

Jan Fook, with Minty (left) and Nellie, was born and raised in Sydney, Australia, and discovered dogs at an early age. In addition to pursuing a career as a social worker and an academic, dogs have always been an important part of her home life. She has a firm belief that the vital role dogs play in our happiness has yet to be fully recognised. In the future, Jan hopes to be able to combine her two greatest loves, dogs and writing.

# Permissions

Terry Wolverton, 'Requiem' first published in *CQ: California State Poetry Quarterly*, 1991. © Terry Wolverton, 1991. Reprinted by permission of Terry Wolverton.

Susan Rhind, 'Kuri' first published in *New Women's Fiction* edited by Cathie Dunsford (New Women's Press) 1986.

Miriel Lenore, 'the visitor' — an earlier version of this poem was published in *sun wind and diesel* (Wakefield) 1977.

Sandy Jeffs, 'The Adoration of Dog's Eye' previously published in *Confessions of a Midweek Lady*, poems by Sandy Jeffs and drawings by Veronica Holland, 2001.

Eloise Klein Healy, 'Holly' previously published in *A Pocket Beating Like A Heart*, Book of a Feather Press, Los Angeles, 1981.

# Photographs

p.ix Allan Kellehear; p.x Annie Irish; p.9 (left) Martyn Jones; (top and bottom right) Hannah Jones; p.13 John Veater; p.16 Renate Klein; p.19 Renate Klein; p.33 Susan Hawthorne; p.35 Allan Kellehear; p.38 Sucharita Sen; p.41 Jan Fry; p.42 Adrian Kennelly; p.55 Carmel Reid; p.59 Lorraine Upwich; p.66 Susan Hawthorne; p.71 (two at left) Karen Shelton; p.76 Robyn Adams; p.81 Annie Irish; p.83 Annie Irish; p.95 Laurel Guymer; p.96 Amanda Owen; p.98 Colleen Rooney; p.106 Laurel Guymer; p.107 Sue Clements; p.114 Lynda Birke; p.117 Lynda Birke; p.119 Tricia Szirom; p.124 David Crofts; p.134 Lyn Valentine; p.135 Lyn Valentine; p.144 Kay Graham; p.150 Adam Mamaj; p.159 Liesbet Geraghty; p.160 Di Brown; p.163 Di Brown; p.165 Sue Barber; p.167 Frances Kelly; p.168 Ellara Woodlock; p.175 (top) Pen Haslett; p.175 (bottom) Pauline Lord; p.186 Morris Zwi; p.187 (top) Morris Zwi; p.187 (bottom) Sharon Zwi; p.189 Cath Dunsford; p.192 (top) Rye Senjen; p.192 (bottom) Kirstie Murdoch; p.199 Pat Clarke; p.206 Allan Kellehear.

All other photographs are from the personal collections of individuals named in the text. The publisher acknowledges kind permission to reproduce these photographs.

## Other books by Jan Fook

*Transforming Social Work Practice*
*Breakthroughs in Practice*
*Radical Casework*
*Professional Expertise* (co-author)
*Critical Social Work in Changing Contexts* (forthcoming)
*The Reflective Researcher* (editor)
*Transforming Social Work Practice* (co-editor)
*Practice and Research in Social Work* (co-editor)
*Breakthroughs in Practice* (co-editor)

## Other books by Renate Klein

*Infertility: Women Speak Out about their Experiences of Reproductive Medicine*
*The Exploitation of a Desire*
*The Ultimate Colonisation: Reproductive and Genetic Engineering*
*RU 486: Misconceptions, Myths and Morals* (co-author)
*Theories of Women's Studies* (co-editor)
*Test-Tube Women* (co-editor)
*Radical Voices* (co-editor)
*Angels of Power and Other Reproductive Creations* (co-editor)
*Australia for Women: Travel and Culture* (co-editor)
*Radically Speaking: Feminism Reclaimed* (co-editor)
*CyberFeminism: Connectivity, Critique and Creativity* (co-editor)

If you would like to know more about Spinifex Press,
write for a free catalogue or visit our Web site.

Spinifex Press
PO Box 212, North Melbourne
Victoria 3051, Australia
<http://www.spinifexpress.com.au>